The South African
Communist Party

The South African Communist Party

Adapting to Thrive in a Post-Communist Age

THOMAS STANLEY KOLASA

McFarland & Company, Inc., Publishers
Jefferson, North Carolina

LIBRARY OF CONGRESS CATALOGUING-IN-PUBLICATION DATA

Kolasa, Thomas Stanley, 1967–
    The South African Communist Party : adapting to thrive in a post-communist age / Thomas Stanley Kolasa.
        p.   cm.
    Includes bibliographical references and index.

    ISBN 978-0-7864-7804-0 (softcover : acid free paper) ∞
    ISBN 978-1-4766-2059-6 (ebook)

    1. South African Communist Party—History.   2. Communism—South Africa—History.   3. South Africa—Politics and government—1909–1948.   4. South Africa—Politics and government—1948–1994.   5. South Africa—Politics and government—1994–   I. Title.

JQ1998.C64K65 2016
324.268'075—dc23   2015033318

BRITISH LIBRARY CATALOGUING DATA ARE AVAILABLE

On the cover: map of Africa and sun rising over savannah, Masai Mara National Reserve, Kenya (© 2016 Digital Vision/Thinkstock)

Printed in the United States of America

McFarland & Company, Inc., Publishers
    Box 611, Jefferson, North Carolina 28640
    www.mcfarlandpub.com

Acknowledgments

I need to thank a number of people who helped me when I originally wrote sections of this book as my dissertation in the late 1990s. First and foremost, the late Dr. Victor Le Vine, my mentor and friend, was invaluable, not only in an academic sense, but also in a personal way. I also have to thank the generous funding of the Department of Political Science of Washington University in St. Louis. I also need to thank the Centre for Ethnic Studies at the University of Witswatersrand (Johannesburg, South Africa) for giving me a research position there. I must also thank everyone in South Africa, both my personal friends and the official contacts, who helped me while I was in South Africa to understand the culture, the people, and the country. Finally, I need to thank my friends and especially my parents for believing in this project and me over the many years.

Table of Contents

Introduction

Dinosaur or Adapter?

1971: As its immediate and foremost task, the South African Communist Party works for a united front of national liberation.... [But] the supreme aim of the Communist Party ... [is] the establishment of a Socialist South Africa, laying the foundation of a classless, communist society [Lerumo 107].

1996: The ultimate aim of the [Communist] Party is the building of a communist society, toward which it is guided by the principles of Marxism-Leninism [Daniels 20].

2012: The SACP and its cadres are everywhere [*Political Report* 1].

2012: We are a party for socialism and eventual communism, that is, the eradication of the capitalist system and an end to the exploitation of one person by another [*Political Report* 8].

The first two quotes are from commentators while the last two are from the South African Communist Party (SACP)[1] itself, but all of them establish the relevance of and justification for this book. Though many scholars, most politicians, and even the general public see "international communism" as a flawed ideology, a failed political system or even just a footnote in history, the SACP still sees communism as a viable and necessary goal for the future of South Africa and the world. A modified version of its traditional structure and ideology, combined with a symbiotic relationship with the African National Congress (ANC), has allowed the SACP not only to survive the collapse of communism but to thrive within the postcommunist era. As two leading scholars on the SACP said in the 1990s, the "SACP is proving itself to be a dynamic organization with a degree of popular appeal" (Ellis and Sechaba 10). Decades later, this comment is still relevant as the SACP's membership has grown from about 3,000 in 1990 to 160,000 in 2012 and as the party helps run South Africa with its larger partner, the ANC (*Political Report* 1).

1

"Communism" may now have little mainstream appeal in developed nations, but it is still too early to write off communism as a viable contender for popular support in select developing countries. Such countries as Peru, the Philippines, India, and South Africa all have communist parties that can make and have made a difference in the past and may yet play a role in the future. With forms of socialism popular in Latin America (Venezuela), communists once again active in parts of eastern Europe (including in Poland and Russia), and communist parties in power in Cuba, Vietnam, North Korea, and China, the many forms of communism are still relevant in the 21st century. Though the SACP is used here as a specific case study, aspects of the model utilized in this book are usable for other surviving communist parties.

Examination of how communist parties fared after the collapse of international communism is also an intellectually robust pursuit due to the many questions it raises: What will these communist parties do given the new environment of the 21st century? How will they continue to adapt? How can they reconcile the imperatives of institutional/organization survival with the new developmental choices found in their countries? How much will they need to revise their ideologies? Not since the collapse of the Napoleonic Empire in the 19th century has there been such an opportunity to study how remnants of a once transnational ideology that ruled an "empire" survive after the core of the system collapsed.

This book examines how a revolutionary organization adapts to both the collapse of an international ideology and to significant domestic change. I posit a model that shows how an organization (the SACP) when confronted with massive environmental changes (the collapse of apartheid and international communism) uses old methods (symbiosis with the ANC) and adapts (conversion to mass party structures and abandonment of Stalinism) to both survive and thrive (party growth and continued influence over both the ANC and the state).

With the SACP's structural and ideological changes, its positions have changed significantly. Ironically, though it has given up on its Stalinist authoritarianism, it has not shifted much on the question of a communist economy (at least in the long term). It has dropped its Stalinism, some of its Leninism, and now relies on a mixture of Leninism, Marxism, and social democracy; a mixture I call "neo–Leninism" and which will be explained fully below. Finally, it has also moved toward the center (from the far left) concerning the pace and extent of socioeconomic change. More than ever it now supports the slow, steady approach being taken by its close and more conservative (though still leftist) ally the ANC.

The SACP's stated goal is the creation of some form of future socialist society. Henry Pike, a well-known anticommunist in his day, was to the point:

> [Communism] uses the language of liberty, while cloaking its unspeakable totalitarianism in the rhetoric of democracy.... The masterminds of Marxism-Leninism have no interest in the plight of any race group of South Africa ... they are concerned, finally and ultimately with only one goal: the complete communist conquest of the world.... Its whole ideology lives and struggles to make the world a communist world ... only a fool will deny these facts [Pike 550].

Though the language is excessively inflammatory, Pike's general message is on target: the SACP does indeed want to see a communist world order come into being one day since it is still made up of true believers. The problem for the SACP is that the ANC is now more of a left-of-center party trying to cope with the heavy responsibility of running a modern, complex, multi-racial capitalist society all within a global competitive system. The ANC has jettisoned much of its "socialist" ideology, even putting off indefinitely its more left-wing public policy goals. It follows that regardless of their currently close alliance, the SACP and ANC will clash more and more, sooner *and* later, both on means and ends. The point is that the SACP faces an unresolved dilemma: to serve the short-term interests by supporting its more centrist ally's policies *or* start to build a socialist agenda and movement now and risk everything it has already accomplished.

This dilemma creates many ideological and practical problems for the SACP. Moreover, this situation is not a strictly "communist party problem," because the SACP is and has been an important actor in South African politics for decades. Because of the SACP's close alliance with the ANC and the Congress of South African Trade Unions (COSATU, the powerful leftist trade union federation), what the SACP now decides can affect South African history. As Heribert Adam, one of the leading writers on the SACP, stated, the "well known historical alliance between the ANC and SACP gives.... African communists particular importance for the future of democracy.... It is only in the Apartheid state that the hammer and sickle emblem proudly flies at mass rallies" (Adam 27). Will the future of South Africa be the left-of-center vision that the ANC holds or the socialist one of the SACP?

Not surprisingly, the communist goals of the SACP were vigorously opposed by the once powerful, but now disbanded, Nationalist Party (NP). Again, Adam stated, "The South African [National Party] government in the past regularly painted communists as militant, KGB-led terrorists" (Adam 27). The NP had not changed its basic assessment of the SACP, even as it faded from power after the All Race Elections of 1994 and then dissolved in the early 2000s. Various other parties and organizations are also avowed enemies of communism and the SACP, including the Inkatha Freedom Party (IFP), the Afrikaner Freedom Front (VF), and the extreme right-wing Afrikaner Armed Resistance (AWB). None of these parties have real, national power anymore (and only the IFP has any regional reach), but the SACP still faces large blocks of the populace of all races that are still anticommunist, seeing the SACP and/or communism as a real threat to South Africa. With so many political enemies watching its every step, clearly the SACP must not only adapt to its hostile and changing environment but also do so carefully.

I submit that this book will not only be useful in understanding the case of the SACP, but also the situations of other communist parties facing similar challenges. This is an end of an era: the so-called communist world has collapsed, with its remnants left without the political leadership once provided by the Soviet Union.[2]

A Dinosaur Party?

A central concept that must be kept in mind as we examine the SACP as it struggles for survival is that it is a "dinosaur party," but what is that exactly? It is an organization that has *seemingly* outlived its own usefulness, though it may in reality have a great deal of life yet. This can mean that like the real dinosaurs, the organization will indeed die out, sooner or later. But it can also mean that though the organization *looks* like a dinosaur, in actuality it is thriving for a number of reasons. Like some dinosaurs that adapted into new forms (birds), the SACP did adapt instead of dying out in the 1990s. From all available evidence, the SACP is not dying, and though its future is hardly assured, it is currently thriving within a challenging environment.

But the SACP has had a great many obstacles to overcome to reach this state of relative success. The domestic challenges that it faces are legion: its tricky alliance with the ANC, a long reputation of being a Stalinist party, and its own factional problems. The international dimension cannot be ignored either.

The importance of the collapse of the world communist movement, both in fact and in myth, cannot be overstated. And though, as Mark Twain might say, the death of communism was greatly exaggerated, the "international communism" known to the world for seventy years is gone forever. Thus, the leaders of the SACP, who were true believers in both Marxism-Lenin *and* Stalinism for more than sixty years, were suddenly left out in the cold. On the face of it, the dinosaur image seemed to fit, at least until the mid–1990s.

Though there is little doubt that the SACP *can* survive for some time in this brave and tough new world, there is no guarantee that it will do so indefinitely. It faces, simultaneously, both domestic upheavals *and* an international paradigm shift. Only a few communist parties have handled this transition well; many have forsaken Marxism-Leninism (often for social democracy), while others have disappeared. The SACP, at this point, hopes to avoid either fate. It may be able to do this because it can draw upon a long history of survival in the face of adversity.

The SACP has its own long history, traditions, and method. In the early 1920s the party was formed from an odd collection of leftist and socialist organizations (Ellis and Sechaba 14). "Established in 1921, the SACP is the oldest Marxist-Leninist party on the [African] continent" (Legum 103). As Sheridan Johns, another expert on the early history of the SACP, pointed out, it was hardly a "black" organization in the beginning, "The Communist Party of South Africa had come into existence on July 30, 1921, with an almost exclusively white membership of several hundred" (Johns 201). Though many more blacks became involved after the crucial 1928 policy changes, "this transformation, however, was not adequately reflected in the party's leadership, policy and perspective" (Lerumo 63). Only in the 1930s did the party become more "black," and even after that, many of its more famous and influential leaders, like Abram Fischer, Joe Slovo, and Jeremy Cronin, have been white (though black ones, like the famous Chris Hani and the current leader, Blade Nzimande, cannot be dismissed). Further, in addition to its problem with the race issue, the SACP has struggled long and hard with its former Stalinist aspects.

For most of its history, the SACP had been considered a mostly unrepentant Stalinist party, though by the mid–1990s it had renounced most of its Stalinist past (Adam 28). Still as Adam explained in the 1980s:

> At present, the [SACP] remains a self-styled elitist group with secret membership.... Will CPSA open up or stayed closed like secret "Broederbond"[3] Afrikaner organizations.... It resembles more an authoritarian Jesuit order for the organic intelligentsia than an open, broad-based vehicle for the self-critical exploration of feasible socialism [Adam 35].

One could argue that it now has shed all of its Stalinist elements, though not its Leninist ones (which it itself admits to still being "Marxist-Leninist"). Thus, the SACP's primary methods and goals have stayed the same: (1) fighting a class war through the use of a national liberation front and (2) creating a socialist state after some period of bourgeois democratic rule under the ANC. Though the SACP has had its victories throughout the decades, it was quite ineffective in helping defeat the nationalist regime, at least until the mid–1980s (Lerumo 77). However it did become quite successful in gaining influence and power within the national liberation movement in South Africa.

By the 1940s, the party had successfully coupled itself with the primary "native organization," the ANC. As we shall see in later chapters, by the 1960s the SACP had begun to play a crucial role in ANC policy creation and execution, plus it helped lead the ANC guerrilla organization Umkhonto We Sizwe (MK). This would last for three decades, until the 1990s when the ban on the ANC and SACP was lifted and world communism collapsed. At that point, though the SACP itself gained from its newly legalized base, it steadily lost influence with the ANC. This has been particularly true since the ANC took state power in April 1994, winning many elections ever since, thus gaining an independent power base. By the early 2000s there were real, public tensions with the ANC (mostly over its centrist public policy), though those have somewhat lessened by the 2010s.

Since its partner the ANC took power in 1994, the main immediate goal of the SACP has been to introduce a leftist perspective within the ANC regime in a number of ways. First, it publishes and distributes literature to other organizations and to the public of South Africa. Such acts have been seen as a serious threat by some (obviously biased) local scholars for decades. "History has proved that nothing can be more disastrous than the effects of communist doctrine and agitation on the minds of simple agrarian people" (Vermaak 104). Second, it still joins in multi-organizational alliances and events by having its members join other organizations; this is an approach it has successfully used for decades. One can see this with the ANC, the Congress of South African Unions (COSATU), and the disbanded MK (the armed wing of the ANC). The ultimate result of this process was the installation of the noted communist leader Joe Slovo as Minister of Housing in the early days of the ANC regime; since then the SACP has held many lesser posts in the government (Jeremy Cronin, the current First Deputy General Secretary of the SACP, is also Deputy Minister of Transport and a member of the ANC National Executive Committee).

The ultimate goal of the SACP has always been to create a socialist regime within South Africa. While the ANC has never embraced the goal of a fully socialist society, some of its leaders have, from time to time, endorsed various socialist ideals (and not surprisingly, this has been especially true of the ANC members that are also SACP ones). The ANC now espouses the goal of a democratic, nonracial regime that may use such public policy tools for the purposes of income redistribution and economic growth. Still, as a matter of fact, "the ideological differences between the ANC and SACP are vast" (Campbell 46). This ranges from problems over the race issue, social policy, and even basic assumptions about the role of socialism in the future. Also, there remains a bloc within the ANC that has consistently mistrusted the SACP (Ellis and Sechaba 53). Still, the fact remains that the SACP influences the ANC considerably because the two organizations have worked together constantly for decades. However, what has been a relatively simple consensus on most matters has been severely tested by the ANC since it took power in 1994.

With the ANC fully devoted to running the country, the SACP has been somewhat relegated to the background, a position difficult for the SACP's leaders to accept. The SACP, having few other choices, has decided to abide by the ANC's decision to take a conciliatory, nonsocialist (though often leftist) path for the time being. To make matters worse, the ANC now formulates public policy with massive corporations (such as the Anglo-American Corporation) that the SACP and its union allies have fought for decades. The revolutionary and socialist goals of the SACP seem to contradict the ANC's leftist but still democratic, capitalist policies.

On strictly numerical grounds, the SACP does not measure up to the other political actors in South Africa with its estimated 160,000 members (the ANC had about 640,000 members in 2012), but it has influence far beyond its numbers. The SACP has turned out to be one of the more reliable and cohesive elements within the Tripartite Alliance (the ANC, the COSATU unions, and the SACP), therefore giving it additional weight. The SACP also has a very clear and respected history of opposition to racism and apartheid. As Nelson Mandela stated in 1964, "For many decades Communists were the only political group in South Africa who were prepared to treat Africans as human beings and their equals ... there are many Africans who, today, tend to equate freedom with communism" (Lerumo 48). Decades later, in 1994, Mandela added, "It is not given to a leader of one political organization in a country to sing praises to the virtues of another. Yet that is what I intend to do today. If anything, this signifies the unique relationship between the African National Congress and the South African Communist Party" (Mandela "Address," 1). This is a very important association, since "freedom" is and has been one of the primary motivations for most activists in South Africa. The SACP builds upon this antiracist reputation by being closely associated with the premier antiapartheid organization, the ANC.

The SACP does play a supporting role to the ANC in the alliance. But the old regime, run by the National Party for decades, often accused the SACP of controlling its senior partner. Strident anticommunists such as Christopher Vermaak referred to the ANC as "the communist-dominated African Nation Congress" (Vermaak 2). Even Oliver Tambo, an old-time ANC leader, admitted, "It is true that the ANC has members of the Communist Party. There has been an overlapping of membership all along the way" (Bardis 104). Finally, Kurt Campbell summed up the old regime's viewpoint well: "The official South African position is that the ANC is controlled by the USSR through white members of the SACP" (Campbell 45). While this is admittedly an extreme and inaccurate view, it was believed by many South Africans.

The SACP has gained strength through its alliance with the ANC and this partnership has allowed the SACP to become more popular than ever. The 1989 SACP Path to Power program declared, "Today the influence and prestige of the South African Communist Party is greater than any time in its history" ("Path to Power" 72). Joe Slovo, famous chairman of the SACP for years, added, "Our party has maintained and increased its popularity [since the ban was lifted]" (Slovo, "Beyond the Stereotype," 1). A noted historian, Colin Bundy, agreed, seeing the SACP as quite adaptive to the changing times (Bundy 6). Some observers maintain that the SACP once comprised anywhere from one-third to two-thirds of the ANC's ruling National Executive Committee. Both neutral and committed analysts state this view as fact:

SACP members are the major force that dominates the theoretical debates and strategies within the broad apartheid opposition [Adam 33].

> Moscow regarded the Communist Party of South Africa as the ideological and organizational leader of the revolutionary communist movement in other parts of Black Africa [Campbell 24].
> In most respects except for sheer numbers, the party came to dominate the ANC.... The Communist Party gradually took over the central role in the ANC policy-making.... The ANC had now adopted a strategy which was virtually identical to that of the party.... Once the party ... had got its grip, it would surely proceed to dominate all other tendencies in the ANC [Ellis and Sechaba 63].

Though the more extreme claims seem odd now, there is still some truth to these statements. How did the SACP achieve this level of influence within the ANC?

"The Party had evolved the technique of forming a caucus with agreed positions which it could push through in meetings of the ANC." Also, SACP methods such as, "the packed meeting, the party caucus, the resolution by acclamation, [and] the techniques of democratic centralism" were effective in securing the SACP's views in the past. Finally, "The ANC's collective style of leadership made this easier" (Ellis and Sechaba 63). All this does not mean, however, that the ANC and the SACP are the same organization, or that the SACP ever even controlled the ANC. As a matter of fact, the leading elements of the ANC have had serious misgivings about the SACP from the start (Ellis and Sechaba 16). "The ANC was singled out in particular as an organization which communists should take all necessary efforts to infiltrate. However, the ANC displayed a historically ambivalent attitude towards the Soviet Union and the CPSA" (Campbell 39). Regardless of the details, it can be argued that the SACP certainly had influence over the ANC. Joining the ANC was the not the only strategy the SACP used to gain broad support.

Throughout the years, the SACP has shifted its emphasis from support of the white proletariat in the 1920s to the championing of the black underclass, a move that broadened both its appeal and membership base (Campbell 26). Over the decades, this has allowed the SACP to gain the respect and admiration of both the legal and (once) illegal black unions. This alliance with the union movement carried over into the formation of COSATU in 1985, with the SACP heavily involved in this leftist federation as it is with the ANC.[4] But the Tripartite Alliance between the ANC, COSATU, and the SACP has been strained since the ANC came to power. The union movement is notoriously suspicious of those in power, even their ally the ANC, and thus the SACP is often caught in the middle, especially if a wildcat strike is called by COSATU which the ANC led regime opposes.

Moreover the SACP's ideological focus, that is, class conflict mixed with a broad "front" policy, has also allowed it to appear more "scientific" and/or professional in its approach than other parties and thus more intellectually attractive. This has attracted European, African, and Asian intellectuals for decades. This ideological clarity, with its mix of Marxist social science and violent rhetoric (and occasional action), has allowed the SACP to gain a deserved reputation of determination. This can be seen in the SACP's support and leadership in the former ANC guerrilla organization MK. If anything, the SACP had more influence in MK than even the ANC, due to the fact that the SACP was the conduit by which East Bloc arms and training were delivered to MK (Ellis and Sechaba 36).

In the eyes of the average African, who has been sometimes put off by the corruption, infighting, and lack of clarity of the ANC, all of this adds up to ambiguity if not wariness towards the ANC, and makes the SACP look that much better. The SACP, on the other hand, has been seen as determined, serious, and ready to act. In other words, the SACP was often seen as both professional and revolutionary, which is a real asset in such a radicalized society. However, the success of these various tactics and strategies notwithstanding, the SACP has been forced to make more changes in its ideology and structure in the last decade than in the previous seven decades.

Adapt or Die

This book also examines why and how the SACP has changed its ideology, strategies, and structure over the past years. At first, it was a standard working-class party, mostly recruiting from the relatively elite South African *white* working class. After the first decade of its existence, it moved to embrace the *black* underclass of workers, a policy pushed by the Comintern (the international communist organization), but also reinforced by the disastrous 1922 miners' strike and similar events, where the SACP was actually seen as an ally of the openly racist white unions. This switch also meant a change in tactics and structure.

The SACP then started to infiltrate unions and black nationalist organizations, a strategy that also meant recruiting more from the large black underclass and less from the white workers' stratum of the proletariat. With such union recruitment, the SACP finally started to gain a greater foothold in its primary target, the ANC. By the 1940s the ANC and SACP had an informal alliance, and once the SACP was forced underground in the 1950s, the two grew ever closer. After the ANC was banned in the early 1960s, they formalized their alliance and created the guerrilla organization MK (Ellis and Sechaba 26). This led to heavy cross-membership and cooperation on a number of projects. For almost thirty years, the alliance fought the racist and rightwing nationalist regime with some success, though it gained no real ground until the mid–1980s.

The latest phase began on February 2, 1990, when the nationalist government lifted the ban on both parties after long negotiations. In part this resulted from the pressure of the ANC policy of "ungovernability" (riots, civil disobedience, and the like), which the alliance had pushed for almost a decade, and from the economic and diplomatic pressure from the international community. Though the SACP was now legal and public again, it still faced many dilemmas, such as preparing for the inevitable All Race Elections (originally to be in 1992, then held in 1994) and coping with the collapse of communism in the East Bloc.

The international relations between the SACP and Communist Party of the Soviet Union (CPSU) are also important for this study. A close look at that relationship allows us to examine the central role played by the former Soviet Union vis-à-vis the SACP. The SACP had strong ties, both ideologically and materially, to the now defunct CPSU.[5] An early communist pamphlet, written by D. Jones and L. Green, stated, "The [CPSA/SACP] will receive great strength and inspiration from its connection with the world communist international, at present led by the Russian Communist Party" (Lerumo 120). In 1969, J.B. Marks, speaking for the SACP, stated, "Above all [the East Bloc nations] have rendered and are rendering valuable practical support to our freedom fighters: money, food, clothing, medicines, assistance in military training and—most precious—arms" (Lerumo 178). In 1989, an expert on the SACP, Panos Bardis, went as far as to state:

> Indeed there are close ties between the Soviet Union and the South African Communist Party, which, to a great extent, controls the ANC. Such influence began as early as 1917, the USSR now being very active in 10 southern African nations [Bardis 101].

As late as 1990, Adam could still state, "The SACP's solidarity with the Soviet Union remained unshaken" (Adam 28). These ties between the SACP and CPSU were deep, extensive, and important. Throughout the years, numerous leaders of the SACP (and ANC) visited Moscow for training, conferences, and even field directives. There were also connections between Soviet-sponsored international trade union organizations and COSATU (Bardis 101). Many communist parties in the developing world did similar things, but the SACP stands out for its closeness to the former Soviet Union.

Because of this, the SACP felt it had to support the Soviet Union almost unconditionally at times. Various scholars have concurred on this:

> The Sixth Congress of the Comintern in 1928 marked the end of the CPSA's autonomy from Moscow and the beginning of absolute discipline to central authority which was demanded by Stalin [Campbell 34].
>
> The Party in South Africa has a notorious reputation for abject servility to Moscow [*Toledo Blade*, August 10, 1986, c2].
>
> A public stance against the sole sponsor [USSR] would have jeopardized the very purpose of the party ... cut off from financial and military assistance ... the SACP would have condemned itself to organizational ineffectiveness and political paralysis [Adam 29].

Soviet support had at times injured the SACP's opposition to apartheid. "[The SACP] glorified and romanticizes the Soviet Union against all criticism and thereby discredited the anti-apartheid cause" (Adams 29). Adam somewhat overstated his case, but he was right to point to black nationalists who have always distrusted Western and Soviet aid, both which were seen as "white charity."

Still, the facts indicate that the SACP and long-defunct Soviet-dominated Comintern had some real differences, especially in the early years, as Soviet and South African historian Kurt Campbell pointed out. "The most striking aspect of Comintern policy ... is the degree to which the ideology of the Comintern diverged from the ideology espoused by the CPSA [SACP]" (Campbell 27). Ironically, the best example was the SACP's resistance to Comintern orders in 1928, concerning the creation of a "front" with the ANC (Ellis and Sechaba 17). "The Comintern's call for multiracial organization ... was met with some dissatisfaction by CPSA members" (Campbell 28). Such disagreements, however, appeared mostly in the first few decades of the SACP's existence.

Since the 1950s, however, the SACP (it formally changes its name at this point from CPSA) has adhered to the Soviet line. Take, for example, statements from the 1969 issue of the party's journal, *The African Communist*: "Experience has proved that socialism is the most suitable method of quickly developing countries which are economically backward" and "Communism is today a great and victorious world movement, embracing more than a third of the human race" (Lerumo 147, 149). The SACP was forced away from these simple but reassuring mottoes and beliefs by the 1990s.

At the end of the day, all these matters point to the SACP's continuing, and problematic, search for the means of its own survival. It must deal with the legacies of its ideological inheritance, the unresolved issues arising from its alliance with the ANC, and the unanswered questions about its role in the new South Africa. Since 1994, SACP members have run for office but always under the ANC banner. In one respect, this makes sense since the ANC is an umbrella organization for various groups, including the SACP. It also means that the SACP, as an organization, is still "hidden" from the electoral process and to a certain extent from the general public. This is in contrast to the statements from the SACP leadership that it wishes to participate fully in the electoral system. Will the SACP move away from the ANC in the near future? Or, will it stay behind the scenes for the time being, as it gains more and more ground? Such questions will be fully explored in later chapters.

Conclusion

Though much of the preliminary and secondary research for this book was done in the United States, it was still necessary to travel to South Africa to do primary research and interviews. Once there, I was able to access primary material both at excellent world-class libraries (at the University of Witswa-tersrand and the University of Cape Town) and at several headquarters of the political parties discussed in this study, especially the SACP itself, which was outstanding in its openness and willingness to aid me in my research (and not just as a former Stalinist party). I was also able to conduct personal interviews with SACP leaders and rank-and-file members to investigate such issues as faction formation, alliance politics, and generally why the SACP is so popular. With the material I gathered, I will be able to mostly answer the major questions asked by this study.

The SACP has already faced serious hurdles and surmounted them. Between the relatively positive (but still jarring) development of apartheid being dismantled and the shocking collapse of communism, the SACP had never been more challenged than in the 1990s. Through its successful strategy of using its symbiotic relationship with the ANC, and by affecting the twin reforms of becoming a mass party and liberalizing its ideology, the SACP has enabled itself to not only survive, unlike many other communist parties, but to also thrive.

The SACP is larger and stronger than ever, at least organizationally. It is also true that, for a number of reasons, it has lost an amount of influence over its ally the ANC. This, however, was unavoidable as the SACP lost its Soviet connections and the funding that came with it, and as the ANC gained state power, the SACP just became less important to the ANC. This is not to suggest that the SACP is about to be expelled from the alliance (though many right-wing and even centrist critics within the ANC have demanded just that for years). The SACP still provides crucial organizational and leadership skills to the ANC through use of the decades-old strategy of "dual membership," by which SACP members also serve as ANC members.

The SACP is preparing well for the hard times to come. It has opened its ranks up and is quickly becoming an effective mass party. It has also ejected the more offensive Stalinist elements from its ideology, while still maintaining that it is a Marxist-Leninist party (avoiding a conversion to social democracy for good or bad). Finally, a new, more liberal generation of leaders is slowly taking office, which will help ensure that these reforms will take root. But this does not mean that the SACP's future is assured.

The next decade of South African history will be a crucial one. After many years of white domination and decades of overt racial segregation under apartheid, the ANC (and its ally the SACP) finally took power in 1994. But they have been forced to rule a deeply divided nation. The cleavages are many: economic, religious, ethnic, generational, ideological, and of course racial.

Can the ANC/SACP alliance surmount these monumental hurdles? Maybe, but many other national liberation organizations have failed in Africa once they took power. As this is written (2014), the future is unclear. One message, however, is clear: the SACP, whatever happens, must adapt or die. The dinosaurs may still have something to teach the SACP.

CHAPTER 1

The SACP and Ideology
The Uncertain Path Between Faith and Pragmatism

Introduction

The importance of ideology goes without saying for most communist parties. It serves as a political tool, a normative backbone, and often as the prism through which to understand political events. This has been true for the SACP, being one of the more orthodox and Stalinist communist parties for much of its existence. However, during this period of massive change of the late 1980s and early 1990s, both within the communist world and South Africa, such rigid orthodoxy became a liability for the SACP. The SACP, unlike many of its communist allies, did adapt its ideology starting in the late 1980s; this allowed it to avoid the fate that overtook so many communist parties throughout the world. Though ideological adaptation is only one of the many ways the SACP has taken to survive and thrive in the 1990s, it is one of the more important.

Why did the SACP's Marxism-Leninism have to be adapted? The more Leninist (and even Stalinist) elements have little useful place in a modern, pluralistic and democratic political arena such as now exists in the new South Africa. Still, what was the catalyst for this significant and painful realization? The SACP faced both the global collapse of "international communism" and the domestic dismantling of apartheid in South Africa. This meant that on the one hand the SACP lost crucial material and moral support from the international communist community on which it had relied for decades. On the other hand, the new South African situation offered rich and rare opportunities for real growth for the party. The SACP rose to this challenge on both accounts, though as we shall see, it took much better advantage of the domestic situation than the international one.

Though the mid–1980s reformist accession of Soviet General Secretary Mikhail Gorbachev may have prompted the leaders of the SACP to consider the need for ideological change, they moved slowly because any such changes would incur real political (and even material) costs, both from internal friction and external opposition. All communist parties struggle with the burden of being branded non-orthodox, "revisionist," or even "deviationist." Though such terms are already mostly part of the past history of world communism, the few remaining viable communist parties still take these words seriously; the SACP itself has utilized such terms in the past. Given the conformity of some forms of ideology, "ideological purity" remains a crucial issue for a communist party like the SACP.

But is the SACP ideologically "pure" by anyone's standards? Of course it all depends on how one defines purity: after more than one hundred years of Marxist communism, there is yet no clear definition. There is so-called Orthodox Marxism, but it has a specific, historical definition that has little to do with the parties and ideologies of the late 20th and early 21st centuries.[1] There is also the problem that almost every "communist party" claims to be Marxist and/or Leninist.[2] As a matter of fact, most modern communist parties claim to be specifically Marxist-Leninist, not just Marxist.[3] The junction is justified, the "Marxist-Leninists" argue, by the assertion that Lenin completed the Marxist canon by joining to it his theory of the vanguard elite, which carries the revolution to its fruition. "Leninism" at once identifies the catalytic agent of change and sets out the operational charter of that change. Still, as Leninism expert and my former professor John Kautsky pointed out in the late 1960s, Leninism is not orthodox Marxism, but more of a form of leftist developmental strategy (Kautsky, *Communism*).

These ambiguities notwithstanding, we shall accept as much as possible the definition of Marxist-Leninism (a.k.a. Leninism) as Lenin himself espoused it.[4] This would include such basic Marxist concepts as dialectical materialism, the class struggle as the engine of history, and the proletarian revolution. However, "Leninism" came to add or emphasize such matters as capitalist imperialism, the need to fight wars of national liberation, the possibility of having a socialist revolution in a "transitional" (developing) nation such as Russia of 1917,[5] and the importance of a vanguard party, which would lead and educate the proletariat. The SACP[6] adopted this form of Leninism in 1921 when it was formed out of a grouping of socialist and leftist organizations.[7] It is also the Leninism that the SACP would begin systematically to deconstruct in the late 1980s to create what I call "neo–Leninism."

To properly understand the role of ideology when discussing the SACP, some historical background is necessary. Though all political parties have some core ideology that changes over time, it is usually not central to understanding most parties' histories. The SACP, like most communist parties, not only has ideology at its center, but there is no way to avoid ideology when examining the party closely. Over the years, the SACP has chosen and has been forced to change tenets of this all-important ideological core.

Historical Context

In 1921, soon after the creation of the SACP, the party already had to adapt to the newly-formed Soviet Comintern's definition of "communism," since many of its new members were part of leftist groups that were hardly Marxist, let alone Leninist. Still, from the very beginning the SACP was one of *the* most orthodox Leninist (and later Stalinist) parties.[8] Dries van Heerden once described the SACP as "the 'most Stalinist' party outside of Albania," with Albania once being infamous in this regard (van Heerden 5). Noted historians Ellis and Sechaba added, "The South African Communist Party has throughout its history closely, at times almost totally, agreed with the brand of Marxism-Leninism applied by the government of the Soviet Union.... South African communists were among the more loyal devotees of Stalin and Stalinism" (Ellis and Sechaba 9).

In 1928, the SACP was bluntly instructed by the Comintern that its policies had been "incorrect" and even "racist,"[9] and that from then on it was to infiltrate the African National Congress (ANC) and use it as a vehicle for an eventual socialist revolution. Though this would become the primary strategy for the SACP for decades, the SACP was initially shocked by the new Comintern policy of "an independent native South African republic, as a stage towards a workers' and peasants' government" (Johns 200). Still, the SACP did make this first major ideological adaptation, and thereafter the ANC "became the target of constant communist infiltration" (Bardis 102). Though the word "infiltration" is somewhat loaded, neither the SACP nor the ANC itself deny the dual-membership nature of many of the people in both parties, even today.

This prescription definitely fit the Leninist concept that indigenous liberation organizations were to be used by both local communists and the Comintern to hit international capitalism at its weakest link: its colonial system. Eventually, the local communist party was either to peacefully co-opt or forcibly overthrow the nationalist (and by definition, bourgeois) native organization and initiate the socialist stage of the revolution. This whole idea would be referred to as the "Two Stage Theory" by the SACP. The two stages would consist first of a bourgeois-democratic nationalist revolution (led by the ANC) and then a socialist one (led by the SACP). "The SACP, and its adherents within the ANC, see the National Democratic Revolution [NDR] as the first step toward socialist revolution" (Bardis 104). Though often condemned by "ultra-leftist" organizations for not pushing immediately for socialism, the SACP believed that a premature leap to socialism would be dangerous:

> To weaken this unity [of the ANC/SACP alliance] by placing the attainment of socialism on the immediate agenda would, in fact, be to postpone the very attainment of socialist transformation...
> Victory in the national democratic revolution is ... the most direct route to socialism and ultimately communism ["Path to Power" 105, 108].

Though those quotes are from 1990, the SACP still holds that position. The SACP has held on to this model, changing it almost not at all, even after the 1994 All Race Elections or at its last congress in 2012.[10]

Though the SACP remained steadfast to its ideas about the *timing* of the revolution, it did move beyond classical Leninism when it adopted aspects of Stalinism (as did the CPSU itself).[11] After being noticed by the Comintern in 1928, the SACP came under its influence in the 1930s. Though it would be a slight overstatement to say the Comintern overtly controlled the parties with which it had contact, it certainly came close to doing so with the SACP in the early to mid–1930s. Just as in the Soviet Union, the SACP "purged" itself of "rightists" and then later, "ultraleft elements," in a vain search for "ideological purity."[12] All of this was under orders from the Comintern (which really meant the CPSU and ultimately Stalin himself) as that organization moved from policy reversal to policy reversal during the 1930s and 1940s, so as to keep up with changing world conditions (due mostly to the rise fascism in a number of countries and eventually World War II).

There is no need to go into details here, but suffice it to say that the Comintern put the SACP and many other communist parties through the proverbial wringer. They were to reject other leftist parties (i.e., Social Democrats) in the early 1930s; then they were to reverse this policy and form "United Fronts" with such parties to fight fascism. Then, they were to support the shocking Nazi-Soviet Non-Aggression Pact of 1939, but soon after, to fight world fascism again after the Nazi invasion of the Soviet Union in 1941.

Finally, the parties were ordered to attack the Western democracies during the beginnings of the Cold War (*SACP 10th Congress* 19). Needless to say, such ideological gymnastics did not help these communist parties' local causes or the chances for a genuine world socialist revolution. The SACP's moral and organizational structure suffered deeply during this period, and it would not regain its strength until the late 1940s.

Though the 1940s saw minor changes to the SACP's ideology and some major structural changes, overall it was not until 1950 and passage of the nationalist government's Communist Suppression Act that the SACP changed significantly. Until then, it had a won a few parliamentary seats in the Cape Province, using its legal status to its fullest. But with its national banning, the SACP was forced deep underground for the next forty years, a period during which and as noted the party changed its name from the Communist Party of South Africa (CPSA) to the South African Communist Party (SACP). It is also when it lost most of its members, especially the least dedicated, due to the strains of underground political activity and the severe punishments the new nationalist regime was handing out to "communists" and other "subversives."

This situation reduced the SACP to a small, hard-core group of leaders determined to continue the fight against the racist and capitalist regime of the nationalists.[13] During the late 1930s and 1940s, the SACP and its members had succeeded in joining (and/or infiltrating) the ANC. The ANC served as *the* front for the SACP, since the ANC itself would not be banned for another decade.[14] During the 1950s various other fronts, such as the Congress of Democrats, would be used by the SACP to help liberate South Africa from what it called "Colonialism of a Special Type."

This term refers to the fact that, unlike other ex-colonial developing states, the "imperial master" of South Africa did not rule from a distant metropole (London or Paris), but from within the very country itself. The whites, both of English and Dutch descent, "colonized" South Africa and dominated the local "tribes" of blacks. Unlike other African countries which had relatively few local whites, South Africa had a large and deeply rooted white population within its borders, most of whom were Afrikaners of Dutch descent. When South Africa gained its independence from Britain in 1910, the indigenous blacks did not gain home rule (as India did in 1949) but the white Afrikaners did, and they continued to rule the native populations for the next eighty-four years. Thus, South Africa, according to the SACP, was still under a form of colonialism, this time locally. The SACP, therefore, dedicated itself to overthrow this special type of colonialism. The historian A. Lerumo explained:

> As its immediate and foremost task, the South African Communist Party works for a united front of national liberation.... The destruction of colonialism ... is the essential condition and key for future advance to the supreme aim of the communist party: the establishment of a Socialist South Africa, laying the foundation of a classless, communist society [Lerumo 107].

Still, this meant aligning with the leftist (but not communist) ANC nationalist organization.

How long this alliance would be needed was not clear either to the SACP or the ANC at that point; only after long decades did this alliance eventually take power in 1994. For most of that time, the SACP would change little of its ideology or structure. The fight for the "democratic national revolution" would last thirty years and would require few adaptations for the SACP. The current generations of communist leaders, even the more liberal reformers, were shaped by this period and refer to it as their ideological benchmark. Therefore, we shall spend some time looking at this "classic" period of SACP ideology, and only then examine the huge changes that would be forced upon the SACP in the late 1980s and brought to final form in the 1990s.

The Long Struggle

By 1960 the nationalist regime had decided that all major forms of opposition to its regime, including the ANC and SACP, must have its roots in "Godless communism."[15] This meant more political bannings, including the ANC this time, and thus both the SACP and ANC would now have to operate underground. This political, and ultimately structural, change also affected the SACP's policies. One of the more significant changes made at the very start of this period was the decision to *overthrow*, not just change, the regime. Thus a new armed guerrilla organization, Umkhonto we Sizwe (MK), was created by both the ANC and SACP to overthrow the regime through the use of violence.[16] As noted in the last chapter, MK was led more by the SACP than was the ANC itself (Lodge 240).[17] With this structural (the creation of MK) and ideological (the authorization of the use of violence to overthrow the regime) change, the makeup of the SACP was to be set for the next thirty years. This baseline became what is now the standard ideology of the SACP.

From 1960 until 1990, the SACP had a relatively standard form of Marxism-Leninism, mixed with aspects of traditional Stalinism. This standard ideology included the already noted Two Stage Theory of revolution, in which it would align with the predominant nationalist organization (the ANC) to overthrow the (special) colonial masters (first the English imperialists, then the Afrikaner nationalists). Then at some later, undefined point, it would move to the second and socialist stage of the revolution. It also perceived itself as a vanguard party that would lead and educate the workers so as to facilitate a revolution—all very Leninist in perspective.

The SACP also bought into other standard Leninist organizational conceptions, doing both legal and illegal activities until 1950, and thereafter with a strictly secret, underground operation that used "cells" and tight security.[18] The SACP also unquestionably bought into the Leninist concept of international communist solidarity. This resulted in unswerving support for Soviet domestic *and* foreign policy for decades, including such controversial acts as the Soviet internal purges and such widely condemned foreign policy moves as the invasions of Hungary and Czechoslovakia.

Like the Eurocommunist parties of the 1970s and later, the SACP did occasionally voice doubts about Soviet policy. However, unlike the Spanish and Italian communist parties, the SACP never really followed up on these doubts about the Soviet Union and its policies until the late 1980s. Even then, long-time SACP leader Joe Slovo may have been rewriting his own history when he stated in 1991 that "as far back as 1970 we rejected the Stalinist concept of a party which was a monopoly of wisdom and a natural and exclusive right to lead its constituency" (Slovo, "Beyond the Stereotype," 2). Later in 1992, he asserted, "My disenchantment [with the Soviet systems] was a long process beginning with Khrushchev's secret speech in 1956" (Daniels 21). But Slovo himself admitted that none of the SACP leaders were nearly critical enough of the Soviet Union (Wren 1).

Still, in 1989, the SACP's important Path to Power program added, "Some of these negative tendencies [of the USSR] also affected communist parties around the world, including our own" ("Path to Power" 79). This all may be true, but I have found no other relevant evidence of these doubts in any other sources, even in the SACP's own archival material (to which I had full access for this book). More to the point, even if some of the SACP's leaders had reservations about the more egregious Soviet acts during this period, the party as an organization did little to condemn or move away from the Soviet sphere, either ideologically or materially.

As for Stalinism, which is an extension of Leninism,[19] the SACP fit this model only to a degree (contrary to what some of its more biased critics would claim). The SACP certainly conformed to it during the 1930s by undertaking internal and often irrational purges, not unlike those in Soviet Union (though to a much lesser magnitude). The SACP also accepted the Stalinist idea of

"Socialism in One Country," which is probably the least Marxist aspect of 20th-century communism.[20] The SACP has even dallied with personality cults, both with Stalin and with its own leaders to a small extent.[21]

Still, in contrast to most other communist parties, the SACP cautiously bought the 1950s Khrushchevian formula of condemning the "excesses" of Stalin and Stalinism while almost never condemning the Soviet system as a whole or even criticizing Leninism.[22] As noted earlier, the SACP did criticize some Soviet actions, but such criticism was always qualified and never of a systemic nature until the 1990s. As Slovo stated in 1992, "You must remember that there is more to the Soviet Union than labor camps. It was the pioneer of free education, free health care, housing for workers and security of employment ... and welfare capitalism was a response to the Soviet example." Slovo also made the point that "the Soviet Union was the only consistent friend we had." He so much as admitted that the SACP was naturally reluctant to be critical of its patron, the USSR (Daniels 21).

Thus, the party did not overtly criticize its patron the USSR, remaining for decades an excellent example of a developing-nation Marxist-Leninist party. Though the SACP was slightly more integrated with its "national liberation ally" (the ANC) than were other communist parties in similar situations, if anything this degree of cooperation was an asset. The party deviated little from the "party line" of international communism during this three-decade period. Even though neither it nor the ANC ever came close to taking power before 1990, the SACP was satisfied that its ideology was appropriate and correct for the "objective conditions" the party faced. But this supreme confidence in its own ideological foundations would be tested and found wanting by the late 1980s. Between the relatively quick collapse of communism in Eastern Europe and the willingness of the nationalist regime in South Africa to negotiate, the SACP quickly faced an entirely new environment in the early 1990s. To face this novel situation appropriately, the SACP saw the need to change both petty and fundamental aspects of its ideology.

The New SACP

Where does all this leave the SACP? It has indeed changed some of its basic ideological planks since its 1990 unbanning by the nationalists.[23] How and why the ban was lifted is for another chapter, as are the effects of the collapse of international communism, but all these factors *forced* the SACP to reexamine some of its basic ideological assumptions. But before we go into the details of these ideological changes, we must ask a more basic question: does the SACP still qualify as a Marxist-Leninist party?

This is not just an academic or semantic question; it is a political issue. Not only does the SACP itself take such terminology very seriously, but so do the party's allies and enemies. For decades, both whites and blacks, liberals and conservatives, were taught that the SACP and/or communism was the "true threat" to South Africa. Though the ANC was often and incorrectly seen as a mere puppet of the SACP, it was still seen as at least less "heinous" than its "communist ally" by both right-wing critics and even the South African mainstream media. With this in mind, the term "Marxist-Leninist" does take on special significance. It is not just a title but a symbol of something much larger. There is also the fact that many former Marxist-Leninist parties have indeed become social democratic.[24]

On the one hand, it appears that the SACP has indeed dropped some pretensions of being a classic Marxist-Leninist party by accepting standard democratic norms, such as abiding by elections and becoming a mass party. As historian Colin Bundy stated, "In policy terms, the party has embraced multi-party democracy freedoms of speech, press, association and worship; its spokespersons champion a mixed economy" (Bundy 62). Joe Slovo said so himself in a 1992 interview: "I have been in favor of a multi-party system for many years now.... I was never impressed by the so-called socialism of Angola and Mozambique ... subjectively, I never thought it worked" (Daniels 21). And as the SACP made clear in its own journal, *African Communist*, "Even the most hostile of our critics were compelled to admit that [the 8th Congress of the SACP] was a Congress that witnessed unprecedented openness and democratic debate" ("Eighth Party Congress" 1).[25]

However, before the SACP is mistaken for a conventional Western-style party, a representative quote from Slovo indicates how much the SACP still admired very undemocratic role models in 1990: "Socialism produced a Stalin and a Ceausecu, but it also produced a Lenin and a Gorbachev" (Slovo 1990, 26). It does no violence to the facts to group Stalin and Lenin as dedicated antidemocrats; even Gorbachev, who helped bring about the collapse of the Soviet system, still sought to preserve the role and privileges of the CPSU. Still, real ideological changes did happen to the SACP in the late 1980s and early 1990s.

In 1992, a writer for the *African Communist* also showed how the SACP still thought. Though he condemned Stalin and "statism," he managed to praise Lenin in the same breath:

The state was seen, no longer as a strategic instrument for the transformation of society, but as an absolute and a fetish.... Ideological tendencies to statism existed in certain Marxists circles in Russia.... Lenin's state and revolution ... [also] reveals some of the features of statism.... [And] there was Trotsky's "militarisation of trade unions." [Finally] there was Stalin's theory of the "revolution from above." The monster of bureaucracy grew.... A warped and distorted type of socialism held sway.... [Still Lenin] was a truly committed, principled and selfless leader of the working people.... He rightly deserves to be singled out and honored.... It is crucial that we look at the Marxist-Leninist body of theory.... to remove the blot of the Stalinist legacy once and for all [Roji 55].

But as late as 2012, the SACP made clear it was still a Marxist-Leninist party that wanted a socialist South Africa, though it fully supported the current democratic model (*Political Report* 1). This split worldview, where Stalin can be a villain while Lenin remains (mostly) a hero, is the formula that the SACP started to use in the late 1980s and is still used today (and to be fair, many other far leftist scholars take a similar stance). Later, after the 1991 Soviet coup, some "liberals" within the SACP did go even further, criticizing Lenin while maintaining faith in Marx.

As we shall see in detail below, the basic tenets of Marxism-Leninism (class struggle, dialectical materialism, vanguardism, and belief in socialism) are still dear to the SACP. Therefore, even though the SACP has indeed begun to find favor with some aspects of Western democracy (i.e., belief in a peaceful, multiparty political system), overall it is still a Marxist party, and in many ways also a Leninist one. It is true, though, that it seems to have removed *all* aspects of Stalinism (purges, authoritarianism, cults of personality, etc.).[26]

It must be admitted that while the SACP itself is the first to point out that it indeed has changed positions on some key issues, this in itself is not a repudiation of its basic Marxism-Leninism. Many communist parties, including the SACP, have often argued that Marxism-Leninism should have never been seen as a dogma but as a guiding ideology and method. As then Deputy General Secretary Cronin stated in 1990:

We must ... take Marxism-Leninism seriously as a science, in other words, a living body of theory.... The scientific basis of Marxism-Leninism does not rest on the infallibility of three outstanding personalities. Marx, Engels and Lenin certainly never claimed to be infallible. They argued strongly that knowledge is always relative.... Lenin constantly revised many of his own perspectives—yes, the very first "revisionist" of Leninism was often Lenin himself [Cronin 1990, 12].

The SACP also invited CPSU members to write in to its journal the *African Communist* on ideological matters. One such correspondence was from Slava Tetekhin, who wrote:

During the Stalin Purges in the 1930s, communists ... were killed. The Communist Party [of the Soviet Union], in the Leninist sense of its functions and tasks, was destroyed.... A set of dogmas presented as "Marxism-Leninism" ... [which then] constituted the ideological backbone of the system. Millions of people were, in fact, denied the knowledge of real Marxism-Leninism.... Marxism-Leninism was never intended to be a set of timeless dogmas [Tetekhin 16].

Thus, from the viewpoint of the SACP, the collapse of the East Bloc was not a condemnation of Marxism-Leninism, but only a rejection of Stalinism and its abuses. Orthodox Marxists would of course go farther, arguing that the Soviet system was never even Marxist per se, though the SACP would not go that far.

Such Marxist-Leninists can and do argue that their ideology is almost infinitely flexible (or, as they would say, dialectical). With this in mind, even fundamental changes in policy are in no way a contradiction but merely the proper readjustment of tactical details to fit the ever-changing objective conditions. On the surface, this all does make sense and has often appeared to ease the minds of the rank and file when major ideological changes are made by the leadership of communist parties, including the SACP.

Nevertheless, there is a point where one must question the claim that some major change is just a "significant tactical maneuver" and not truly a fundamental ideological change. It is not just a matter of degree, but a question of what Marxism-Leninism *is* exactly. The point was made earlier that there is no one set definition for Marxism or Leninism, but as already shown there are some basic tenets of both systems, and these have been upheld by the SACP since the 1920s. With that in mind, I will argue that regardless of the fact that Marxism-Leninism does admittedly have some built-in flexibility, one can in fact argue whether a communist party has (or has not) deviated from a common and historical ground.

The SACP's Marxist elements have changed the least. If anything, the SACP has rediscovered Marxism without its Stalinist, and at times Leninist, additions. Slovo made this clear. "Marxism in all its essential respects, remains valid and provides an indispensable theoretical guide to achieve a society free of all forms of exploitation of person by person" (Monteiro 29). This is nothing new. The Social Democrats of the 1920s and the Eurocommunists of the 1970s did the same ideological and political maneuver as they jettisoned the more violent and radical elements of their ideology for the sake of adapting to new environments, and not coincidentally to gain more votes, as the SACP may do one day.

Such terms as "class struggle," "dialectical materialism," and the like have taken on a seemingly greater importance for the SACP. Not unlike President Mikhail Gorbachev when he denounced Stalinism and rejuvenated Leninism in the collapsing Soviet Union, the SACP has taken similar action while stressing its Marxist (and sometimes its Leninist) credentials that much more. SACP leaders argue that this is not a cynical political move to cut their losses after the collapse of international communism, but just an adaptation to new conditions while still maintaining basic Marxist and Leninist tenets. This does seem to be the case. Still, though the SACP and all communist parties have claimed to be Marxist, they have rejected (or "modified") key concepts of orthodox Marxism.

One of these tenets, that the world proletarian revolution would begin in the industrialized West, was obviously discarded by Lenin himself when he led a socialist revolution in backward, developing Russia (though he would argue that he was starting a worldwide socialist revolution that would spread to the West, thus only modifying the Marxist prediction; Stalin would disregard even this with his theory of "Socialism in One Country"). Another, that the party would be a facilitator of an already class-consciousness proletariat, was also dropped as Lenin developed his "vanguard party" to *lead* the proletariat. The SACP also adopted these positions.

Leninists claim that a socialist revolution can indeed occur in a less developed nation like Russia, because of the factors that make it the weak link in the system of international capital. This does make sense, and did indeed happen, but still this turns orthodox Marxism on its head, since Marx unquestionably argued that his form of socialism could only occur, let alone continue, in a highly industrialized nation; it was the next step after fully developed capitalism. It must be added that Marx made it clear that the *material* conditions had to be just right for a proper socialist revolution to succeed; such conditions existed only in the highly industrialized West.

This means that Leninists not only disagree with Marx on where a socialist revolution can happen, but also under what conditions. The SACP still holds that a socialist revolution can indeed (and will) still occur in a less developed nation such as South Africa, but it now argues that the ANC needs to lead a capitalist stage of development to improve the material/objective conditions of the nation so as to allow for an eventual socialist transformation. Other orthodox Leninist parties have also started to admit that indeed Marx was correct when he argued that material conditions were ultimately the foundation for what he called the "objective" needs of a socialist revolution. As the historic ANC/SACP Morogoro Declaration of 1969 stated so clearly:

Untimely, ill planned or premature manifestations of violence impede and do not advance the prospect for revolutionary change and are clearly counter-revolutionary. It is obvious therefore that policy and organizational structures must grow out of the real situation if they are not to become meaningless clichés [Morogoro Document 5].

This is where the SACP is indeed correct to point out that this is no change in policy or ideology. It has almost always believed in the Two Stage Theory. But the change in emphasis is still important.

Earlier, the first stage, consisting of ANC-led democratic-capitalist rule, was seen as more of a necessity, a political reality that would be done and forgotten as soon as possible. Now the SACP stresses the economic-developmental aspects of the first stage, arguing often how only when objective conditions are met can a socialist stage begin.[27] There is no fundamental ideological change here, but the emphasis is much different and important. The SACP is now one of the major supporters of the current capitalist regime of the ANC. Is this a betrayal of the socialist revolution? Though some ultra-leftists (anarchists, Stalinist split-off groups, radical unionists, etc.) definitely believe it is, the SACP correctly points out that the objective conditions are not currently conducive to a socialist transformation of South Africa (and also argues that if it were tried prematurely, unwanted party dictatorship and eventual collapse would result, like in the old Soviet Union). This takes us is to the SACP's modified views on the party and the proletariat.

Again, a more orthodox Marxist position has been taken on this touchy issue. Though all Leninist parties claim to be following the wishes of the workers they are attempting to liberate from capitalism, they also add that the party must lead the proletariat (and often the peasant masses, thus the hammer and sickle) because their consciousness has not yet sufficiently developed. Some Leninists, especially the Maoists, go further and state that such consciousness can be created and enriched through proper party leadership and policies. As a matter of fact, China's infamous Chairman Mao went so far as to argue that "will" can overcome objective conditions; this obviously turns orthodox Marxism (and its materialist basis) totally on its head (Mao 2012). But most Leninists, including the SACP, do not agree with this aspect of Maoism (and due to the Sino-Soviet Split of the 1960s had very little to do with "Red China" until the late 1990s).

Marx argued that a proletarian revolution could only occur when the workers did indeed obtain enough class consciousness through their struggle with the bourgeoisie and thus could see their own class interests in overthrowing the capitalist system. To argue that a party needs to lead, let alone imbed, class consciousness into the proletariat is hardly Marxism. According to Marx, this consciousness can only be created or shaped by the material conditions to which the workers are exposed to, such as the factory with its harsh conditions, concentrations of fellow workers, and the like. Neither a communist party (nor anyone else) can create or even stimulate consciousness within any class. Only the objective conditions, as the Marxists themselves call them, can create this new consciousness.

Yet this is where the "new" SACP fits in, for it too now stresses the need to allow the proletariat in South Africa to gain more of a class consciousness. This will be accomplished by allowing the ANC to enact its capitalist (though still leftist) public policies, which will in turn force the workers to see the need for a true socialist revolution (or "transition," as the SACP now calls it). And while process unfolds, the SACP's function is to recruit this slowly awakening proletariat into the party.

While the Russian Bolsheviks recruited only the most dedicated among the proletariat, the SACP has begun to do mass recruiting much like the German Social Democrats of the late 19th century. Then Deputy General Secretary Cronin of the SACP has also argued that the party will remain a vanguard while becoming a mass party:

> Lenin never ceased conceiving of [the party] as a vanguard formation. But what character it should assume in order to fulfill this role was something on which he changed his perspective.... In July 1990 we launched the SACP as a legal formation under two main banners: "build the workers' vanguard," and "build the mass party" [Cronin 1990, 17].

Technically, Cronin was right: a current party of 160,000 can be as much a vanguard party as one of 3,000 back in 1990. But it seems somewhat counterintuitive to argue that a vanguard party can also be a mass party: is the party leading the masses or does it consist of them? The SACP, since 1990, is definitely moving toward the mass model. Though it is hardly equal in size to its ally, the 640,000-member ANC, the shift to mass recruiting is certainly a sign of significant ideological (and structural) change.

Since 1950, the SACP had been a traditional, developing-nation communist party in structure. This meant that it was a mostly underground, highly secretive, cell-based party with little interparty democracy and a full belief in Leninist "democratic centralism." Most of this changed by the 1980s. In 1990, the no longer banned SACP boldly decided that it would once again become a mass party (which it technically was before 1950), openly recruiting members and supporters. Mass parties form to compete in a democratic system, something the "old" SACP would not have tried to do even if it had been legal.[28] Jumping from a few thousand members to more than 160,000 is not only a genuine accomplishment but also a reflection of the SACP's popularity in South Africa (Lodge 1983, 172). It also shows that though the SACP still remains somewhat secretive,[29] overall it does appear to be devoted to participating openly in a pluralistic, democratic system (albeit with some justified reservations due to the still polarized South African political culture).[30]

The party leadership has not only decided that a small, underground party is not necessary, which is probably true, but that instead of "leading" the masses, it must cultivate them. In general, this fits the more democratic emphasis that the party is now pushing. But it also means that it is relying on a more Marxist view of what a communist party should do, and less on a Leninist model of its role. Finally, we shall also see that the adoption of a mass party model will allow the SACP to fully incorporate itself, one day, into the electoral system (which it again debated doing in 2012, a matter to which we will return to in later chapters). These structural changes are only some of the many changes the SACP has started to make, including the adoption of interparty democracy, open membership lists, and the like.[31]

Such democratic reforms will likely bring in more and more members from the working class, but will they allow the party to remain a *Leninist* vanguard party? In other contexts, "vanguard" can mean almost anything, but in the Leninist tradition one must question if the current transformations will allow the party to keep this designation. Now, losing such a title could be an asset, as the party takes on an identity with less of an elitist and dictatorial stamp and returns to Marxist roots. But sacrificing any tradition has its costs, especially during a period of upheaval. Moreover, high-ranking party members have disagreed with this trend (Roads 1992). The late Harry Gwala, a so-called Stalinist within the SACP, summed it up well:

> Thus we have come to a crossroads. Either a Marxist-Leninist party has the vanguard role of mobilizing all the working class and its allies the peasants and the middle class and leading them into a National Democratic Revolution headed by the African National Congress, or it becomes an amorphous mess which allows in all and sundry and works towards reforming capitalism into "democratic socialism" [Gwala 1991, 10].

Gwala was not alone in making this critique. As a disgusted leftist critic (who later resigned from the SACP) stated, "I think that our leadership has degenerated into a petty bourgeoisie aspiring to get into a bourgeois parliament at all cost…. The leadership sees negotiations as the only terrain of struggle" (Molaba 16). Even the term "democratic socialism" is dreaded and even the more liberal members of the SACP now avoid the term, if not the ideology and policies associated with it. Why that is will be explored below.

So, what does the SACP now hold as its canon? First, in spite of the dissenters, the party still holds that it is indeed the "vanguard of the revolutionary proletariat." This classic Leninist position, though, has always been tempered by the Two Stage Theory of the SACP, and has now, if anything, become even more conditional. The SACP may be the so-called vanguard of the proletariat, but it has always stressed that the ANC is the leader of the national liberation movement, and that the ANC is made up of many classes, including the proletariat but also middle-class liberals, poor farmers, and so on. Now that the ANC has been in power for decades, to say that the ANC is in charge is literally to state the obvious. But the SACP still sees itself as the special protector of the proletariat (workers) and the would-be midwife of the socialist stage of the revolution.

Thus the SACP still sees itself as the vanguard of the proletariat, but with so many conditions and qualifications that one must still question what "vanguard" really means. Is it the workers' voice in a coalition government? The SACP's answer is yes, but some workers seem to disagree. In the early 1990s, the National Union of Mineworkers (NUM; the largest union in the SACP's ally COSATU) actually suggested that the unions leave the Tripartite Alliance of the ANC/SACP/COSATU. NUM argued that the unions could be co-opted into betraying the workers' interests once the ANC ruled the nation and would begin to placate all the classes within South Africa. NUM's conclusion: that a new "workers' party" might be necessary to represent the proletariat's needs.

The SACP carefully and respectfully disagreed, making the straightforward, though simple, argument that it was the only party the workers needed. More recently, the National Union of Metalworkers of South Africa (NUMSA) made similar arguments against the ANC, its centrist economic policies, and even the SACP, suggesting the need for a new and true "workers' party" (Masondo 29). However, the fact that NUM or NUMSA even looked into such an option indicates that the SACP either took seriously its pledge not to interfere with the unions, or that it was unable to stop the debate in the first place (Lodge 1983, 174).

These incidents demonstrated that the SACP's rather close and sometimes messy relationship with the ANC can obscure its role as the workers' "vanguard party." There is a core contradiction in the SACP's many roles that cannot readily be ignored. If the SACP is a loyal ally to the ANC, it will use its influence with the unions and workers to get them to agree to the ANC regime's line (which may not always serve the working class, since the ANC is a multiclass party ruling a multiclass nation). But if the SACP pushes class politics as a proletarian vanguard party and stands by the workers' needs, it will inevitably come in conflict with the ANC government and its need to balance various economic and class interests, as any ruling party must within a democratic-capitalist context.

Granted, even the Bolsheviks themselves had to align with parties and forces that were not in favor of the early Soviet regime. When the Bolsheviks aligned with the left Social Revolutionaries against the more bourgeois Kadets and Kerensky regime, Lenin had to balance his priorities carefully. Also, during the 1930s United Front Period, the very Leninist (and even Stalinist) German communists also had to work with the (then hated) Social Democrats against the Nazis and other conservative parties. Still, few communist parties have had to work closely with a radical but still nonsocialist ally for decades, as the SACP has done with the ANC; even fewer have taken power with said ally. The SACP, in contrast, is in the very unique situation of actually working with a victorious national liberation organization.

One of the few times that this kind of collaboration happened previously was when the Chinese Communist Party (CCP) worked with the Chinese Nationalists (KMT) in the 1920s, but this eventually resulted in a slaughter for the communists in China by 1928 (Checa 151). This is not to suggest in any way that the ANC plans to attack the SACP. But it is true that though both parties reaffirm their alliance at various times, both also reserve the right to disagree with each other's policies. It is fair to suggest that these disagreements will only grow as the ANC settles into its role as the leftist (but not socialist) ruling party of a multiclass society. The SACP, if it is to remain a worker's party and not just the ANC's radical left-wing (which it itself denies is its role), must move away from the ANC's ever-more-centrist policies (and, some even argue, right-of-center). How these contradictions are working out will be covered in the next chapter in detail. For now, it needs to be kept in mind that the SACP itself is playing a balancing act between its role as the workers' vanguard and as the ally of the multiclass ANC. However, in doing so, it lessens its claim to be a true "vanguard party." With that noted, what of other classical Leninist positions, how does the SACP stand on them?

On the question of imperialism, the SACP is on stronger ideological ground when it claims it is still Leninist. Though it has used a modified version of Lenin's theory for many decades, as noted above as "Colonialism of a Special Type,"[32] the SACP continues to accept, unmodified, the core tenets of Lenin's imperialism theory ("Path to Power" 88). The SACP still sees capitalist imperialism as *the* problem for the world, as has every communist party since the early 1920s. Though Western economics and political science have dismissed much of Lenin's ideas on "economic imperialism,"[33] communist parties have never accepted these critiques. Some communist parties more than others have bought into the theory of imperialism,[34] but all of them to one degree or another have accepted the premise that international capitalism has caused much of the ills of the planet, from climate change to gross poverty to wars that kill millions of people.

The SACP has always and still sees capitalist imperialism as the major cause of human suffering in most of the world. The SACP explains most human events through the internationalization of the class conflict that Lenin's thesis on imperialism proposes. Though such references have somewhat lessened in recent years, this is more due to the fact the SACP has concentrated more on domestic affairs due to its sudden rise in influence within South Africa. Still, the SACP explains many domestic events within an international context, as do many Marxists and Leninists. Though this traditional form of Marxist internationalism does have its advantages over many other simplistic and often conspiratorial theories that various developing nation's leaders often espouse (see Venezuela or Iran for most of the 2000s), it still has its limits.

Some of the more salient points of Marxist ideas on economic imperialism are relevant for the SACP today. One of them, that the "North" (West) really does exploit the "South" (developing world), is crucial for the SACP and South Africa. Both white and black citizens seemingly distrust "international capital." Connections between the old nationalist regime and international capitalism, especially with the diamond trade, have often been cited in the media.[35] Even many white, conservative Afrikaners see conspiracies behind every multinational corporation, both domestic and (especially) foreign ones.[36] So whether the theory of economic imperialism is objectively "correct" or not, it must be addressed since it is a popular idea in South Africa, and not just among SACP members.

Still, none of this is why the SACP holds onto this seemingly outdated economic theory (at least within Western academia). Adherence to an economic theory that has been rejected by most Western countries tells a lot about the SACP and South Africa. It indicates that though the SACP has modified and/or dropped some basic tenets of Leninism, it still holds onto others quite tightly, regardless of the facts and theories held by most (though not all) Western economists. Why? This is where South Africa and its situation come into the picture. Many nations seemingly fit the Leninist model of economic imperialism and South Africa is one of them. Though external "imperialism" was minimal, the fact that "white" (i.e., Western) companies dominated the country for centuries cannot be disputed. Anglo-American, the largest conglomerate in the country, still holds a huge block of the capitalization of the Johannesburg Stock Exchange (Anglo-American 1). This is what the SACP calls "Special Colonialism," and it appears so self-evident to many people that the SACP would have a hard time convincing its own members, let alone the masses, that economic imperialism was *not* a reality. Black/white economic disparities are just that stark in South Africa. Thus, the political and economic environment reinforces whatever pre-existing ideas the SACP had on the issue of imperialism. But there is another reason, related to the international situation, the SACP has held on to theories of imperialism.

As will be detailed below, the SACP was part of an international network of communist parties. Though some communist parties were more integrated into this network than others (say, the Vietnamese Workers Party versus the Nicaraguan Communist Party), as discussed the SACP was one of the more loyal Stalinist parties of the Comintern, and after the Comintern's dissolution in 1943,[37] the SACP remained extremely close to the Union of Soviet Socialist Republics (USSR) and the Communist Party of the Soviet Union (CPSU) that controlled it. Its ties to the Foreign Department of the CPSU are well documented and uncontested by all involved.[38] How does this relate to the SACP's theories on imperialism?

First, the Soviets required the Comintern member parties to accept the theory.[39] This went beyond simple requirements, however, for under Stalin the Soviets began to use the Comintern and its later manifestations as a blatant Soviet policy tool. This would mean that Soviet-aligned parties like the SACP tended to back Soviet foreign policy, which naturally in the Cold War years opposed "Western imperialism" throughout the world, including South Africa. Thus, both the domestic and international situations reinforced the SACP's position on imperialism.

Still, by the early 1990s such loyalty to what was left of "international communism" was not relevant. Starting in the mid–1980s with Soviet President Gorbachev's accession to power in the Soviet Union and ending with the coup against him in 1991, old-style communism in the East Bloc just ceased to exist. Though communism certainly still existed elsewhere (various parties in the developing world but also as states in Cuba, North Korea, Vietnam, and China), Western media and academia somewhat prematurely styled this as the "collapse of communism."[40] What it did mean for the SACP is that loyalty to Soviet communism became a moot issue. The SACP does still maintain ties to various leftist, socialist, and communist parties and organizations throughout the world; at its last congress in 2012, it had both Cuban and Chinese delegates at the forefront (*Political Report*).[41] Though this may one day constitute the embryonic core of some new form of the historic "International," the simple fact is that since 1991 the SACP cannot be accused of being an "agent of foreign powers," as it had been for so many years.[42]

So, the SACP still sees itself as a vanguard party and it believes in Lenin's imperialism theory. But does the SACP still adhere to one of the most basic beliefs of Marxist-Leninism, opposition to capitalism? The answer is an unqualified yes, but *how* it opposes capitalism is the key difference between the old and new SACP. The SACP has always and probably will always oppose capitalism, domestic and international, in principle. Even if it someday becomes some form of social democratic party, which it considered and rejected at the 8th Party Congress in the early 1990s,[43] it will still oppose what it perceives as the cruelty of the "free market." All far leftist parties critique and/or oppose capitalism to a degree, and all communist parties oppose it on a number of different levels, including its stress on private property, wasteful and cruel competition, and the commoditization of human beings. The SACP deviates from none of this.

For decades, the SACP has openly and strongly rejected capitalism as a way of organizing human society on economic, philosophical, and even racial grounds. Racism is not unique to South Africa, but apartheid was blamed on capitalism, which the SACP claims used race as a means to divide the proletariat.[44] As a matter of fact, the SACP's resolute opposition to capitalism had probably been the most consistent ideological position it has taken.

The real story, though, is how the SACP has opposed capitalism throughout its long history. This is where the SACP has most adapted its ideology to allow for its own survival in the democratic 1990s. At first, in the early 1920s, the SACP took the classical social democracy approach of organizing industrial workers (mostly whites at the time) against capital. Once it joined the more radical Comintern, the SACP became somewhat more conspiratorial but basically remained a workers' party. Only later did it become the stereotypical Leninist/Stalinist party, with its secrecy, international connections, and internal purges. This more Stalinist form emerged in the 1930s,[45] which meant that overall the rhetoric against capitalism also took on ever more radical and often violent forms. This radicalization on this issue would continue until it reached its logical conclusion in 1960, when the SACP and the ANC created the Umkhonto we Sizwe (MK) guerrilla organization that militarily fought the regime for thirty years.

From 1960 until 1990, the SACP officially backed the violent, revolutionary overthrow of the capitalist regime in South Africa. This involved various forms of guerrilla actions and terrorism, fighting in regional wars,[46] and infiltrating various domestic organizations.[47] In the 1960 declaration that created MK, the ANC/SACP alliance stated that the banning of the ANC "forced" them to move the fight from the legal dimension to a more covert, illegal one. For the SACP, this would involve more than just supporting and supplying MK, it would mean all sorts of domestic activities that could clearly be labeled "subversive" by all parties involved, not just the ruling nationalists. In any event, the move to create MK and all that it involved was not a simple one.

The ANC's decision to create a guerrilla organization was qualified, but as one author made clear, "In the SACP there was no equivocation on the issue.... Shortly after the lifting of the post–Sharpsville August 1960, the SACP leadership had resolved to create an armed force" (Barrell 5). In any case, both parties decided that the "bombings" would center on economic targets (power lines, factories, etc.). This conformed to Lenin's dictum that conventional terrorism was counterproductive (Laqueur 62). As terrorist expert Samuel Francis noted, "The communist statement endorsing violence but rejecting individual terrorism and refusing to reject non-violent forms of struggle is also perfectly consistent with the classical Leninist theory of revolutionary strategy" (Francis 60). In later years, though, MK would hit more and more human targets (though still not innocent bystanders, at least on purpose), not just economic ones. Still, this allowed the regime the predictable response of branding the SACP and ANC as "bloody terrorists" (Lodge 1983, 234). For the next three decades the SACP and its ANC ally would fight a classical Marxist-Leninist battle against a repressive, capitalist "colonial" regime.

Can it be said today that the SACP is still fighting such a battle? Of course not; everything has changed. The ANC/SACP officially suspended the violent aspect of their national liberation struggle soon after their unbanning in 1990, which meant that MK would soon be disbanded (and elements brought into the South African Defense Force, as it too was reformed). As the ANC/SACP alliance negotiated with the nationalist regime, the SACP made it clear that though the democratic path seemed to be the future for South Africa, it "reserved the right to resort to violence" (Cronin AT Interview 1995).

Why did the SACP agree to suspend this crucial trump card? The main reason is that its ally, the ANC, had been secretly negotiating with the nationalist regime for years and for the sake of further progress, the SACP decided to call off the "violent revolution," at least as the SACP had conceived of it for decades. Though there is no proof that there was a quid pro quo between de Klerk and Mandela, the fact that the ANC suspended the violence option soon after its unbanning by the government is probably no coincidence. The SACP could have split from this new nonviolent ANC, but this would have been a highly unlikely option for the much smaller SACP.[48] However, there was another reason that both the ANC and SACP moved away from the idea of a violent revolution against capitalist South Africa.

One word could sum up the ANC/SACP "revolution": failure. After almost thirty years of fighting a revolution against the nationalists and gaining little ground, at least militarily, they finally decided that another strategy was necessary. This is not to deny the crucial role that the 1980s policy of "ungovernability" played in forcing the regime and non–Africans in general in realizing that apartheid was doomed. But ungovernability, in fact, had little to do with MK, or any formal plan of the ANC or SACP. Not unlike the *Intifada* of the 1980s in the Occupied Areas in Palestine, where the Palestinian Liberation Organization (PLO) may have claimed credit but had little initially to do with it, the ANC nor the SACP could claim the uprisings in the townships were planned or even started by them (Contreras 39). So did the alliance really succeed in affecting the outcome of the struggle through violence?

Ultimately, the answer has to be no. It is true that as with ungovernability, MK attacks within South Africa did wear down the regime to a degree over the years, but never enough to come close to forcing the nationalists out of power. As analyst Michael Radu stated as late as 1987, "[MK] is still ineffective and numerically small" (Radu 68). Another critic commented, "The so-called struggle 'waged' by [MK] proved to be a charade" (Mokonyane 129). It is true that the military activities of MK in Angola did have an impact on the nationalist regime by helping the Angola government to bloody the vaunted South African Defense Force (SADF). Yet even this success was not unqualified.

First, the SADF was most severely damaged by Cuban and/or Angolan forces, not those of the MK. Also, MK units, at least initially, did poorly against the SADF. Finally, regardless of who did what to whom, the SADF never came close to being defeated by any of its opponents. While it is true that the Angolan War could be seen as a political defeat for the nationalists, it was not a defeat in strictly military terms. Like the American forces in Vietnam, the SADF never lost a significant military campaign, though in the end political pressures back home forced them to pull out of a quagmire ("Umkhonto we Sizwe (MK) in Exile" 1). What does this all mean for MK?

After all the funding and effort put into MK and their revolution, the SACP got little in return.[49] The violent revolution had not come and did not seem likely to come in the near future. As terrorism expert Walter Laqueur stated, "What are the political prospects of the Third World communist parties in the years to come? By and large, their chances seem dimmer now than in the mid–1960s and 1970s" (Laqueur 1983, 7). This was as true for the SACP as elsewhere. Both the ANC and SACP must have realized this by the end of the 1980s, so the peace feelers extended by the nationalist President de Klerk after his accession to power in 1989 were welcome indeed.

This meant that the SACP decided to drop its thirty-year commitment to the violent overthrow of the capitalist regime to make a go at peace. This was a serious concession for the Stalinists within the party, and many still regretted going along with it during the early 1990s. But the liberals of the SACP did indeed win their most serious struggle within the party when the SACP, along with the ANC and MK, "suspended the revolution." Soon enough, this suspension would become the indefinite status quo for the SACP, even though, as noted, it formally reserves the right to resort to violence if necessary (Cronin AT Interview 1995).[50]

By the 1994 All Race Elections, the SACP had decided not to run directly in the elections: its members would run under the ANC banner (and continue to do so to this day). This meant that, at least indirectly, they had opted for the nonviolent defeat of the regime, which did succeed, at least politically. In other words, the SACP, which had once decried the social democratic option of a parliamentary and gradual evolution to socialism, was taking that very option for itself after seven decades of struggle. Though, as noted, then–Deputy General Secretary Cronin told me in 1995 that the party always reserves the option of a violent overthrow of "the regime," he made it clear that the SACP fully supported the new ANC regime, even its centrist capitalist policies. Analyst Dries van Heerden believed that in most important ways, the SACP had become a social democratic party; this was an overstatement, especially compared to such parties in Europe, but it had a ring of truth (van Heerden 5). Does this mean that the SACP is now a social democratic party in all but name?

The answer has still to be settled fully, but for now it would have to be a qualified no. Officially, the SACP is not a social democratic party. As Comrade Blade Nzimande, a former "Stalinist" in the SACP and its current leader, stated, "[Democratic socialism] wipes out by a stroke of a pen the entire Marxist critique of liberal and bourgeois democracy.... The concept of democratic socialism was firmly rejected at our party's 8th Congress..." (Nzimande 42).

He is correct in that such a proposal was indeed rejected formally at the 8th Congress. At the 9th Party Congress, the SACP again debated these and other issues and concluded that though there would be some real changes in its basic ideological assumptions (i.e., acceptance of multiparty democracy), it would remain a "Marxist-Leninist Party"[51] committed to the Two Stage Theory and therefore to a "Socialist Revolution" (9th Congress AT 1995).[52] Though the political decisions of the congress will be examined elsewhere, some of its broader ideological positions need to be mentioned here.

The most significant change is the final and full commitment to a multiparty system and the desire to participate in it openly as a mass party, all within a democratic, capitalist system. This move began as early as 1989 at the party's 7th Congress in Havana, Cuba. Here, the party finally came around to recognizing what was happening throughout the world as international communism itself had begun to come into question. The party adopted the new program Path to Power, which replaced the 1962 Road to South African Freedom. The new program called for a renewed commitment to democracy *and* "the struggle," obviously hedging its bets even in 1989 (Lodge 1983, 172). As it turns out, the SACP did not need to struggle (at least violently) much longer against the regime; by 1994, the ANC and SACP would be in power.

The fact that the SACP is now committed to a democratic regime is not shocking in a theoretical sense. Though the SACP, like the ANC, thought the nationalist regime would have to be overthrown violently until the late 1980s, *after* its overthrow the alliance had always been committed to creating some form of Western democracy.[53] Therefore, the SACP has always supported the democratic option for South Africa. Of course, this does not contradict the SACP's official position of the Two Stage Theory, which as noted always had the SACP supporting some form of bourgeois, democratic regime after the overthrow of apartheid, but only until socialism could be built.[54] Even though this change in position is apparently not an ideological contradiction for the SACP, it is a significant modification. Still, the implications of this decision are far-reaching, since it also reflects on the SACP's former support of the very undemocratic regimes in the communist East Bloc.

It is also true that except for the CPSU's constitutional guarantee within the Soviet Union of power within the state,[55] no communist party has to adhere to the idea that any future communist regime must be a one-party state (Slovo 1990). However, considering the authoritarian, let alone totalitarian, aspirations of many communist parties, nothing but a one-party regime would seemingly do for the SACP until the late 1980s (though it is possible they would allow a multiparty option). But the situation did indeed change and so did the SACP.

As a matter of fact, as early as 1989, the party stated, "Fundamental to the socialist political system is the introduction of the widest democracy" ("Path to Power" 109). Adam commented, "Slovo defines Stalinism as 'socialism without democracy'" (Adam 28), and the SACP itself stated in 1992:

> It is not possible to sustain and develop socialism in an authoritarian environment.... Civil society was absorbed into the gambit of party and state politics. But a thriving socialism requires a whole network of mass democratic formations and organs of popular power.... Nevertheless ... positive results were achieved in the socialist countries ["The Way Forward..." 41].

The SACP was seemingly unable to condemn the Soviet system without also giving it some praise. Still, by now these totalitarian tendencies have also officially disappeared from the SACP manifesto. As Slovo stated, "[T]he 'mission' to promote real democracy under a one-party system is not just difficult but, in the long run, impossible ... it becomes a short-cut to a political tyranny" (Slovo 1990, 41).[56]

As a matter of fact, for quite a while the SACP has favored the creation of a multiparty system that promotes a vibrant civil society. The history of the "civics"—public associations operating at the nongovernmental levels of society—in South Africa is for another volume, but ever since the United Democratic Front (UDF) became the predominant organ of protest in the 1980s, civil society had become the focus for both the ANC and SACP. The SACP's official position is that the civics will prove to be the transmission belt for relaying the needs of the people to state agencies (Mayekiso).[57] Though even the SACP admitted that communist parties in other countries have "abused" such organizations in the past, Slovo argued, "We do not regard the trade union or national movement as mere conduits of our policies. Nor do we attempt to advance our policy positions through intrigue or manipulation" (Slovo 1990, 47).[58] He added that the party stresses how "such leadership must be won rather than imposed" (Slovo 1990, 45). More recently, at the 13th Congress in 2012, the SACP even debated whether the civics umbrella organization, the South African National Civics Organisation (SANCO), should be formally brought into the alliance (*Political Report* 36). This all fits neatly with the SACP's new interest in bottom-up democracy.

It is true that decades ago the SACP fully supported the Stalinist regime in the Soviet Union, especially during the darkest and bloodiest days of the Show Trials and the Great Purges of the 1930s. As a matter of fact, the SACP often purged itself of whatever "elements" were "the class enemy" that year.

They also supported, when other communist parties started to pull back, such controversial Soviet foreign policies as the 1956 Hungarian and 1968 Czech invasions.[59] Thus, as noted earlier, the SACP could rightfully be called a Stalinist party in the past, to which Joe Slovo even admitted in an interview with the *New York Times* shortly before his death (Wren 1993). Also, Slovo openly stated:

> There are certainly some rather murky skeletons in our historical cupboard....
> We went through a period during which we absorbed what was described as
> "Leninism" without realizing that much of it was wrapping paper for Stalinism.
> Lenin was undoubtedly the greatest revolutionary this century.... But many of
> Lenin's propositions which referred to special moments in the history of a spe-
> cific struggle were perpetuated to serve the Stalinist bureaucracy [Slovo 1991, 1].

Then Slovo went from attacking Stalinism to criticizing his own party:

> [The SACP] was a party which was, at the end of the day, was not even answer-
> able to the class it claimed to represent.... Democratic centralism was denuded of
> its democratic content and become centralism, pure and simple.... The relation-
> ship between the party and social organizations was degraded.... The single
> party state came to be accepted as a permanent feature of society and not as a
> passing historic phase. A style of ideological polemic emerged which prohibited
> any questioning of the wisdom of the leading organ.... We cannot deny that
> these distortions ... also impinged themselves on our own practice. It led us to a
> degree of intolerance, exclusiveness and elitism. Our external policies were dom-
> inated by a blind adherence to the decisions of the Soviet Communist Party
> [Slovo 1991, 2–3].

Moreover, as Slovo had stated earlier, any deviation from Stalinism "led to isolation or excommunication," a terrible fate for loyal party members (Slovo 1990, 34).

Thus, party members either were kept from the truth by both the SACP and the CPSU or personally avoided it, but either way they did support Soviet policy almost unconditionally at times.[60] As Slovo said so well, many communists were "blind worshippers in the temple of the cult of the personality" (Slovo 1990, 35). Even as late as 1990, the SACP Stalinist Gwala could dodge the Stalin question per se, while praising the Soviet system (Gwala 1990, 39). He even added that General Secretary Andropov, a former KGB chief, "contributed" to socialism. This is a sad overstatement, since one of Andropov's largest contributions to the Soviet system was a failed antidrinking program (though it must be admitted that at least he was for some type of systematic reform, unlike his last two predecessors). Regardless, he died before any of his would-be reforms took off ("Yuri Andropov" 1).

All this changed as the Soviet Union first began to reform in the mid–

1980s, and especially after the 1991 coup when the SACP finally broke from the disintegrating Soviet Union (Slovo 1990). Slovo pointed out that communists throughout the world should have been critical long before that, "We cannot disclaim our share of the responsibility for the spread of the personality cult and mechanical embrace of Soviet domestic and foreign policies, some of which discredited the cause of socialism" (Slovo 1990, 44). Pallo Jordan, former ANC National Executive Committee member, certainly agreed:

> Any regular reader of the SACP's publications can point to a consistent pattern of praise and support for every violation of freedom perpetrated by the Soviet leadership both before and after the death of Stalin ... the political culture nurtured by the SACP leadership over the years has produced a spirit of intolerance, petty intellectual thuggery and political dissembling [Bundy 61].

But that was before, since by 1990 the SACP had begun to question *all* the Stalinist premises it had accepted for decades. In the end and as noted, the SACP kept its Marxist roots and many of its Leninist ones, but did discard the Stalinist stress on totalitarianism and the rejection of "bourgeois" democracy. As Slovo made clear in this critique of Stalinism:

> Socialism is undoubtedly in the throes of a crisis greater than any time since 1917 ... these [revolts in eastern Europe] were popular revolts against unpopular regimes; if socialists are unable to come to terms with this reality, the future of socialism is indeed bleak ... the mounting chronicle of crimes and distortions in the history of existing socialism, its economic failures an the divide between socialism and democracy, have raised doubts ... as to whether socialism can work at all ... for our part, we firmly believe in the future of socialism [Slovo 1990, 25–26].

Whether the party undertook this critique for tactical and publicity reasons, or whether it was genuine in its desire for reform, is still not fully clear, though at this late point, the latter seems more close to the truth. All the evidence available suggests that Slovo and his "liberal" faction within the SACP seemed genuine in their strong but long delayed repudiation of Stalinism.

Because of these changes, the SACP returned to its more Marxist roots in the early 1990s and began to stress a bottom-up democratic model though still being critical of capitalism. It did this by publishing the key work of its post–Stalinist period, "Has Socialism Failed?" by Slovo himself.[61] Slovo summed up the new party line well: "We believe, however, that the theory of Marxism, in all its essential respects, remains valid"—but he went on to criticize openly the former Stalinist East Bloc regimes, asserting that "the deformations experienced by existing socialist states were the results of bureaucratic distortions" (Slovo 1990; 33, 35).[62] Analyst Meryn Frost added, "Slovo argues that Stalinism cannot be excused, nor can it be attributed to some feature of socialist theory that makes failure inevitable.... The deformations experienced by existing socialist states were the results of bureaucratic distortions that were rationalised at the ideological level" (Frost 2).

Chris Hani, a longtime leader of the SACP, hero of MK, and the second most popular leader in the ANC before his death in 1994, added, "The SACP wants to take into account the problems socialism has faced in the Soviet Union ... the fact that socialism was never able to solve the key requirements and demands of society" (Goodman 12). The Slovo/Hani faction jammed through these reforms against such Stalinists as Gwala and others of the far left. Though they were defeated on the question of social democracy, all their other important propositions were adopted by the SACP, transforming this Stalinist party into something different and seemingly better, at least in terms of survival.

The phrase "socialism without democracy" had become common in the SACP's mounting criticisms of the old Stalinist regimes, including the former Soviet Union, the regime that at one time seemingly could do no wrong in the party's eyes. Slovo stated in the early 1990s:

> The fact that socialist power was first won in the most backward outpost of European capitalism, without democratic political tradition, played no small part in the way it was shaped ... over time the [CPSU] party leadership was transformed into a command post with an overbearing centralism and very little democracy [Monteiro 30].
>
> Existing [East Bloc] socialism failed because it was separated from democracy. We believe that democratic socialism is the only rational future for humankind [Slovo 1991, 8].

In 1992, Hani also condemned the Soviet system for similar reasons: "We feel there were a number of serious violations.... There was violation of democracy and an arrogation of power and control by the [Soviet] communist party" (Hani 6).

The SACP then officially declared that without bottom-up, grassroots democracy, socialism cannot work. Again, Slovo added, "Marxism clearly projects a system anchored in deep-seated political democracy" (Slovo 1990, 37). He went so far as to say that the term and concept of the "dictatorship of the proletariat" was no longer applicable, much to the disgust of the Stalinists within the party (Slovo 1990, 37). The more liberal Cronin agreed, arguing that the new South Africa needed bottom-up, grassroots-based democracy. He explained, "In other words, we need to build socialism in the interices of the present system" (Cronin 1994, 42). This new stress on democracy, while still denouncing the abuses of capitalism, is a fundamental and genuine change of emphasis for the SACP.[63]

These momentous changes were not unopposed within the SACP. As one party member put it, "What ever happened to the dictatorship of the proletariat?" (Molaba 16). Then and current General Secretary Blade Nzimande also attacked the dismissal of the "dictatorship of the proletariat." He claimed that Slovo saw the problems of the East Bloc as basically stemming from the separation of socialism from democracy, but such theories must be based on social democratic ideology. Nzimande claimed the SACP needed to be critical in its revisionism, not just because of the collapse of communism. He explained that the dictatorship of the proletariat failed in the East Bloc because it was a "dictatorship of the bureaucracy," and nothing more; civil society, democracy, and so on had little to do with it. He concluded with the interesting point that if the dictatorship of the proletariat can be "thrown out" so easily, why cannot other "sacred assumptions" of Marxism-Leninism be trashed also (Nzimande 42–44)? Nzimande did have a valid point: once such basic assumptions are attacked, one's entire belief system can collapse. In other words, was all of Marxism-Leninism being questioned (Slovo would argue no) or just Stalinism (which would turn out to be the case)?

Gwala, Nzimande, and others attacked Slovo for seemingly "selling out" the revolutionary history of the party. Gwala stated in 1990, "It is a common thing today for many theoreticians on the problems of socialism to open their writings with the denunciation of Stalin. This sort of nihilism only clouds the issue and does not deal with problems of socialism scientifically" (Gwala 1990, 39). It would appear Gwala would rather just not deal with the real issues of Stalinism (and its collapse), though he did admit, "There were many excesses committed during the time of Stalin" (Gwala 1990, 39).[64] Even Brian Bunting, another leader of the party but not as Stalinist as many others, argued that some aspects of Stalinism were necessary; thus Slovo was going too far in his denunciation of that era (Lodge 1983, 175).

Some, however, argued that the SACP had never gone far enough in rejecting Stalinism:

> The SACP, over the years, supported Stalin's mass murders and other subsequent massacres and refused to accept the brutality of state capitalism in Russia.... Russia was not a socialist state but a capitalist one, and that the Bolshevik revolution was a belated bourgeois one.... Russia had nothing to do with "socialism" [Mokonyane 84].

Mokonyane added that the "new SACP" was dropping its old allies and constituencies, like the youth of the townships:

> Hani suggested that they [the youths] should form a peace corps but at a recent
> conference of youth even more draconian "solution" were proposed amongst the
> most popular (perish the thought) a la Master Stalin, the youth should be sent
> to labor camps! These valiant young men and women ... are going to be
> rewarded by the "Sun of Freedom" dawning for them behind prison bars ... how
> low can the quislings stoop [Mokonyane 135]?

Hani is now dead, no "youth camps" ever were created, but such fears among some "comrades" show that the new SACP is no longer trusted by all its old adherents. Regardless of these inevitable critiques, the party continued to reject its Stalinist past.

These changes were also opposed by other communist parties. The Communist Party of the USA (CPUSA) disagreed that Leninist terms or even Leninism was ever part of the Stalinist rejection of democracy. A CPUSA spokesperson put it thus in 1990:

> The essence of Lenin's legacy with respect to democracy, however, is that under
> socialism every question to be resolved requires more democracy, more partici-
> pation, more freedom.... The survival of socialism, Lenin vigorously insisted,
> demanded democracy.... Perestroika re-establishes and strengthens in practice
> this necessary correlation. However, its roots are Leninism [Monteiro 32].

This is closer to Gorbachev's rejection of Stalinist traditions and attempts to renew Leninism, unlike the SACP's move toward a more purist Marxism, which expels both Stalinist and some Leninist elements. This becomes clear as the CPUSA spokesperson goes on: "While in 'the long run' the one party system does not serve democracy, it is often an inevitable stage in the consolidation of revolutionary power.... [But] Comrade Slovo correctly points out that the over-centralized commandist and bureaucratic running of the socialist economy alienates workers..." Yet this author still must add, "The whole of Soviet history is dismissed as anti-democratic, which is all wrong..." In conclusion, "Comrade Slovo has gone a bit overboard.... The criticism of socialism must occur within the boundaries of defending it... [And] there is no evidence to suggest that the historic trend away from capitalism and toward socialism has been reversed" (Monteiro 33–34). This is somewhat unfair to Slovo, at least in 1990, because he and his party did occasionally criticize the Soviets, albeit in a guarded way. This would not change until right before and especially after the Soviet coup of 1991.

None of these democratic-leaning reforms exactly fits Leninist vanguardism, which (as argued above) is innately elite driven,[65] but is not contradictory to the basic, mass-based premises of Marxism, which assumes that the "workers" would take power. The SACP has gone so far in this strain of thinking that even the ANC has been criticized by the SACP for ignoring its former "civics" allies and various grassroots organizations. Hani commented on this elitism, which he claimed still resides in the SACP: "I think party elitism is a dangerous tendency and I believe the party must step in to stop it" (Hani 15). This new stress on bottom-up democracy also led the SACP to other changes as well, though as always, it stayed critical of capitalism both at home and globally.

Slovo argued that "a multi-party post-apartheid democracy, both in the national democratic and socialist phases, is desirable" (Slovo 1990, 48). Hani added, "Firstly, we must ensure that we support pluralism as a party.... We are moving away from the situation where once the party is in, it has got to entrench itself" (Goodman 12). However, a critic of the alliance accurately predicted in 1994, "Voting alone ... will not work; the society will, at best, be ruled by an exchange of elites" (Mokonyane 82). This may be an overstatement, but thus far there has been no sign of a social and/or socialist revolution. Still, the rejection of Stalinism by the SACP was only the first step; the party has also accepted of the Western idea of "human rights."

Until recently, the SACP, as a Leninist party, never bought into the "bourgeois" concept of universal human rights. The Soviet Union often did use the term "human rights" in its rhetoric, especially in speeches before the United Nations, and then to condemn Western imperialism and/or various abuses by Western nations, especially America (segregation, homelessness, lack of universal health care, etc.). Ironically, not only did the rulers of the USSR obviously not practice a respect for universal human rights within their own country (systematic use of torture, the gulag system, mass killings, etc.), ideologically speaking they did not and could not even believe in them. Marxist and Leninist theory both argue that all morality, including conceptions of human rights, is historically class-based and thus ultimately relative (and thus not universal). This is only logical, considering the materialist and dialectical basis of Marxist-Leninist philosophy.

Since classes are ultimately shaped by their different material surroundings during different historical stages, their component populations would therefore have different material environments and therefore different moralities. This would also naturally result in different conceptions about human rights. Thus, a worker may see the "right to have a job" as a human right, but an owner may think differently. The dialectical nature of Marxist-Leninist philosophy also undermines any belief in universal human rights. Since all dialecticians believe that the universe is literally always in flux, no one set of material conditions will last indefinitely. Thus, no one set of morals or ideas about human rights will last either, since they are based on such material constructs. Therefore, the basic premise of human rights, that they are in some way "universal" and thus always applicable (let alone God-given), is unacceptable to Marxist-Leninists. The SACP agreed with this view on morality and human rights until the 1990s.

However, the SACP has now accepted the need to espouse the need for human rights in all societies. This is probably one of the *least* explained changes in its ideology. Though the SACP claims that it always believed in some form of human rights (rights for the workers, rights for the majority, more education and health care, etc.) and that now its views are more public and more similar to the conventional definition, this is not good enough as an explanation. Even if the SACP now truly does accept the need for "human rights," can it honestly claim that this will be a final position? According to its own philosophy of dialectical materialism, can it believe human rights are either universal or eternal? (9th Congress AT, 1995). It cannot. This is not necessarily to question the party's sincerity, but its intellectual integrity for holding this seemingly contradictory position is questionable. Then there is also the fact that factions within the SACP oppose this new trend.

One communist dissenter commented, "[The last Central Committee report] was so liberal, so moral, so completely devoid of class analysis ... in essence, it was insulting" (Molaba 16). Another critic complained:

> When squatters decided to seize empty, good and well-constructed houses, it was the ANC/SACP which was the first (not to help—no!) but to condemn ... the ANC/SACP was quick to condemn this because it makes it difficult for them to negotiate the betrayal of the black people of South Africa by telling them that the solution will arrive with the going to Parliament, whereas, in reality, all they are doing is to sell out the struggle of the people already pursued with storm of blood [Mokonyane 127]!

These critics are gaining popularity among the masses in the huge squatter cities that still surround all the major metropolitan areas of South Africa. Though the SACP is still admired by many in such areas because in the past it was the most radical and effective of the many parties fighting apartheid, it risks losing such support. The SACP is sometimes perceived to be "selling out" its base, the very poor of South Africa, by helping run the country with its ally the ANC.

As communist expert Tom Lodge made clear, "The South African Communists are ... deeply divided" on such issues (Keller 1992). Stalinist stalwart Gwala never did adopt many of these new positions, like multiparty democracy or human rights, and even supported the 1991 coup against Gorbachev led by the KGB, Red Army, and Stalinists (Lodge 1983, 175). As a "liberal," Cronin puts it:

[Gwala] sniffs at the right to "freedom of criticism" within the party....
The freezing of Marxism-Leninism into a closed and unchanging doctrine ...
is dogmatism. It is, of course, this ... tendency that is so evident in Gwala's intervention.... Gwala treats Marxism-Leninism, not as a science, but as a holy script.
He is like a religious fundamentalist....
  Gwala wants to transform the SACP, not into a vanguard, but a rearguard, an
inward looking cabal, desperately defending a dry and dusty dogma [Cronin
1990; 12, 18].

Ironically, Mokonyane, also a critic of the SACP, partially agrees with Cronin's condemnation of Stalinism, claiming that, "History plays no part in [the SACP's] understanding or praxis of either Marxism, or, indeed, capital-ism.... The system is ahistorically and undialectically treated" (Mokonyane 25). Gwala, though, had his own views which were mostly critical of the new path of the SACP:

These new times with their new ideas have led to the disarming of the working
class and the demise of socialism in the face of aggressive imperialism.... We find
the same [revisionist] thinking in our modern South African Marxists [Gwala
1991, 8].

Another leftist critic also condemns the SACP's close ties to the "bour-geois" ANC (Molaba 16). Yet even if such thinking were popular, which it is not, this more Stalinist faction led by Gwala has been neutralized politically. Gwala himself was suspended from the party soon before his death,[66] and one of his closest allies, Blade Nzimande, broke from Gwala years ago, and has since become the top leader of the SACP for many years by moderating his far leftist views.

However, political issues such as democracy were not the only ones rethought by the SACP. As analyst David Goodman noted, "The ideological blueprint for a post–Apartheid South Africa has long been the Freedom Char-ter, an essentially socialist platform...," but "critical re-thinking about eco-nomics has been forced upon the SACP and ANC by the grim realities of present-day South Africa ... [Slovo] now speaks favorably of a mixed econ-omy." Hani added, "We have not said the mines would be nationalized, but we are calling for state participation in the mining industry." Tito Mboweni, then the ANC's chief economist, asserted, "State participation ... between the public and private sectors [is best]" (Goodman 12).

All this should not be interpreted to mean the SACP has given up its socialist aims or has embraced capitalism. It does demonstrate that in this "stage" of the new South Africa, the SACP has moderated its demands and has come to accept the necessity of a democratic-capitalist stage on the path to socialism. Goodman agreed:

> For the African National Congress (ANC), the shift has brought with it some about-faces on once-sacred economic positions. Simply put, the ANC is abandoning much of its socialist program for familiar Keynesian formulas.... What was "inconceivable" is now official ANC policy: the movement is now backpedaling from its insistence on nationalizing major industries [Goodman 12].

Still, the ANC is not always in agreement with the SACP, especially on this issue. The ANC does seem to have forsaken its socialist positions for a more left-of-center public policy, but there is no evidence that the SACP has made any "about-face" at this point. As a matter of fact, the SACP has constantly pushed the ANC on such issues (though with less and less success as time passes). Goodman added, "The ANC describes its overall economic policy as 'growth through redistribution,'" and described an ANC and COSATU paper that said the state, "would assume the leading role in the reconstruction of the economy" (Goodman 12).

In other words, though the ANC may be backsliding vis-à-vis its more leftist tradition, it still has a social market orientation, while the SACP still pushes for a more social democratic solution now, and later will push a pure socialist one. Cronin's criticism of the Soviet economic system was to the point: "The Bolshevik project becomes the attempt to deploy capitalist techniques while controlling/coercing them through a powerful party/state apparatus." He added that the SACP agreed with Cuban revolutionary Che Guevara that socialist regimes that use capitalist methods are dangerous (Cronin 1994, 37)—although, more recently, this sort of argument has been dropped, as the SACP becomes closer to communist China, which indeed does use a form of state capitalism, often quite successfully.

Goodman was right when he went on to describe some of the pressures under which the SACP operated. "The SACP, which enjoys strong labor support and is said to be the only communist party in the world whose membership is still growing rapidly, has been re-examining its economic policy in light of the collapse of socialism in eastern Europe ... [Slovo] now speaks favorably of a mixed economy" (Goodman 12). This is still basically true, but there is more to it. Though the SACP does not approve of capitalist production, it admits that it is necessary for now, due to the current stage of development. Slovo and the rest of the leadership claimed to have adopted these "capitalist tools" only for the time being; but it is almost two decades into

ANC/SACP rule. Some leftist critics of the SACP would disagree with this evaluation, seeing the alliance giving up on socialism. All of this is like the position of the Chinese Communist Party (CCP) since the 1980s, when it argues that the path to long-term socialism is indeed a lengthy and deep capitalist stage (and no one can deny that the Chinese have wholeheartedly embraced this for now as China races to become the largest economy in the world).

Still, one of the more vocal critics of the alliance in general was the leftist Dan Mokonyane. In his book *The Big Sell Out*, he examined how the alliance has betrayed the people of South Africa on a number of different levels. In general:

> The SACP/ANC parvenu, however, has opted against the seizure of land ... for a type of "accomodationism" where they, as the petty-bourgeois, capitalist crumbs, while goading the black masses away from their real demands: the land wealth, housing, education, etc., to the fetish of one person one vote as the solution of all our woes and problems.... The illusions they cultivate are the usual bourgeois stock-in-trade ones [Mokonyane 6].

His critique of the new economic policies of the alliance, most of them a moderation of former ones, was even more scathing:

> The ANC/SACP are no longer debating issues as far as capitalism is concerned. They have accepted it in toto.... What the ANC/SACP stood for, even in 1990, has long been forgotten or quietly dropped. What became of one unitary South Africa, or nationalisation or whatever, including the so-called Freedom Charter? The SACP wing of the Congress Alliance now specializes in drawing up "sunset clauses" for white rule [Mokonyane 67].

While this is all an overstatement and somewhat simplistic, it did reflect a sentiment growing among some former communist cadres, black nationalists, and the poor. With poverty still *the* problem in South Africa, it is understandable why people are asking such questions. So far, however, the SACP is still seen as the most influential far leftist organization in South Africa. Thus, its commitment to democracy and economic reform remains a serious issue for all the political actors in South Africa.

Conclusion

Many of the arguments presented here will be further explored in later chapters, but some concluding thoughts are still needed. First, the SACP has genuinely changed in a number of ways to adapt to its new environment. Its ideology and structure have modified. Some of these changes were due to external pressures and/or expediency, but many of them resulted from genuine soul-searching on past mistakes by the party's leaders, changing both the ideology and structure of the party in a number of ways, and probably irreversibly. I mostly agree with Frost: "I fully expect the SACP to emerge as an ordinary political party.... It will contain no distinct Leninist methods of operating" (Frost 2). This, though, will be in the long run. At this point, not only are there still traces of Leninism in its practice, but the SACP still holds on to the title of "Marxist-Leninist" party.

In any case, it is worth reiterating some of my doubts about the reforms that the SACP has initiated. Some of them, such as the SACP's new belief in human rights, are philosophically problematic and contradictory for the party and therefore less solid than other reforms. The party, due to the fact that it is currently going through a complex transition, is faced with many such contradictions.

An example of this is the SACP's support for the ANC regime, which is troublesome both ideologically and practically. Given its ideology, any Marxist-Leninist party must be careful about supporting nonsocialist nationalist regimes such as the current ANC-led one of South Africa. Though there are important, practical advantages in doing so, the party risks ideological incoherence by following that path (for example, when *exactly* does the SACP's ideology call for a break with the ANC regime?). The SACP also has practical problems with this and other issues.

The SACP also confuses its core constituency, the workers of South Africa, when it states that it supports their economic and class demands but then also backs the moderation of such demands for the sake of "the regime" or worse, the needs of "international capital" to attract needed foreign investment (which is indeed often the ANC position). Why the SACP does this is self-evident due to the give-and-take of such situations, but how long can it continue this juggling act effectively? And how much does it have to distort its ideology to justify such juggling? At its 2012 congress, the SACP itself asked similar questions, so I am not alone in this train of thought. The SACP also faces the practical challenge of integrating all its new members into its once small and secretive structure. Though having more members has many advantages, any sizable increase in its membership also creates liabilities for what was once a small and coherent party.

For one thing, these new members are not well versed in Marxism-Leninism, let alone the SACP's somewhat special and complex brand of the ideology. Moreover, most of the new members do not hold, nor understand, the Leninist "party discipline" that the old cadres had. Though moving to a mass party structure may have been necessary because of ideological changes, and may have real advantages, the very real problems just mentioned will not just go away. These problems will undoubtedly cause more, not less, ideological strife as time passes. Whether the SACP is ready to handle these core ideological (and practical) issues is unclear at this time.

CHAPTER 2

The Alliance
Who Is in Charge?

Introduction

The alliance between the SACP and the ANC has been a significant element in South African politics since the 1930s and has been a dominant one since the 1960s. By the 1980s, it was clear that all other opponents to the regime would have to take a backseat to the alliance and its agenda. "'Long live the ANC/SACP Alliance!' This became one of the most popular and ubiquitous slogans at mass rallies during the second half of the 1980s" (Bundy 52). By the late 1980s, there was little doubt that the ANC would eventually take power, which meant, by definition, that the SACP would also share power in some manner. This also meant that the alliance had to figure into the SACP's socialist plans for South Africa.

Though it seems obvious that the ANC leads the alliance, many right-wing critics have argued that the *real* power in the alliance is the SACP. Some make the assertion for political reasons; others truly believe it. In any case, as we shall see, there is a small kernel of truth to such claims. Nevertheless, appearances notwithstanding, this chapter will demonstrate that though the SACP at times has had overwhelming influence at both the highest and lowest levels of the ANC, *the SACP has never outright controlled ANC*. In fact, to even call this sort of influence on the ANC "control" would be an overstatement. Finally, the SACP itself and ANC agree that the ANC has always been the dominant partner. Still, there is no denying that the SACP has indeed exercised considerable influence on the ANC for decades (which, again, both parties agree upon).

The SACP has fully acknowledged that at this stage, "The African National Congress is the spearhead of the national democratic revolution"

("Path to Power" 110). A former national chair of the SACP, Dan Tloome, underlined this: "We are perfectly clear on the point that the stronger the ANC is the stronger the SACP becomes.... The imperialists and racists would dearly love to split the alliance between the ANC and the SACP" (Tloome 69). In other words, from the point of view of the SACP, what is good for the ANC is good for the SACP (in most cases). This was generally true in the past, and may be mostly true for the present, but it could change in the foreseeable future.

When exactly the alliance began is still debated. Samuel Francis believed that "by 1958 the communist influence in the ANC had reached such an extent that the [black] nationalists in the organization broke off and founded the Pan African Congress (PAC)" (Francis 55). Colin Bundy claimed the official alliance started with the "Road to South African Freedom" program in 1962 (Bundy 52). Still others date the formal alliance from 1969 with the Morogoro declaration (Legum 109). Whatever the exact date, analyst Philip Nel argued that

> during the 1940s relations between the ANC and CPSA improved considerably.... Both realised that unity lay in strength ... the ANC and the CPSA entered into an informal alliance in 1947.... After the dissolution of the CPSA on 20 June 1950.... The pragmatic co-operation of the 1940s between the ANC and the CPSA quickly developed into an increasingly ideological cohesion [Nel 8].

Nel was probably as close to the facts as anyone. The point is that whenever the alliance began, it has mostly worked for many decades. In the final analysis, it was the alliance which brought apartheid down once and for all (though other factors did contribute to the fall) and which now rules South Africa.

In the past, the SACP has played a number of roles within the alliance, including being "one of the main pillars of the national liberation movement" ("Path to Power" 72). For much of the time before 1994, its main role was that of the ANC's steadfast ally against the common enemy the racist nationalist regime. Initially, under the Two Stage Theory, the SACP saw itself supporting the "national democratic revolution" against the Colonialism of a Special Type that existed in South Africa. As noted, it was directed in 1928 by the Soviet-led Comintern to join (and/or infiltrate) the ANC and to aid it in overthrowing the nationalist regime, first through legal means, then through revolution. In the end, of course, liberation came by way of the ballot box in 1994, and this, too, got the SACP's support.[1] Through the decades, the SACP has also taken on a number of other roles vis-à-vis the ANC, changing them as the situation warranted.

The SACP currently has had two primary roles: to be a supportive ally of the ANC and to represent the (leftist) interests of the working class. These roles can both complement and contradict each other, depending on the context. The SACP has played the former with little reservation since the 1940s, and it has tried to do the latter as much as it could as an illegal, underground party with conflicting interests. In other words, there were few problems for the alliance until it took power because the SACP was more of a revolutionary organization than a traditional "workers' party." Thus, it could concentrate on working with its partner, the ANC, to bring about the overthrow of the nationalist regime. However, now that the ANC has taken power, and has held onto it for two decades, this has all changed.

Not only is the SACP now in a position to aid the working class but it also cannot claim the exclusive role in that task, since trying to do so alone would be bound to antagonize its ANC partner, which needs to placate many classes within the country. Herein, of course, exists both a dilemma and a paradox. First, the dilemma involves the dual mission of the ANC. As a left-of-center partner, it too is supposed to help the poor (mostly black) masses of South Africa. As the government, though, the ANC must ultimately represent *all* classes in South Africa, including the capitalist (often white) interests that have dominated the country for decades. Therefore, the large and poor working class will inevitably come into conflict with the government—that is, the ANC. Thus, as the workers' champion, the SACP will be forced to oppose, to one degree or another, ANC policies that do not give primacy to workers' interests, from worker safety to wage demands. The paradox lies in the new role into which the SACP's own fidelity to the alliance has cast it: it cannot be both true to itself and continue to share power with its ANC ally which must, for the sake of its own survival, ultimately reject some of the SACP's positions.

How the conflict unfolds will be fascinating since the two organizations are so intertwined and usually in agreement on the "big picture": that South Africa needs to be a democratic-capitalist society, if not one with a leftist public policy. The point is that conflict is unavoidable unless: (a) the ANC "betrays" all other class interests for the sake of the workers (highly improbable); or (b) the SACP "sells out" the workers and aligns with the ANC (possible but very unlikely). Since neither of the two outcomes is likely, the two partners must clash (and have); to what extent is the more relevant question. It is possible that they may be able to find some formula for continued collaboration, but as things stand today, they cannot continue to occupy the same ground without confrontation. So that we can better understand this conflict, we must explore the relationship between these two organizations.

The SACP Aids the ANC

A modern revolution needs both money and guns; this was also true for South Africa. In the late 1920s, the young SACP merely joined ANC activities (such as marches), but this soon changed, and by the late 1930s more and more SACP members also became members of the ANC.[2] On its face, this represented either a serious conflict of interest or a plan to infiltrate the ANC. The SACP denies both even today. It has always claimed that even though "dual membership" was and still is standard practice for many of its members, there was no conflict of interest since both organizations wanted the same thing: the overthrow of the nationalist regime and a leftist public policy (both of which have happened). The SACP always adds that its members within the ANC have always obeyed ANC authority. As a matter of fact, it has claimed that such members have never even formed informal caucuses or cliques. On the evidence, the SACP protests too much.

It would be naive and just plain incorrect to assume that these SACP members had no formal mission within the ANC. If nothing else, they discuss their ANC duties amongst themselves at their SACP meetings (which, in fact, have been quite secretive at times). Though there is no evidence of some sort of SACP "master plan" to take over the ANC,[3] everything up to that point is not only possible but also quite likely. This should not be surprising: in any political partnership, the partners struggle to gain dominance at one time or another. In any case, as the alliance became more and more formalized, the interdependence of the partners also increased. This is where the SACP's money and guns came in (or at least the supplies it channeled from the Soviet Union and its allies).

As the SACP became increasingly integrated with the ANC, the latter gained assets from its much smaller but more internationally well-connected partner. The ANC obviously provided the operational assets of a large, relatively powerful nationalist organization for the small but dedicated SACP. In return, through its international connections via the Comintern and later Soviet organs,[4] the SACP consistently provided funding, training, and money for the ANC (and later COSATU). As Colin Bundy made clear:

> The Communist Party provided a ready-made network of links—with the Soviet Union, with East Europe, and with "fraternal organisations" in capitalist countries.... Over time, the Soviet Union and other Socialist Bloc countries became major supporters of the ANC in terms of military equipment and military training [Bundy 54].

Colin Legum agreed:

> The USSR offered itself as a major ally of the ANC.... All the negotiations
> between the ANC and Moscow were conducted by, and through, the SACP....
> Moscow transferred funds through the SACP Treasurer.... Slovo became the
> principal conductor of the orchestrated efforts to widen the ANC-SACP
> Alliance.... The ANC Secretary General, Alfred Nzo, became the negotiator
> between his party and Moscow [Legum 109].

There was more than just money and arms for the ANC: the communist East
Bloc's expertise was also being transferred. The training the East Bloc gave to
the alliance was significant. As Peter Vanneman explains, ANC camps were
created in Tanzania, Uganda, and Ethiopia, all with communist Cuban and
East German trainers. There was even the use of "Center 26" in Moscow for
advanced training, including the party "cell building" (Vanneman 21). These
facts are not debatable, with both the SACP *and* its most dedicated enemies
agreeing on the basics. Amounts and motives are of course contested, with
the former being especially unclear.

The actual financial contributions have never been calculated or revealed
by any sources, but some estimates put it as high as many tens of millions of
dollars; if it is that high, that would be a great deal of money for the then
struggling and illegal ANC. Former ANC president Oliver Tambo stated in
1987 that the ANC received 24 million British pounds in 1987 alone, much
of it from the Soviets. Tambo believed the Soviet Union resolved to contribute
everything within its power, but as we shall see, that was definitely and ironically not the case. A 1982 U.S. State Department report estimated that Soviet
aid amounted to 60 percent of all ANC monies and 90 percent of ANC arms
(Vanneman 19).

However, the exact amount is not important, since again, both sides
agree that the amounts were large and crucial for the alliance. "It was easy for
the NKVD [Soviet intelligence] to pass sums of money, literature, intelligence
and information of any kind back and forth from South Africa" (Pike 320).
In 1990, Soviet expert Peter Vanneman also indicated how much continuity
there was in the relationship:

> The new Soviet pragmatism has mitigated the rigid ideologically pre–Gor-
> bachevite SACP, but its dependence on the USSR for military and financial assis-
> tance is almost total.... Although the Soviets often deny it ... most of the ANC's
> military and financial aid has come from the USSR and its allies. The USSR fun-
> nels most aid to the ANC through the Liberation Committee of the Organiza-
> tion of African Unity (OAU) [Vanneman 20].

It should be added that Vanneman himself questions the reliability of the
ANC as an ally, despite what it owed the Soviets: "Moscow does provide
much of the military and economic support for the ANC, but few of the

ANC's leaders are completely reliable instruments of Soviet foreign policy....
Moscow [nor the SACP] certainly does not control [the ANC]" (Vanneman
25). Still, all this material and aid did influence the ANC.

The SACP has often praised its international communist allies for being
generous with their aid. Alfred Nzo, a former ANC and communist leader,
said as much in 1984, "We recognize that the Soviet Union and other socialist
countries are our dependable allies" (Francis 57). The East Bloc was the primary ally and donor to the SACP cause, with East Germany and the Soviet
Union being the biggest contributors (Lodge 1983, 174). As Radu pointed out:

> [SACP] links with the Soviet Bloc ensure ANC funding, military supplies, train-
> ing, and word-wide propaganda sources.... Practical cooperation between coun-
> tries of the Soviet Bloc and the ANC started in the mid–1950s.... Weapons
> deployed by or captured from the MK in South Africa are uniformly Soviet-
> made [Radu 67–68].

Legum agreed, adding, "[The Soviet Union] gives diplomatic and political
support at the international level.... It provides financial support ... weapons
to MK ... substantial help in military training ... financial and technical facilities to produce ANC publications" (Legum 109). The Central Committee
of the SACP itself stated in 1990, "The socialist countries gave practical aid
to freedom fighters in all continents" ("The Crisis in the Socialist World"
14). It should be added that many other leftist organizations and regimes
throughout Africa (some close to the Soviets, some not) also aided the ANC,
but none of it was close to the Soviet aid given (Francis 61).

What, exactly, was the nature of this aid? First and foremost, there were
large monetary fund transfers, probably one of the *least* documented aspects
of the relationship. This author has yet to find any real details on such transfers. Thus, how much will remain a mystery unless a well placed SACP or
ANC official produces credible and hard factual evidence.[5] No one denies
that this monetary relationship between the Soviet East Bloc and the ANC
existed for decades, but we know little more than that. Other types of aid
have left a somewhat better trail to follow.

The other main material support was weapons. As a matter of fact, the
Umkhonto we Sizwe (MK) could not have been a viable force without
Soviet/SACP military supplies.[6] East Bloc weapons played a crucial role in
the economic sabotage of the early years and later in the bush wars in Angola,
Southwest Africa, and elsewhere. And though the war that MK waged was
not successful in the final analysis, this still allowed the SACP to gain a great
deal of influence over both the ANC and MK. Unlike with the ANC, the
SACP did dominate MK: long-time SACP leader, Joe Slovo, helped lead MK.

Lodge claimed that "[SACP] members were especially entrenched in the command structures of Umkhonto we Sizwe" (Lodge 1983, 174). Bardis agreed: "[MK] was ... under the South African Communist Party's control" (Bardis 83). So did Francis. "In 1966, Abram Fischer, a leader of the SACP, testified at his trial that the leaders of MK had given assurances to the [Communist] Party that no terrorist action would be carried out without prior approval of the [Communist] Party" (Francis 59). Nel argued that "the initial reluctance with which ANC members involved in MK accepted Soviet assistance gave way to greater ideological cohesion between the ANC, SACP and the CPSU" and "the ANC ... has become increasingly dependent on the Soviet Union for weapons and training facilities" (Nel 12).

Though the weapons supplied were often low-tech and of poor quality compared to the South Africa Defense Force's (SADF) arms, they were still better than nothing. Without the potential represented by these weapons, the alliance probably would have never launched MK in 1961, for at that point, the amount of weapons in the hands of the ANC and SACP were insignificant. Thus, these East Bloc arms were a crucial morale booster and did aid to pressure (if not overthrow) the Nationalist regime and was yet another method by which the SACP aided the ANC.

Though it is almost impossible to measure, the boost in morale that the SACP's support gave to the whole national liberation movement in South Africa must not be underestimated. The money and arms contributed directly, but so did the organizational ability and general experience of the SACP cadres that joined the ANC (Ellis and Sechaba 26). Tom Lodge said it best: "What distinguishes the communists in the ANC and the reason so many have risen to leadership positions, is that they've done the fighting and dying.... What they do have is a moral authority that others may lack" (Keller 1994, 19). Such authority has been crucial for the SACP in its role within the ANC: though it has used organizational maneuvers at times to gain influence within the ANC, it has mostly relied upon this hard-to-measure but still powerful moral influence. It is based upon the SACP's reputation for courage, experience, ruthlessness, and cunning. Compared to the average ANC member, communist cadres often stand out in all these qualities.

There was also the fact that the SACP used youth organizations to get closer to the ANC. As Francis commented, "One source for the increasing closeness between the ANC and the communists was a militant faction within the ANC Youth League which came under the influence of the communist leader Yusef Dadoo" (Francis 56). As Vanemann added, "ANC youth may be quite nationalist, but ironically they see the 'internationalist' SACP as the best means by which to vent their militancy" (Vanemann 28). Vanemann also stated that though many black youths were aligned with the SACP by the 1980s, this younger generation gave little allegiance to the Soviets, and even saw them as an alien influence (Vanemann 32). This stand fit the positions taken by the ANC Youth League, where even Mandela himself showed some anticommunist/Soviet tendencies in his early years.

In sum, the SACP took advantage of the ANC's *lack* of organizational strength. Leading communist Joe Slovo commented on the situation in the early 1960s: "At the time, the ANC's underground structures were virtually non-existent" (Bundy 57). With the ANC being forced into the underground existence in which the SACP had already lived for a decade, the SACP had much to offer to this newly covert ANC. Needless to say, at this point the ANC was more than ever open to SACP influence. "The [SACP's] clear advantage over the ANC in funding, mobilization, organization, and propaganda gave it increasing influence within the ANC" (Radu 61). The SACP also compensated for other weaknesses in the ANC.

The ANC was and is an "umbrella" organization of many classes, occupations, and even ethnic groups (Wheatcroft 4). Though this broad front approach had its advantages, especially within a multiethnic and splintered South Africa, it also weakened the ANC's cohesion. This approach also made it difficult for the ANC to develop its own coherent ideology. Vanemann agreed. "Ideologically, the ANC embraces a wide spectrum of opinions" (Vanemann 26). As a matter of fact, other than a dedication to overthrow the nationalist regime and an underdefined, left-of-center public policy platform, the ANC had no real ideology per se. The SACP compensated, as a kind of backbone for the ANC, by providing a core of cadres armed with a clear Marxist-Leninist ideology (as detailed in the previous chapter). An examination of the composition of the National Executive Committee (NEC) of the ANC shows that though it has only been "dominated" by the SACP a few times, communists have sat on it at all times, demonstrating that the ANC did appreciate the communists' abilities by promoting them to high positions (Lodge 1983, 174). These highly placed communists undoubtedly provided a needed core of stability for the faction-ridden alliance of civic organizations, women's groups, and ethnic parties that comprises the ANC.

Interestingly, no one denies that the ANC and the SACP are close; the only questions are how close, who controls whom, and at what point does the SACP hold more or less sway. As a matter of fact, as early as 1928 the SACP was quite open about its intentions to "align" with the "local national liberation organization" (i.e., the ANC). For the next few decades this alliance not only became more open but also was finally formally and clearly announced in the Morogoro declaration of 1969. As Legum added:

> A formal alliance was established between the ANC and SACP under the terms of the Morogoro Agreement.... This agreement gave the SACP status within the ANC.... For the first time, non–Africans were allowed to join the ANC ... the majority of non–African recruits appear to have been Communists [Legum 109].

Right-wing elements in South Africa condemned this alliance with vivid (if not entirely accurate) language: "The Black Peril thus finally fused with the Communist Peril" (Nel 3). "Fused" may be too strong a word. Chris Hani, longtime leader of the SACP, stated in 1991 that the ANC and SACP do indeed have differences:

> Where [the ANC and SACP] disagree, of course, is the ultimate goal. The objective of the Communist Party is the building of socialism; the ANC does not see itself going beyond the post–Apartheid period, where there is a mixed economy.... [But] there are no tensions at the moment because we are bound by the [post–Apartheid] program [Goodman 13–14].

Finally, though this alliance was reaffirmed on public television by none other than President Mandela when he gave a speech at the SACP's 9th Party Congress in April 1995 (which this author watched), he hinted that the two organizations may indeed part ways one day. He stated that the alliance was never stronger, though he added (as the ANC does more and more) that the two organizations do have different agendas at times (9th Congress AT, 1995). Both sides agree that though they must stay aligned for the duration, ultimately there are fundamental differences. These "different agendas" will be more fully explored below, but for now the evidence indicates that the alliance is still solid (though it did have a very rocky patch in the early 2000s). Soon before this death, Slovo agreed, "The alliance between the SACP and ANC is, we are convinced, more solid than it has ever been" (Slovo 1991, 5).

So where does this leave us? If the evidence shows, at least, that the alliance has been solid and will be for the immediate future, then it is the nature of the alliance that needs more thorough examination. Is the SACP the seemingly silent and less powerful partner it likes to portray itself as? Or, as the South African right-wing would have it, is it the "spider" at the center of an ominous web, controlling not only the ANC but now also the government through covert mole-like agents? Or, finally and more probable, is the situation something in between these two unlikely extremes? Even Slovo saw these extremes as inaccurate. "It is alleged that we have the ANC in our pockets. The ultraleft, by the way, attacks us for being in the pockets of the ANC" (Slovo 1991, 5). As we explore the details of the alliance, we shall discover that something between these extremes is indeed closer to reality. We shall also briefly look at the role of the Congress of South African Trade Unions (COSATU) within the alliance.[7] Finally, we shall examine the relationship between the ANC and SACP since 1994, when the alliance finally took power. Three models of the ANC-SACP relationship suggest themselves: the "parasite" model, in which the SACP is depicted as a weak, even unwelcome, organism on its ANC host; the "front" model, in which the ANC is seen as a mere cover for the SACP and its communist plots; and the "symbiote" model, which most likely reflects the reality of the situation by depicting a more interdependent relationship.

The Parasite Model

This model argues that the SACP is basically an organizational "parasite," feeding off its host, the ANC. It assumes that the SACP is indeed the weaker of the two, and that its time, at least within the alliance, is limited now that the ANC no longer needs the SACP. It also means that the SACP may be willing to "sell out" its ideology and/or mission to stay in power. Leftist critics of the SACP "charge that the party has diluted or jettisoned its Marxism, abandoned the working class, and opted for petty bourgeois nationalism" (Bundy 53). Dries van Heerden agreed that "[the SACP's] policies have been greatly diluted, nowadays closely resembling democratic socialism…. The party's most radical theoretician, former Chairman Joe Slovo, has developed into the foremost critic of old style communism" (van Heerden 5). In other words, the SACP changed itself so as to continue to siphon strength from the ANC.

Though those who share this view admit that at one time the SACP may indeed have been crucial for the ANC's success, the period of communist importance is over. They argue that the communist era ended in the early 1990s when communism collapsed in the East Bloc. Since then, as its funds dry up, the SACP has been lucky to keep what influence it has with the ANC (van Heerden 5).[8] Bundy explained how bad the international situation became:

> Above all, there is the crisis of "actually existing socialism"—the collapse of late Stalinist regimes in Eastern Europe, and the confusion and conflict mounting in the Soviet Union. The negative impact of these developments is considerable. Most directly, it has led to the disruption of material backing and weakening of support and solidarity. It also set adrift some of the ideological and emotional moorings of the party; this is perhaps most obvious in the rightwards shift on economic and social policy…. There could in short hardly be a more adverse

international context for the task of building socialism in a mid-sized industrial power [Bundy 60–61].

There is also the fact that even if the SACP still had money or guns for its ally, the ANC no longer needs such assistance now that it is the ruling party in South Africa, with the entire state apparatus behind it, not some underfunded, underground party which once needed the SACP.

In all, there is a little bit of truth to this parasite model. The East Bloc of communist nations collapsed in the late 1980s and early 1990s[9]; the SACP then lost its international funding.[10] Though it is true that the SACP still has ties with various leftist, socialist, and communist parties throughout the world,[11] these are usually smaller organizations, which are even more impoverished than the SACP itself (such as the Communist Party of India, or even the Communist Party USA). One would not want to underrate such international connections, but they are almost meaningless when it comes to the ANC alliance. Since the SACP did indeed lose its international funding source over two decades ago, does that also mean that the party must now become some sort of parasite on the ANC?

The answer to this question ultimately must be in the negative. There are indications that some factions within the ANC see the SACP as some sort of troublesome parasite, but that hardly makes it one. It might be added that some elements within the SACP also see the ANC becoming the new class enemy (van Heerden 5). All of these arguments mean that there is no love lost between the extreme elements of both parties, but this is common between any two parties that have an alliance.

At the very least the SACP would have to be dependent on the ANC to fit this definition of being a political parasite, but is it? Though there are indeed interdependences on both sides, in the final analysis the SACP is not that dependent on the ANC and thus is not a parasite. First and foremost, though the SACP no longer supplies funds for the ANC, there is no evidence that the ANC finances the SACP's operations. If anything the two organizations are now financially *independent* from one another, the opposite of parasitism for either. But what of other factors of influence? Are they important?

Another major asset shared by the two organizations was arms. As detailed above, the SACP supplied many of the weapons for the liberation movement and thereby gained additional influence over its partners. Now that the ANC literally controls the armed forces of the state,[12] it obviously no longer needs the covert arms shipments it used to obtain from the SACP,[13] nor, of course, the use of foreign bases for guerrilla training. Also, the SACP no longer has leftist states it can readily get arms from (and no longer needs to anyway). In sum, even though some of the traditional vectors of the SACP influence, like money and arms, have indeed diminished to a great extent, that still does not make the SACP a parasite of the ANC.

The simple fact that the ruling clique of the ANC in 1994, led by Mandela himself, but also supported by then-deputy president Mbeki,[14] still openly and fully supported the alliance means that the SACP was not treated as a mere parasite at that crucial transitional period. Nevertheless, communist leader Raymond Mhlaba felt that there was a growing "procapitalist" element within the ANC that could one day pose a threat to the SACP (Lodge 1983, 176). Obviously one cannot know what these ANC leaders privately thought of their SACP allies, but their public comments in 1994 and 1995 make it clear that the SACP would remain a necessary and valuable ally (9th Congress AT, 1995). Still, and as detailed below, there have been serious and public tensions between the two parties, mostly over the ANC's move towards to the center on economic policy. This came to a head in the early 2000s under then-president Mbeki, but has since lessened under the current president, Zuma, who is more of a leftist and is a former communist leader. Of course, there may be elements within the ANC that see the SACP as a liability, but this faction has yet to gain power or even a strong voice within the ANC. It is possible that the SACP faction within the ANC has silenced this would-be anti–SACP clique, but there seems to be no evidence of this. But even if that were the case, that only demonstrates the influence, not dependence, of the SACP. Before passing to the other models, one last significant way that the SACP could be considered a parasite must be addressed.

If the SACP is dependent at all on the ANC, it is in regard to the electoral system. Though the SACP is independent from the ANC in most ways, it still seems to need to run under the ANC banner in all elections, from small local ones to the national ones.[15] Since 1994, all SACP members who have run for office ran as ANC members. Technically this presents no problems, since as pointed out elsewhere such SACP members are indeed also ANC members (Ellis and Sechaba 26). Dual membership is common for many SACP members (though not vice versa) and this is no exception. Still, one must ask why the SACP *chooses* to run under the ANC banner, when it could (and maybe should) run as an independent party, at least locally (as the Communist Party of India has done for decades, with some success until recently). The obvious answer most often cited by those who see the SACP as a parasite is simple: if the SACP were to run independently in the elections, it would receive very few votes.

Whether this is true or not is obviously a matter for conjecture, but there is some data to help us examine the situation. For the crucial 1994 All Race Elections, it would seem the SACP was wise to run under the ANC banner. A 1992 poll showed that even though, in general, there was reasonable respect for the SACP, very few (3 percent) of those polled indicated a desire to vote for the SACP as independent party (Keller 1992, 12). But since then, has the situation changed? Not really, and this is coming from the SACP itself. As detailed below, the SACP has looked not only at South Africa but communist parties in other developing nations. It concluded that for complex reasons, no communist party has won outright in a national election—though, as with the SACP, there have been other parties that have served within an alliance in power (*The South African Road to Socialism* 12). Though this may change in the future, the SACP is aware of this telling fact.

Why is this? It probably has to do with the SACP's size, its reputation, and most important, the fact that the ANC has a special place in the hearts of the electorate. Though the estimates differ, most scholars place the SACP's size at the end of the 1980s at around 3,000 members. This was a good size for a party that stated just in 1989 that "the SACP should remain a working class party composed primarily of professional revolutionaries" ("For a Democratic Victory..." 11).

After the ban was lifted in 1990, as one of the SACP's more significant reforms, it decided to become a mass party. Earlier, "the SACP never succeeded in attracting a large membership" (Legum 105). After the ban was lifted, a heavy recruitment drive was begun, and by 1992, the party had 25,000 members (Lodge 1983, 174). At the 9th Congress, in 1995, the number 75,000 was mentioned (9th Congress AT, 1995).[16] By the 13th Congress, in 2013, the SACP claimed to have 160,000 members (*Political Report* 1). In 1990, the Central Committee explained why such growth in membership was needed:

> Today our party is emerging from the underground with massive prestige and popularity.... Communists will remain prime targets for all kinds of repression.... A major objective of the coming months will be the building of a strong, legal SACP rooted among the working mass of our people ["De Klerk's Challenge Must Be Answered" 12].

Still, the SACP is a small party compared to the ANC, which had about 640,000 members in 2012.[17] This, though, is not just a matter of numbers because the SACP does not also have the extensive and often rural political network that serves the ANC; in a country like South Africa, that is a serious liability. In the SACP's favor there is the fact that it is a national organization with five regional offices. It is also true, then and now, as Lodge added, that "most communists are young, in the 25 to 30 age group, the street Jacobins of the 1980s ghetto revolts" (Lodge 1983, 174). This can be a valuable asset for a party with a radical agenda, especially in a few years as these youth become, in theory, dedicated cadres for the SACP. Still, the SACP is weak in other ways that prevent it from running independently in elections.

Another of the SACP's liabilities is its reputation for being a radical, dangerous, and, ironically, a "white" party. The fact that this "reputation" has currency among whites, even liberal ones, should surprise no one, after decades of anticommunist nationalist propaganda under apartheid.[18] But this view of the party is also held to some extent among black voters because the SACP *is* a radical party and because it does espouse communism, which is still seen as extremist and often alien by most people in South Africa. The SACP, at least to some extent, is still seen as "dangerous." When I was in South Africa in 1995, I asked about the party, and people of all races and classes on the street were often unable to say how the SACP was a "threat," but they certainly believed it was at some level.[19] This undefined apprehension was truer for whites and wealthier people, but many blacks and poor people also saw the SACP as a threat.[20] Since then, this has undoubtedly lessened: the SACP has openly helped rule South Africa for two decades. Still, whites, of course, have a very specific reason for their distrust of the communists: for many of them communists were and still are "terrorists" and "atheists."[21] This admittedly impressionistic but still negative aura around the party will be hard to shed, though the party tries to do so constantly.[22] With its membership way up, it seems to have partially succeeded.

Finally, the SACP still struggles at times with the odd and inaccurate impression that it is a "white" party, though this image is much weaker than it used to be. The fact remained that "the party elite, always heavily dominated by whites and Indians, succeeded in attracting few influential black leaders" (Legum 106). This racial image of the SACP may have arisen in the early 1920s when the SACP was mostly a white party, with few black members. Also, the infamous decision to join in the undeniably racist Rand Strike of 1922 still occasionally haunts the party.[23] However, it is more than the distant past that plagues the SACP.

For years, the nationalist regime labeled the SACP as a foreign party with a foreign ideology, emphasizing the European (and Russian/Jewish) origins of communism and of some of the SACP leaders.[24] Though blacks hated the old racist regime, they did inadvertently buy into some of its propaganda, including this crude and inaccurate material. There has also been a whispered but very real anti–Semitic angle to this whole ugly affair. Some of the leaders of the SACP have been white *and* Jewish and the regime naturally exploited this.[25] The attacks on Abram Fischer are probably the most famous case of this form of dangerous propaganda, and because anti–Semitism is alive in South Africa, this too was an effective strategy. Also, having Joe Slovo, a white person of Lithuanian Jewish roots, as a prominent leader for so long added to these rumors. Still, as pointed out elsewhere, Chris Hani and Blaze Nzimande, both blacks and important leaders of the SACP, have helped reverse this trend. Plus with many blacks joining the SACP for decades now, this racial issue has lessened a great deal.

In sum, it can be concluded that the SACP depends on the ANC due to its unique electoral needs. But does this make the SACP a parasite? Not really, and not only because the SACP has matters other than elections on its agenda (which it has stressed more recently),[26] but also because the ANC gets something important from having SACP members running as ANC members: competent and experienced leadership. In fact, this may be the aspect of the relationship that keeps the alliance alive.

Even the average SACP cadre is a valuable commodity to the often splintered and poorly structured ANC. These individuals often make the best agitators, union organizers, and leaders throughout the whole ANC organization. There is also the fact that when it comes to elections, many former MK/SACP veterans are quite popular with the black masses (the late Chris Hani being the most outstanding example of this phenomenon). So the SACP, though seemingly dependent on the ANC in elections, actually contributes a great deal to the ANC in this respect. Overall, the Parasite Model, by and large, does not accurately describe the long, complicated relationship between the SACP and ANC.[27] So, does the Front Model explain the alliance any better?

The Front Model

This model is almost the exact opposite of the Parasite Model in the way it depicts the relationship between the ANC and SACP. Instead of the SACP being seen as a weak (if not tenacious) parasite, here it is portrayed as akin to a spider in the middle of a complex political web, manipulating all within its reach but especially the ANC. This is an obviously popular model for the right-wing in South Africa (and elsewhere) since it gains political capital from depicting the ANC as a "communist pawn" of the "nefarious SACP." "[The SACP's] right-wing critics see [the alliance] as an opportunistic marriage of convenience, a cynical manipulation by the communists" (Bundy 53). Is any of this true? Not overall, but the full answer is somewhat more complex.

Most authors who have written on the subject, especially the more right-wing ones, see it all in quite simple terms. One author claimed:

> The ANC has been transformed into a Marxist-Leninist organization.... While claiming to be a "national liberation" movement it is actually revolutionary movement.... Communist penetration of the ANC proper is six decades old, and infiltration of the MK has been the case since its creation [Radu 74].

Another author stated:

> The ANC, in fact, has been under the effective control of the South African Communist Party (SACP) since the late 1940s.... Although not all of its leaders are communists, enough of them are members of the party to exert a controlling influence in the organization and hence render the ANC in a effect a Soviet-controlled satellite [Francis 55].

In the 1980s, this may have been marginally truer, since as pointed out the ANC was still quite dependent on the SACP's monies, arms, and international ties. However, decades later, the ANC is in control of the very state whose government it was trying to overthrow for so long. Thus, though the simple vision of the relationship, as Radu or Francis portrays it, has appeal even today, the reality is far more complex.

Still, it remains that an entire school of thought and ultimately a state ideology was built around this Front Model. A right-wing author who exemplifies this perspective is Chris Vermaak. His infamous 1966 book *The Red Trap* summed up a popular Afrikaner perspective on communism and the SACP.[28] He saw an amorphous but all-powerful "international communism" using local communist parties (SACP) to infiltrate and corrupt various local organizations (the ANC, the Congress of Democrats, etc.). Other authors such as Panos Bardis claimed the SACP was trying to control the United Democratic Front in the 1980s (Bardis 102, 106). Colin Legum added details: "The SACP's main targets for infiltration were the African National Congress (ANC), the Indian Congress, the Labour Party, the Congress of Democrats, the Springbok Legion ... and the labor unions" (Legum 107). Once this was completed, the SACP was supposedly to use these "fronts" to slowly take over South Africa. This was and is a popular view of the ANC/SACP alliance among whites, and has some purchase among the black nationalist organizations such as the Pan Africanist Congress (PAC) (PAC Interviews AT, 1995). This whole idea of a communist party hiding behind leftist fronts is not just a South Africa issue; the far right in America has claimed similar things since the 1950s. Regardless, is this an accurate or more paranoid view?

In the final analysis, this view was and is somewhat paranoid and thus inaccurate for a number of reasons. Starting from the first premise about "international communism," those who accepted this notion were wrong. The whole idea of a "communist bloc" was always only partially true and by 1960 it was not correct at all. The Sino-Soviet split was known of, if not extensively, by the mid–1960s when Vermaak's book was written, and the Soviet-Yugoslav split was over a decade old. By the 1980s, when the South African regime saturated the country with anticommunist propaganda that still talked of "international communism," the whole idea had little correspondence in the real world. The complex situation in Cambodia once the ultra–Maoist Khmer Rouge took over in 1975 showed how split the "communist bloc" was by the late 1970s. Still, it seems, many South Africans *wanted* to believe such things.

For Afrikaners, the entire notion of a "world communist plot" fit their sometimes xenophobic worldview. Ever since their national identity began to form after the Dutch farmers moved out of the Europeanized Cape Town area into the "wilderness" of the South African interior in 1832, the Afrikaners have seen themselves as a persecuted minority, which has indeed been true at times. They saw enemies everywhere: first it was the Dutch Cape governor, then it was the indigenous Africans they encountered as they penetrated into the interior, and finally it was their British overlords during the late 19th century. What new enemy was there to fear after formal independence in 1910? Conveniently, in the early 1920s a new one did appear: the SACP.

Since its conception, the SACP has been seen as a threat by both the English and Afrikaners. Though communists were persecuted before 1948, it was only after the Nationalist victory that anti-communism became a literal state ideology. The Nationalists saw the communists as the threat, even greater than the "native" (read: black) one (Vermaak Chapter 1). Though the sheer numbers of blacks was frightening, many whites saw the SACP as (a) a "white" (and often "Jewish") organization and thus (b) the true "brains" behind the alliance and therefore the real threat; this was not only racist but also inaccurate.[29] The Afrikaners, unlike most whites of English descent, also saw the SACP as a representative of "foreign" international communism. The British, long the Afrikaners' most hated enemy,[30] would be slowly replaced by the "foreign communist element" as the number-one enemy of their new order.

So as the Afrikaners became more and more convinced that domestic communism was a threat because of its international ties, a political myth began to form. This myth saw communism as a world bloc of diabolical and powerful communist parties that worked in near perfect unity for the downfall of the "Christian White West," which Afrikaners saw themselves as part of. Ironically, unlike in America and parts of western Europe where the "communist threat" was seen primarily as an economic and/or political one (i.e., anticapitalist and antidemocratic), most Afrikaners also saw the threat as a religious one (though at the height of McCarthyism, the religious factor was also used in America). Not only were the communists seen as officially atheists[31] but they also were accused of undermining the National Christian Education foundation of apartheid (Goodwin 262). This indeed was a serious charge, since the Christian fundamentalist foundation of the school system was an important component of the Afrikaners' racist regime. Thus, the SACP appeared to the nationalists and their supporters as foreign, atheistic revolutionaries being directed from foreign lands.

Ironically, this image contains some truth. There were "foreigners" in the SACP, both perceived (i.e., Slovo) and real (i.e., Wolton), but they were hardly the majority in the SACP, especially by the 1980s. Moreover, most of them were hardly true "foreigners," at least no more than most white South Africans, like the Italians, the Portuguese, and so on, who were all relatively recent arrivals.[32] On the religious front, it is hard to say how many of the communists were true atheists, especially the rank and file (as elsewhere, agnosticism seems common in the ranks of this communist party), but again, since the SACP itself has (a) not stressed the issue for decades, and (b) has no real power yet to enforce any religious policy, the matter remains moot. It is true that the SACP (and ANC) did threaten the Afrikaners National Christian Education system, but this is only to be expected, since this program was more political and racist than religious. Finally, to complicate matters, the SACP was and was not an agent of international communism.

As has been detailed elsewhere in this book, the SACP certainly was close to its Soviet allies for most of its existence. During certain periods, the SACP could even be considered a "pawn" of the Soviet-dominated Comintern.[33] However, it would be a gross overstatement to insist on that characterization after the 1960s and especially by the 1980s (and of course it is a nonissue after 1991 and the collapse of communism). Not only did it deviate from the official policies of Moscow, though admittedly not often, but it also did have genuine domestic support both within the ANC and the black masses as well as in white radical circles. Thus, even given the SACP's extensive foreign affiliations, it could still boast of extensive roots in South African soil. As a matter of fact, those foreign connections often turned out to be less useful than the SACP's real domestic support. Arms and money are always important in a revolution, but without the disgruntled masses to actually fight the revolution, arms and money do any organization very little good.[34] So though the SACP could be accused of having "foreign ties," the point is that even without them the SACP had real South African constituencies. It proved this in the last two decades, as the SACP has gained domestic support for its socialist program.

Another popular idea about the SACP is that its primary tactical goal was to infiltrate and dominate the ANC. As discussed in the previous section, there is some truth to this allegation, but again, the devil is in the details. It is certainly true that in 1928 the SACP was literally *ordered* to infiltrate the ANC by a foreign body, the Comintern. It is also true that the SACP did indeed do just that during the next three decades. However, was this the insidious plot that some believe it was, or was it just smart politics? The SACP did not secretly "infiltrate" the ANC: it was quite open about the need to align with the ANC[35] and had an entire historical model to explain why (the Two Stage Theory). This was hardly some "secret, international plot," but rather a sensible, declared political plan. That being said, it still remains to ask if this plan succeeded. That will be answered in the next section, but before we explore that issue, we need to examine the last premise of the Front Model.

With the alliance fully formed, the right-wing Vermaak school of thought assumed that if given the opportunity, the SACP would use the ANC to "take over" South Africa covertly and establish a totalitarian communist state. Vermaak was only partially right and only on one point: the Nationalist regime did eventually lose power to the ANC. He got all the other details wrong, sometimes excessively. As noted, the SACP did indeed infiltrate/align with the ANC, it did fight against the Nationalist regime for years, and the ANC did win in the end. However, that is where everything else Vermaak (and others) predicted was incorrect. First and foremost, though the ANC did indeed win power, it was through the ballot box, not through some "communist revolution." Vermaak could never have predicted the ANC's electoral victory since he had always been for the policy of the nationalist regime to deny the vote to blacks. Yet, the Nationalists even supported the 1994 elections, knowing full well what the outcome would be.[36]

The fact that the ANC never won the revolution through violence also means that whatever alleged totalitarian plans the alliance may have had (and it is unclear the ANC had any and the SACP had few), they became impossible to implement. As a matter of fact, the Government of National Unity (GNU, headed by the ANC) was a rather unstable edifice until its disintegration in 1996; it was hardly a prototype for a traditional East Bloc communist regime. Further, this all assumed that (a) the ANC did indeed want communism, or (b) if the ANC did not, the SACP so dominated the ANC that it would create a communist system through the ANC. On the former point, there is little evidence that the ANC ever wanted a "communist" regime. On the latter point, there is little evidence it is true.

The ANC Freedom Charter of 1955 did call for some nationalization of resources and industries,[37] but that hardly qualifies the ANC as a "communist" organization.[38] If nationalization does indeed equal communism, then most of western Europe has been "communist" since the end of World War II, since such nations as Sweden, Norway, France and even England have had nationalized industries for decades (though privatization campaigns have picked up momentum since the 1980s). Moreover, some, like David Goodman, felt the ANC had already abandoned its socialist orientation:

> For the African National Congress (ANC), the shift has brought with it some about-faces on once-sacred economic positions. Simply put, the ANC is abandoning much of its socialist program for familiar Keynesian formulas.... What was "inconceivable" is now official ANC policy: the movement is now backpeddling from its insistence on nationalizing major industries [Goodman 12].

Nevertheless, Mandela went on record as late as 1990 stating, "The nationalization of the mines, banks is backed by the ANC, and a change or modification of our views in this regard is inconceivable" (Goodman 12).[39] Ultimately, the proof of the ANC's intentions is in its actions. So far, not only has the ANC *not* nationalized any industries since 1994 but it has actually started to "restructure state assets" (read: privatization) ("No to Mindless Privatisation" 1).[40]

Regardless of the ANC's macroeconomic policies, since many ANC members are also SACP members, this means many individual members of the ANC are "communists" by definition.[41] Still, the ANC as an organization has stated over and over that it is not communist, and more to the point, it has certainly done nothing remotely "communist" in its public policy since taking power.[42] If anything, the SACP and other leftist groups have attacked the ANC, especially under Mbeki, for being too centrist.

Finally, does the ANC's communist ally, the SACP, somehow have a totalitarian card up its sleeve? Obviously, the question can ultimately only be answered by the passing of time, but at this point the SACP has shown no desire to "take power," let alone set up some all-powerful state. As described earlier, for decades the SACP has held that there will be two stages to the revolution, the national democratic one led by their ally the ANC, and the later socialist transformation led by the SACP and the working class.[43] Therefore, "Communists are careful to reaffirm the ANC's senior status in their partnership" (Lodge 1983, 176). Until the proper objective situation exists, which the SACP claims has certainly not yet arrived, the party will support their multiclass ally, the ANC, while building up both class consciousness and political structures within the working class.[44] Lodge stated, "The SACP retains a vanguardist conception of its role" (Lodge 174). The SACP Central Committee made the same point earlier: "The ANC ... recognizes the leading role of the working class.... However, the ANC is not a workers' vanguard political party" ("Path to Power" 110). Slovo himself stated this:

> The ANC remains a mass nationalist movement ... the ANC does not and should not demand a commitment to a Socialist South Africa as a precondition to membership. [The SACP, on the other hand,] is not a mass-movement; it represents the aspirations of a single class—the proletariat [Bundy 54].

The stress on avoiding "mass-movement" status has been lessened, as a huge membership drive was initiated soon after this statement was issued, but the SACP's emphasis on its identity as a class-based party is consistent with decades-long party policy.

Since the socialist transformation stage is discussed in only the broadest of strokes in party circles, *when* it will come is not really an issue for the party now (or, as a matter of fact, the ANC).[45] The SACP's reading of Marxism-Leninism makes it quite clear that the proper moment for the revolution ("the transformation")[46] only comes when the objective forces have progressed and aligned to the proper point and the subjective factors, such as the communist party, leadership issues, and the like are also ready to act; then and only then can the revolution be successful. This is actually more Orthodox Marxism than Marxism-Leninism, which has always hedged its bets on whether a revolution can happen "earlier" than it would first seem possible.

Now even if the SACP had plans to create a totalitarian and/or communist state, such an event would occur at some distant time. This is not to suggest that the party leadership is cynically using the promise of a "communist paradise" to somehow dupe the masses. All the evidence indicates that when Slovo stated, "Let me reiterate our complete confidence that ultimately South Africa will arrive at a socialist system," he meant it (Slovo 1991, 7). The rest of the SACP's top leaders seem to agree with this policy, at least publicly. Still, the party was and is clear that this "socialist future" is far off and there is no clear way to know when it will come. Certainly not while an ever more centrist ANC still runs the country, as it has for decades.

Finally, there is also the fact that, officially, the SACP does not now believe in the merits of the "totalitarian state." The term is put in quotes only because the East Bloc regimes never officially saw themselves in that light either. No one could deny that before the rise of Eurocommunism in the 1970s most communist parties did approve of the Stalinist model of rule, which, if not truly totalitarian in all ways, was certainly close to it. All of this has changed since the collapse of East Bloc communism. Most remaining communist parties, including the SACP, have now officially accepted the merits of a democratic, plural system of some sort. The integrity of these claims was explored earlier, but the general conclusion is worth recalling: the SACP is seemingly honest in its claims, if not totally ideologically coherent when it makes them.[47]

How do these conclusions affect the Front Model? Overall, the evidence shows that in some ways the SACP has indeed "used" its ally the ANC to gain influence and popularity. However, that hardly proves that the ANC is a mere front for a communist takeover of South Africa. The main reason the Front Model is unpersuasive is that it is not only tainted by a right-wing bias but that it ignores evidence about the SACP's actual influence over the ANC. As we shall see, the SACP has done a great deal with very little over the decades to gain seemingly powerful positions within the ANC. However, have these positions actually translated into real power for the SACP? They have, but only in some limited and rare cases. However, much of the time the SACP's plans and desires are stymied by the ANC and its surprisingly centrist approach to rule since taking power two decades ago. If the ANC is to the right of the SACP on the ideological spectrum, that must mean the SACP has obviously not "controlled" ANC policy for quite some time.[48]

In 1989, the SACP itself denied any aspirations to make the ANC into a puppet. "Communists have never sought to transform the national democratic movement into a front of the Party" ("Path to Power" 112). Though one would expect such an answer from the SACP, the statement has the ring of truth. If nothing else, there is no evidence that the SACP ever overtly tried to make the ANC into a communist organization. Nevertheless, even if it did not go that far, the SACP did seem to influence the ANC considerably for decades; the extent of that influence is the question to which this entire chapter is devoted.

Whereas in the Parasite Model the SACP's influence is understated, in the Front Model it is severely overstated. As we shall see, the SACP is neither a weak parasite nor a scheming political spider, but something rather unique, in between these two extremes. This is also not to say that the alliance's official and simple explanation of their relationship should be accepted without some reservations:

> The two partners in the alliance refute all these charges [of secret agendas]. They emphasize the voluntary nature of the alliance, and its reciprocity ... [and] the alliance does not obliterate their separate identities [Bundy 53].

What, then, is the nature of the relationship, if the SACP is neither parasite nor spider? I suggest that the term that best describes the SACP is "symbiote."

The Symbiotic Model

As shown, the SACP hardly controls the ANC, let alone dominates South African society as the Front Model would have us believe. Though the SACP indeed has had a great deal of influence over the ANC at some points during their long alliance, this does not mean that it ever "dominated" the ANC. This is especially true of the current period, as we shall see below. So though the right-wing "Vermaaks" of the 1960s might be shocked that the new South Africa has a black president and is ruled by the ANC, they might also be disappointed to learn that the "dreaded" SACP has left a surprisingly small footprint, so far, on the public policy of this new regime (and ironically, the SACP would partially agree on this point).

With both of the more extreme models (parasite and front) mostly discredited, the answer to the question of "who is in charge" is already partially answered: neither the ANC nor the SACP is really in control (though the ANC is undoubtedly the dominant partner). As in all symbiotic relationships, *they use each other*. However, that simple formula hardly does justice to the real and very complex situation that exists within the alliance and spills over into the government, civic organizations, and unions. Since the alliance does touch on so many different areas, many of them still need to be explored to determine who, in any given context, has more influence, the SACP or ANC.

The most important area where the two organizations "share" power is the government. As noted earlier, the two organizations, while not merged, do share their membership. Though few ANC members are in the SACP, many SACP members are in the ANC. Thus, this membership overlap, especially from the SACP perspective, is extensive and naturally applies to how the SACP shares power with the ANC in the government. To begin with, the SACP holds no public offices as the SACP, due to the fact that the SACP did not run separately in the elections. Therefore, though there are many SACP members throughout the government, even at the highest levels, none carry the SACP label. All of them are officially ANC members, represent themselves as ANC members, and basically act like ANC members (if not leftist ones); but still, are they truly ANC?

The question, then, is one of role conflict and the possibility of divided loyalties. Officially, the SACP has stated repeatedly that its members who are also part of the ANC must obey its discipline and decisions (though lately it has also stressed that it means not violating core communist values). Slovo himself made this clear:

> [Our alliance] is an unusual relationship ... on the face of it, there are undoubt-edly risks of double discipline ... [but] the strength of the alliance lies in the fact the communists in the ANC have always totally subjected themselves to ANC discipline and authority.... The party leadership has on no occasion instructed party members to adopt specific positions on any aspect of ANC policy [Slovo 1991, 5].

Is this in fact true? I admit I cannot cite one piece of evidence to indicate that the SACP ever tried to undermine the ANC's authority through its members within the ANC.[49] Therefore, to a certain extent, we must take the SACP's statement at face value. In fact, this may all be somewhat of a nonissue in the first place, because of the very fact that the SACP occupies so many positions within the ANC. Since the SACP has a voice literally at the highest offices of the ANC (and government), does it need to undermine the very policies it itself helped to develop and execute?

This is one of the keys to the alliance's success. The SACP, while the admitted "junior partner" at this stage, still has a great deal of influence, some argue an undue amount, because its members hold so many key posts. The SACP hardly ever seems to overplay its hand; if anything, just the opposite is true, in that it is often so subtle and evolutionary in influencing the ANC that it has been accused by other leftists of selling out. By most accounts, that charge is generally incorrect.

A long list of experts and scholars agree that the SACP has indeed been successful in influencing the ANC. By the early 1960s, "the Communist Party gradually took over the central role in the ANC policy-making" (Ellis and Sechaba 41). Radu went farther when he stated:

> Some [members of NEC] are first and foremost ANC cadres; others are cadres of the SACP specializing in front organizations, indoctrination, and propaganda.
> [The ANC] has changed from a semi-nationalist organization dedicated to the pursuit of civil and political rights for South Africa's blacks, to a "vanguard" type of organization with strong Marxist-Leninist elements, operating on the Leninist principle of "democratic centralism," and pursuing anti-capitalist, "anti-imperialist goals" that are congruent with Soviet foreign policy objects [Radu 58–59].

Vanneman also agreed: "In evaluating SACP prospects, it is important to remember that the ANC presidential staff had been almost a SACP preserve for some time, that the SACP had recruited the cream of the Soweto genera-tion of refugees into the SACP ranks, and it virtually controlled the education of key cadres for over a decade" (Vanemann 23). As Lodge added, "Members of the SACP continue to occupy leadership positions within the ANC disproportionate to the relative sizes, in terms of membership, of the two organizations.... Party members were especially entrenched in the command structures of Umkhonto We Sizwe.... We know that party members played a central role in defining ANC strategy in the 1980s" (Lodge 1983, 172). Francis added:

> Public confirmation of the powerful communist influence in the ANC in recent years was provided by Bartholomew Hlapane [NEC member] ... in testimony [to Congress].... No major decision could be taken by the ANC without the concurrence and approval of the Central Committee of the South African Communist Party. Most major developments were in fact initiated by the Central Committee [Francis 57; 59].

Dries van Heerden also saw the SACP dominating the ANC:

> The real strength of the SACP has always been its ability to wield power and influence in the ANC above and beyond its numerical strength.... During the exile years senior communists managed to gain control of key positions in the ANC's top structure.... At least one third of the ANC's governing body ... are also members of the SACP.... The situation is exaggerated on the lower levels of the organization where SACP activists have often managed to gain control of local and regional structures [van Heerden 5].

Finally, Philip Nicolaide and Richard Gibson claimed:

> The ANC has been dominated by communists for years.... Cooperation between the African National Congress and the South African Communist Party began long before they were driven underground.... South African Communists are today a major influence on the ANC.... They hope eventually to make a typical one-party communist dictatorship ... communists are essential in obtaining Soviet arms and training ... the party in South Africa has a notorious reputation for abject servility to Moscow [Bardis 102].

The testimony of these authors and the few witnesses who have stepped forward was conclusive: *the SACP has been extremely effective in influencing the ANC.*

It should be noted, though, that former president of the ANC Oliver Tambo denied any "domination" by the SACP while he admitted a close relationship: "The ANC-SACP relationship has blossomed into a close alliance.... The South African Communist Party, in particular, is inextricably woven into the fabric of our struggle" (Legum 110). The former chairperson of SACP himself, Dan Tloome, made the same point: "The communists hold some leading posts in the ANC and are active in the people's army, Umkhonto we

Sizwe" (Tloome 69). The actual numbers behind these descriptions are also quite telling.

Peter Vanneman claimed that "when the NEC was expanded to 35, 3 of the 7 new members were also SACP members" (Vanneman 23). Lodge stated that the SACP held twenty-one of thirty-five NEC seats in 1985, and later in 1991 ten of twenty-six of the ANC's National Working Committee, nineteen of thirty-five NEC seats in 1991, and eight of thirty-two ex officio posts of the ANC's Executive Committee (Lodge 1983, 174). Colin Legum was more conservative: "On the available evidence there seems little doubt that Communists form a substantial minority [of the NEC]" (Legum 111). Philip Nicolaide estimated, "At least half the present members of [the NEC] ... have been SACP stalwarts" (Bardis 102). Richard Gibson added, "As many as 14 of [Slovo's] black colleagues may also be secret communist party members" (Bardis 102). Dries van Heerden put the number at about twelve NEC positions held by the SACP (van Heerden 5). Finally, Ben Keller of the *New York Times* estimated that ten NEC positions were controlled by the communists (Keller 1992).

Francis listed likely SACP members in the ANC of the mid–1980s: Yusef Dadoo, vice president; Alfred Nzo, secretary general; Dan Tloome, deputy secretary general; Joe Slovo, deputy chief of MK; Josiah Dele, director of international affairs; Mziwandele Piliso, chief of personnel and security; Reginald September, NEC; Moses Mabhida, NEC; Stephen Dlamini, NEC; Hector Nkula, NEC; John Nadimeng, NEC; Thabo Mbeki, chief of political department (Francis 157). Later, Vanemann also listed some prominent SACP members among the ANC: Mzwai Pilaso, ANC intelligence; Dan Tloome, undercover operations in Botswana; Joe Slovo, MK leader; Stephen Dlamini, COSATU leader; Mac Maharaj, leading Indian official; Chris Hani, MK leader; Aziz Pahad, expert on SADF; Ruth Monpati and John Nkadimeng, SACP Politburo; Ronnie Kasrils, NEC; Cassius Make, head of training in Angola (Vanemann 32–33). Finally, while we do not know the exact number of SACP members who ran in the 1994 All Race Elections, Keller has argued that thirty-four of the two hundred ANC candidates were also SACP (Keller 1994). More recent estimates have been much harder to find, since there has been much less interest in this issue both domestically and globally, and the SACP has not released a comprehensive list of its members that serve in the ANC and/or the state (maybe for obvious reasons). Still, all these numbers and facts, though somewhat debatable at the margins, still appear on target.[50] In any event and regardless of the exact numbers, it is obvious that the SACP has had considerable influence at the highest levels of the ANC.

This means that most important ANC decisions, from the grassroots level to the National Executive Committee, has had some communist input as they are made and carried out. Though it would be wrong to argue that the SACP "controls" this process, it certainly seems to have the opportunity to shape and guide it. This influence, though, is hardly limitless. Lodge agreed: "[T]he Party did not enjoy complete intellectual dominance within the ANC.... The ANC was promoted by individuals who were independent of the Party and sometimes critical of it" (Lodge 1983, 174). The SACP also denies that it has any form of caucus within the ANC, though Lodge seemed to disagree with this assertion (Slovo 1991, 5; Lodge 174). Moreover, lately the SACP's power has indeed been reduced. "[The SACP's] influence has been lessened by the new openness within its ranks thanks to the collapse of world communism, and by the growing differences between the ANC and its old ally" (Lodge 1983, 172). This assessment was correct in 1992, and is becoming more true as time passes, especially after the national election in 1999 when the ANC cemented its electoral mandate once again (though with SACP help as usual) and President Mbeki took power. Mbeki was noticeably more cool towards the SACP, unlike President Zuma, who would come later in 2009 and was an ex-communist himself.

There is seemingly no formal SACP caucus of any kind within the ANC. Though the ANC is such a large and amorphous organization that such bodies could easily come into being, the SACP is far too politically savvy to do something that overt. Plus, there is also no evidence that it has done so. There probably are not even informal caucuses of any sort (though it is hard to tell since there is little information on any of this). Ultimately, the SACP does not need such crude, and easily discoverable, political tools to maintain its influence within the ANC. SACP leader Cronin argued that the SACP did not need formal bodies within the ANC, since its members helped the ANC itself develop and execute policy; this was and is true (Cronin AT Interview 1995).

As detailed elsewhere, the SACP is a highly disciplined organization with a clear ideology and political strategy. Critics on both the right and left agree that all members of the party know this, because they are trained in it through various party education efforts (Vermaak 1966; 9th Congress AT, 1995). Even the lowest and least educated communist party members have some idea what the future holds as the party sees it. Unlike ANC members, who at times seem unclear on what the organization stands for other than opposition to racism and "building a new South Africa" (both admirable if amorphous goals), the cadres of the SACP do have a "mission," both political and personal. Party members know that building socialism is the SACP's ultimate goal, and though some may disagree about how it is being done, the members who have stayed with the party are still devoted to it.

On a personal level, these party members seem to gain real satisfaction from what they see almost as a (secular) "messianic mission" (9th Congress AT, 1995). Though the religious metaphor has been overdrawn in the past, Marxist-Leninist parties do appear to give their members more than just political fulfillment (if not literally a spiritual one, at least a psychological one). With all this in mind, the SACP members in the ANC are usually far more devoted, focused, and ultimately more effective than most other ANC members, though there are of course exceptions on both sides (especially as the SACP has grown; at its last congress in 2012, it talked of improving the quality of its new recruits) (*Political Report* 1).

Even if the SACP had its members report on ANC efforts from the lowest to highest levels, the SACP would still gain a huge advantage in dealing with its partner, since the ANC has no similar intelligence capacity vis-à-vis the SACP. Moreover, despite what the SACP says about "ANC authority" and the lack of caucuses, it would be naive in the extreme to think that SACP members do not inform the SACP about ANC activities. Obviously, they could even do this as a service to the alliance, since a properly informed partner can be a more effective one. How does this subtle strategy aid the SACP's goals?

Even granting the improbable, that the SACP may have "diabolical" plans or even a caucus within the ANC, its agenda is not necessarily that different from the ANC's at this stage. Neither the ANC nor the SACP denies this, often even citing this "two agenda" situation, but always making it clear that this is not a problem, especially during this democratic stage of the revolution. Both agree that the ANC is to lead, both in government and in the alliance, and that a "mixed (capitalist) economy" is best for now, due to the current "objective conditions." What will occur in the SACP-proposed socialist Second Stage is much less clear, but that has been seemingly put off indefinitely. Therefore and for now, there is little friction on this point within the alliance. The ANC accepts that as long as there is no formal SACP faction within the ANC, individual SACP members within the ANC are free to voice "their" positions, as can any ANC member. The fact that these SACP members are inevitably pushing, to one degree or another, the SACP's position as theirs, is the principal way the SACP influences the ANC.

Since the ANC has always had some form of internal democracy with its many members,[51] this has allowed the SACP to push its agenda openly and quite legitimately. As a matter of fact, the SACP is not the only organization that does this within the ANC, in that many groups are aligned with this large organization, often with the same dual-membership system that the ANC/SACP shares. These smaller organizations (known as "civics") also try to establish their agendas within the ANC (van Heerden 5). The only difference between these organizations and the SACP are in size and effectiveness. The SACP is one of the larger aligned organizations, with only the Congress of South African Unions (COSATU) being larger (though it is not nearly as organized or effective as the SACP within the ANC). Yet even here the SACP has its fingers, for the SACP also effectively influences COSATU policy, as we shall see below.

In the final analysis there is nothing insidious about the SACP's role within the ANC. This belies the Front Model, with all of its assertions of international "red tentacles" and "moles" (Vermaak 1966). Note that term "mole" implies some sort of secret underground penetration, but as noted the SACP is and always has been open about its cross-membership with the ANC.[52] Even before the lift of the ban in 1990, when security was much tighter, it was still obvious to even the casual observer which of the ANC leaders were also part of the SACP. Slovo would, of course, be the best example, but Chris Hani, Jay Naidoo, Jacob Zuma, and many others would also fit. It is true that during the long struggle against apartheid some of the SACP members within the ANC kept their communist loyalties secret. But all evidence indicates that this was to keep the national regime in the dark, not the ANC.[53]

Now we need to return to the question of the alleged "separate" SACP agenda. The SACP sees itself in a number of different roles and one of them is the "consciousness" of the alliance. It does this by pushing a leftist economic agenda, usually centered on workers' issues but also involving other progressive causes.[54] These can range from women's and children's rights, various environmental causes, anti-globalization, and so on (*SACP 10th Congress* Resolutions. SACP Home Page, July 1998, 20–21). None of this should be surprising, since such causes all fit the general socialist agenda (and even a general leftist one), especially for a party still fighting the international capitalist system.[55] However, the SACP is now in an odd and often uncomfortable position: though it is pledged to fight the injustices of capitalism, it is also aligned with the ruling party that now presides over just such a system. When the alliance members were outsiders, it was easy to attack the racist and capitalist nationalist regime. But now that the ANC is the ruling party, the situation is far more complicated, for itself but also for the SACP.

Though much of the ANC leadership still appears to oppose the abuses of the capitalist system, for various political reasons it has not heavily pushed any of its former "socialist" (more left-of-center) agenda. The welfare programs it has started are often inadequate (though this is not certainly always the ANC's fault). There is also a general perception among the poor masses that the ANC is cutting deals with the "big corporations"; though overstated, it is true that any ruling party within a capitalist country must work with the corporations residing within it. It must also be granted that the ANC has little choice but to cater to the business sector due to a fear of capital flight, economic decline, and international economic pressures. Such factors are faced by any ruling party in the developing world. Thus, the ANC is even put into the unenviable position of pressuring the unions (the ANC's allies) into not disrupting the weak economy: ("South Africa Affiliates Seek End," 556–557; 9th Congress AT, 1995). This last issue is especially sensitive for the SACP, because of its workers' rights agenda and its close ties to COSATU. Though the SACP has so far balanced these conflicting roles well, it cannot do so indefinitely.

For now, the SACP pushes its workers' agenda within the ANC and the government. As the SACP itself claims, there is no evidence that it does so in some covert or even synchronized way, but it is clear that SACP members do push their party's agenda every chance they get at all levels of the ANC and the government. Does the ANC resent this? Officially, former president Mandela saw the SACP's "vigilance" as a useful asset that could help the average South African's life (9th Congress AT, 1995). It would appear that Mandela himself, and probably most of the ruling ANC clique he led at the time, believed this too.[56] But since the late 1990s, there has been ANC pushback on this issue, sometimes strongly:

> Deputy President Thabo Mbeki on Thursday added his voice to Wednesday's criticism by President Nelson Mandela of the South African Communist Party.
> Addressing the SACP's 10th annual congress, Mbeki berated the party for the ease with which it has leveled "charges of treachery" against the African National Congress, adding that the ANC does not need the SACP as a watchdog over its policies as government.
> Said Mbeki: "None of us should go around carrying around the notion in our heads that we have a special responsibility to be a revolutionary watchdog over the ANC."
> At the heart of the attacks by Mandela and Mbeki is criticism by the ANC's allies the SACP and the Congress of SA Trade Unions of government's Growth, Employment and Redistribution (Gear) macroeconomic programme [Maharaj 1998].

It might be added, however, that even the influential Cronin of the SACP feels that if the alliance is to last, the two parties must constantly work together, sometimes in a critical way, to stay united (van Heerden 5; 9th Congress AT, 1995). He stated in 1998:

> that the SACP is not a "revolutionary watchdog ... snapping from the stands," and that the party's criticism of the ANC was made in good faith. He reiterated the SACP's opposition to GEAR. He said the SACP intends to remain in the Tripartite Alliance, and to be "communist, autonomous, independent and have the courage of our conviction" [Maharaj 1998].

Cooperation is one thing, but unanimity of views is another.

The ANC members farther to the right, those who work within the Finance Ministry (therefore with "big capital"), all tend to see the SACP differently. At best, they view this "leftist critic" as an embarrassment for the ANC and the country. Now that the ANC has finally taken power, they claim privately that they could get some real work done if they did not still have the "communist albatross" around their necks, limiting foreign aid and diminishing the respect of international capital. At worst, they suspect the SACP to be a generally subversive element within their own ranks, one that could prove disastrous for them one day (Manamela 2013). They also rightfully ask when the SACP intends to start its "socialist transformation" of South Africa, and what role the ANC would play in this "Second Stage." The SACP is keenly aware of these critics within the alliance.

The SACP has been aware of this right-of-center threat from within the ANC for quite awhile, though it played it down. As former National Chair Tloome stated, "Our enemy is still hoping to find 'moderate African nationalists' who would come out against the communists" (Tloome 69). Since then, and after almost two decades in power, there are indeed moderate and rightist ANC members who have little use for the SACP. It is also likely that this more conservative element in the ANC can only increase and become more prominent as time passes; this can already be seen by the more conservative changes in ANC policy since the late 1990s and early 2000s.

As the ANC settles down as a "responsible ruling party," it will come under more and more pressure on it to enact the centrist and/or right-of-center policies that the SACP opposes (privatization, austerity, opening trade policy, etc.). But how much influence do these right-of-center ANC elements have now? In the early 1990s, the Nationalist regime did *try* to separate the ANC and SACP by exploiting this rightist element within the ANC, but the attempt failed, mostly due to Mandela's quick and full domination of the ANC after his prison release and his immediate declaration of full support for the SACP.[57] This is not to say, however, that such a rightist opposition to the SACP does not now exist within the ANC, which gained its high point under Mbeki but has receded since Zuma took office.[58]

In 1992 Pallo Jordan, then ANC communications director, waged a "war" against SACP influence within the ANC. This, too, failed, with Jordan being fired in early 1996 over another similar power struggle with Mandela ("Crossing Madiba..." 1). This indicates that some leaders within the ANC are indeed in opposition to the SACP; as a matter of fact, some fear the SACP's considerable influence (Radosh). As Vanemann explained:

> Although the ANC and the SACP have been formally allied for years ... there has been continuing friction between the two.... ANC suspicion of the SACP emanates from three sources: fear of communist domination, resentment over the predominance of whites in the SACP, and concern that the SACP, despite recent rhetoric, shares Moscow's present aversion to revolution [Vanemann 29].

Most of these specific fears of the SACP have subsided or disappeared since the early 1990s, especially and obviously those concerning the Soviets and their influence. Yet if anything, as the ANC gains its own separate power base within the state, elements within the ANC have increasingly come to resent the SACP's role in the alliance.

It should also be noted that historically even the longtime ally of the SACP, Mandela, was once reportedly against the communists. Legum explained:

> The main stumbling block to the Communists' united front tactics was the black nationalists.... The SACP's persistent attempts to win alliance of the ANC were strongly resisted not only its more conservative and bourgeois leaders but by young militants like Nelson Mandela and Oliver Tambo.... Mandela and Tambo proposed the expulsion of Communists from the ANC in the late 1940s [Legum 107].

However, that was many decades ago and Mandela is now dead. It is ironic that during this period, the nationalists constantly tried to argue that Mandela *was* a communist. By the 1960s, Mandela and Tambo were allies of the SACP and worked closely with it within MK. As Legum himself admitted, collaboration aside, "Mandela and Tambo did not, however, accept the doctrines of Marxism." Mandela himself underlined the point during his 1963 trial: "It is true that I have been influenced by Marxist thought ... but this does not mean [I am a] Marxist.... The Communist Party sought to emphasize class distinctions while the ANC seeks to harmonize them. This is a vital distinction" (Legum 108). That is still very true today as the ANC is burdened with running a multiclass, multiethnic South Africa. This distinction remains important and, I will argue later, could become the dividing issue between these two organizations.

To make matters even more complicated for the SACP, it is not only right-wing critics in the ANC who are antagonistic to the SACP. *Leftist* critics, some within the ANC, accuse the SACP of not being serious about a revolution. "ANC Marxists are critical of the SACP as well as its Soviet patron" (Vanneman 29). The Soviet patron itself has disappeared, but the criticism continues. It should also be mentioned that some ultraleftist critics claim that there is no significant difference between the various cliques and factions of the alliance. One such critic of the alliance claimed:

> It must be stated ... that the so-called difference in the ANC/SACP between hard-liners on the one hand, and pragmatic moderates on the other, is a thorough delusion.... We are dealing with quislings where opportunism and careerism feature more importantly than policy, programme and principle. The ANC has always been a quisling organisation.... Nothing has changed and much has got worse. The worst are the so-called leftists in the executives of the ANC and SACP who exist comfortably in this rotten corpse [Mokonyane 68].

The facts are mostly otherwise, but the charge still has some bite. In the final analysis, to say there is no significant different between the ANC and SACP is to miss some of the most important factors in this complicated relationship.

In any case, the SACP sees itself as leftist critic and conscience vis-à-vis its powerful ally, the ANC. However, the evidence suggests it wants far more. As discussed above, the SACP is building a mass base as fast as possible and has gained a number of powerful positions in the central and provincial governments of South Africa: Slovo was briefly Minister of Housing, Cronin recently became Minister of Transportation, and the head of the SACP itself, Nzimande, is Minister of Higher Education and Training. Though at this point it is seemingly serving ANC needs, what if this situation ever changed? Could this small but formidable party be a threat to the ANC regime? Would it ever want to be?

The answer can only lie in the realm of speculation since the two parties are still close allies, but after examining the extensive SACP penetration of both ANC party and state structures, it is clear that the SACP has the potential to be a major disruptive force in the alliance. Again, the proponents of the Parasite Model would argue that the SACP has bluffed the ANC and South Africa for more than a decade, as its power decreased during the collapse of communism. The Front Model proponents, however, would argue that if anything, the whole idea that the SACP was going to "strike" at the ANC was absurd, since the communists already control their larger ally in the first place.

Both these views miss the mark. The SACP did not and does not control the ANC and therefore it is not ridiculous to ask if the SACP might one day break the alliance and attack the ANC. It is also true that the SACP should not be underestimated. It does have many of its members within key positions inside the ANC and the state, and if there were ever a break, these people could disrupt the ANC. Their mere resignation could damage the ANC, and if they remained within the ANC and fought as a faction, they would probably lose, but by then the ANC would be disrupted. This anarchy would surely translate into trouble inside and outside of the alliance, possibly causing a rift between the ANC and COSATU and/or chaos pouring into the streets. But for any of this to happen, one must assume that these SACP members within the ANC would stay loyal to SACP. Is this safe to assume?

The answer actually came from then deputy general secretary Cronin in a candid interview with me in 1995. He was asked about the "Stalinists" within the party and what happened to them when the party sided against the 1991 coup in the Soviet Union. He answered that some quit, others came around, but then continued, saying that after the ban was lifted in 1990, it was not only the Stalinists who left the party. He commented that many "hangers-on" and "careerists" also left the party, once legality brought the spotlight of publicity down upon them. Many just wanted to quit "the struggle after so many years," but others saw new careers in the more "respectable" ANC. He claimed that most of the "unreliable elements" had left the party years ago (Cronin Interview AT, 1995).

Is Cronin to be believed? It is hard to check such things (and he may not fully have known either), but his analysis did make sense and explained much. After years of covert and underground struggle, it is easy to imagine why many formerly dedicated cadres would want just to settle down in the new South Africa, maybe as ANC members or even as normal citizens, instead of fighting battle after endless battle. As for the so-called careerists, the SACP had denied such members even existed. But the mere fact that the party itself admitted to them after 1990 now lends some credence to the claim that they have left or been expelled. But how does this all relate to the reliability of the remaining members, especially the leaders in key positions?

It seems that the SACP members who have stayed and have taken on this last struggle for the creation of a socialist South Africa are probably quite serious. It is of course possible that a few may indeed defect to the ANC, or quit politics in general, if there is a split in the alliance. But after literally decades of being loyal communist cadres fighting for an idealistic cause, it would be odd indeed for them to forsake it all when the actual struggle for socialism was just beginning. The communists I talked with while in South

Africa did honestly and fully believe in the Second Stage of the revolution, when socialism will be built.[59] Such cadres will probably not betray their party, the SACP, if the alliance breaks down. But before we go on to what might cause this breakdown, we need to examine the often ignored third partner in the Tripartite Alliance, COSATU.

COSATU: The Silent Partner

The Congress of South African Unions (COSATU) has always been the junior partner in the larger Tripartite Alliance, which also includes the ANC and SACP. As the SACP's current program, Path to Power, stated in 1989: "[T]he national liberation offensive is led by the African National Congress in revolutionary alliance with the vanguard workers' party—the South African Communist Party—and the South African Congress of Trade Unions" ("Path to Power" 72). It added that the unions, though strong, needed a party (i.e., the SACP) to become politically effective ("Path to Power" 111). Basically, this is again another case of overlapping memberships and agendas, with a degree of friction mixed in (though less so than with the ANC). The core of the Tripartite Alliance is of course the ANC/SACP alliance with COSATU orbiting around this center. This makes it less involved in the alliance and also much less influential in the running of the government now that the ANC has taken power.

Still, COSATU is not without its resources. It has over a million members, numerous unions as part of its federation, and a real respect from much of its rank-and-file (9th Congress AT, 1995; Baskin ix). Its power to strike is not only economic; as in most South African strikes, there is a serious political dimension (Baskin Chapter 25). And strikes are a serious matter in South Africa: they have rocked South Africa for a century, before, during, and now after apartheid. Although the ANC now rules the country, strikes remain a stark reality due to the abysmal economic status of most workers (9th Congress AT, 1995; "The World Factbook..." 1). COSATU knows this all and often implicitly uses the threat of chaos to push its agenda with its alliance partners (van Heerden 5). However, its power is still ultimately limited by a number of factors.

The first and probably strongest constraint, ironically, is its own self-restraint. COSATU is a relatively loyal member of the alliance and shares much of its "reconstruction" agenda, though in the last decade this has decreased, as some of the more radical unions within COSATU (like NUMSA) feel change has come much too slowly to South Africa. In 2011, the once more radical Blade Nzimande, who has been general secretary of the SACP since 1998, opposed mass nationalization within South Africa, even though it was proposed by COSATU ("Nationalization Won't Help the Poor" 1). To be fair, the SACP, as far back as 1995, showed real doubts about such nationalization schemes ("No to Mindless Privatisation" 1). Still, COSATU generally agrees with the ANC and SACP that though the workers' plight must be improved, change can only come relatively slowly due to the economic realities in and outside the country. It too generally accepts the ANC motto, "growth through redistribution."[60] Though this position has often caused friction within this union federation, it has usually followed the path of the ANC and SACP by defusing rank-and-file complaints.[61] How long it will continue to mute its own potential is hard to say, as more and more wildcat strikes are staged by more militant locals, especially since the mid–2000s. Regardless, other factors also constrain COSATU.

The origins of COSATU are important in understanding the basis for its loyalty. It was formed at the initiative of various ANC and SACP activists; as a matter of fact, many COSATU leaders are also SACP members. As Goodman pointed out, "The SACP ... enjoys strong labor support" (Goodman 12). Lodge added, "Communists make a strong showing in trade union hierarchies"; the SACP holds many, often a majority, of positions in union leadership circles (Lodge 1983, 172; 175). Vanneman has also argued that COSATU is heavily penetrated by the SACP (Vanneman 16). The former SACP national chair Dan Tloome claims that the SACP has a great deal of power over the unions (Tloome 69). Jay Naidoo, a longtime SACP and COSATU leader, and one-time leader of the once important Reconstruction and Redevelopment Program (RDP), shows again the intimate connections between the SACP and COSATU (Baskin 6). It can be concluded that, not unlike the relationship the SACP shares with the ANC, it influences COSATU, if not dominates it. Of course, the SACP claims that COSATU is fully independent. As communist leader Hani stated, "I think the independence of COSATU is very essential" (Goodman 14). Thus not only is COSATU officially free to do as it pleases, but the SACP's influence on it does have its limits.

Still, cross-membership between the ANC, SACP, and COSATU obviously leads to a rather surprisingly effective cohesion between such seemingly disparate organizations.[62] When union rank-and-file do want to strike or denounce some new governmental (ANC) policy,[63] these impulses are often defused or deflected by either ANC or SACP members within the union. They are able to do this because they won the trust of the average member after years of struggle. However, as a disgruntled leftist critic of the alliance complained, "These [spontaneous] activities are said by the ANC/SACP to introduce chaos and anarchy" (Mokonyane 126), which any ruling party, even the ANC, would prefer not to have.

But are such strikes "chaos," or genuine complaints of the working class that the SACP claims to represent? Undoubtedly they are both: strikes do present the possibility of the chaos a government fears (and rightfully so), but most strikes also represent economic demands that the SACP should address and even support as the "working class party of South Africa." Again, *the SACP is caught in the middle.* More to the point, one must wonder how long the ANC (or even the SACP) can hold down these rebellious impulses by union members. Or, better yet, how long will the SACP continue to side with the ANC (and its "capitalist" allies) against COSATU (its natural ally made up of workers)?

For the foreseeable future, COSATU will probably continue to take its lead from the ANC and SACP. This will not change for the time being, since all the partners realize that political players outside the alliance are still the primary threat and not each other's agendas. However, as the ANC solidifies its hold on the state and society, this carefully balanced situation may well be replaced with one where the different agendas may come to the front. When this happens, COSATU will surely authorize strikes against industries that the ANC may not want hit. Moreover, even if COSATU backs down indefinitely, the threat of rank-and-file rebellion will still exist and surely grow.

As for the SACP, it will be caught in the middle between the ANC and COSATU (and the workers it represents). On the one hand, the communists' agenda is much closer to COSATU's; that is, workers' empowerment. On the other hand, no one can deny that the long history of the ANC/SACP alliance means quite a great deal for both parties; such organizational and personal ties are not easily broken. Still, with SACP members in both organizations,[64] the party will indeed be in a highly uncomfortable position. It remains, however, that whatever the SACP decides in relations with COSATU, its primary concern is its future with its longtime ally, the ANC.

After Mandela

The SACP faced many challenges after Mandela left office in 1999, mostly concentrating on the rocky changes in leadership in the ANC and the country (from Nelson Mandela to Thabo Mbeki to Kgalema Motlanthe to Jacob

Zuma) and the ever-present fight to keep a leftist public policy, especially on South Africa's all-important development plans, including the Reconstruction and Development Programme (RDP) to the Growth, Employment, and Redistribution plan (GEAR) to the current National Development Plan (NDP). The last-named issue will be covered in detail in the next section, but we need to examine how the SACP handled the various leaders of both the ANC and South Africa after Mandela.

The SACP's relationship with the ANC has faced many hurdles over the decades, and though the ones they encountered since 1994 have been real and at times caustic, overall too many observers have overstated how serious they are. All of the issues push the SACP to decide when they will stake out more independent territory from the ANC, but none of them seem to be causing that "breakup." This is not only true nominally, since the SACP has made various statements reaffirming their commitment to the ANC, but also practically, since the SACP is not yet ready to be wholly separate from the ANC (and, it might be added, the ANC still needs the SACP and COSATU).

Still, the ANC's (and thus South Africa's) leadership transition from Mandela to others was rightfully feared by those within the ANC, the SACP, and the country as a whole. It was not nearly as disastrous as some on the far right or left predicted, sometimes with dire projections of civil war. But Mandela was a highly stabilizing force that many on all sides could at least somewhat rally around. As *The Economist* stated in 1997 on both Mandela and Mbeki:

> The soothing of white apprehension has been the hallmark of Mr. Mandela's government, the price of achieving a peaceful transition from apartheid. But Mr. Mbeki, who treads the same delicate line between black hopes and white fears, navigates a different path. He weighs the acknowledged risk of scaring off whites against a greater need to thwart a black rebellion if, five years hence, nothing much has changed ["Who is..." 1].

Once Mandela was gone from office (though not the spotlight at times), this soothing and stabilizing "rock" would be absent, thus exposing some of the more rough edges of the ANC and its rule of South Africa.

But Mandela's leaving office in 1999 was a loss to the SACP, since he had been a close ally of it for decades, before and during the time he spent in prison. Though an anticommunist as a youth, he switched this position in the early 1950s, never joining the SACP but becoming a "social democrat" for the rest of his life and working closely with both the SACP and MK (Mandela 1994, 172–177). Mandela always emphasized working closely and collaboratively with his alliance allies, and later even the National Party, during the early to mid–1990s, to prepare for the 1994 All Race Elections and then joint rule after that. Though this meant ultimately a mild leftist-to-centrist approach to public policy, he made sure the famous communist Slovo headed the Housing Ministry and that other SACP members got posts in his government, and he pushed social reforms while in office. General economic liberalization starting in 1996 would become an issue for the SACP under Mandela, but would not become a real problem until Mbeki's time in office (Meredith, 521–522). As a matter of fact, not until Mbeki took office in 1999 would there be serious tensions between the SACP and the ANC.

The (sadly) normal accusations of corruption got worse under all three post–Mandela leaders, a serious debate about neoliberalism and a bizarre revisionism about AIDS came with Mbeki, and finally more debates about the role of the state but also overt personal issues arose. The SACP was often (reluctantly) in the middle on all of this. It officially stood for good and rational governance with a real handle on personal scandals; this, sadly, could not be always said about its ally the ANC.

This volume is not the place to detail the leadership transitions of the ANC since it took power, but some of the issues directly affected the SACP and COSATU and do need to be noted. In the broadest of strokes, the Mbeki administration started a push towards a more centrist public policy (some would argue neo-liberal), especially on economic issues such as privatization programs that have only recently been slowed (though not reversed) by Zuma. This move towards the center from the more leftist policies of Mandela was opposed by both the SACP and COSATU (especially some of its more radical unions, like NUMSA).

The SACP pushback against centrist policies will be detailed below, but by the end of Mbeki's time in office (1999–2007), the SACP was openly attacking him, his leadership style, and his policies:

> In an unprecedented attack, the South African Communist Party has lashed President Thabo Mbeki, accusing him of undermining parliament and alienating African National Congress members.
>
> The attack is contained in a discussion document that also strongly hints that the SACP is considering a future without the ANC.
>
> In what is another salvo in the battle for control of the ANC, the SACP —a key alliance partner and staunch supporter of ANC deputy president Jacob Zuma—has charged that Mbeki's presidency is alienating the ANC leadership from its ordinary members and making it difficult to eradicate unemployment and poverty...
>
> In the discussion document, to be debated at the weekend's central committee meeting, the SACP has accused Mbeki's presidency of dominating all aspects of government and the ruling party, thus weakening the ANC as an organisation.

The document, described by SACP general secretary Blade Nzimande on Wednesday as frank and "sparing no holy cows," says Mbeki has undermined the functions of ANC secretary-general Kgalema Motlanthe, reducing his job to an "administrative" position.

"This has involved, among other things, a certain presidentialising of the ANC itself ... reducing the secretary-general's office and organising work to administrative tasks, while 'politics' is housed in a separate, more or less parallel, ANC, dominated by the president," the document states [Monare 2006].

The SACP would soon back Zuma (who joined the SACP in 1963 and become a SACP Politburo member in 1989, though he left the party soon after in 1990), lending support both within the ANC and then later as president. Thus this rift between the ANC and the SACP would be mostly alleviated after 2009 (Gevisser 2007, Beresford 2009, Trewhela 2009). There were rumors that the SACP was mostly supportive of Zuma during his corruption charges and his rape trial (he was acquitted of both charges) and later of the ANC faction that ousted Mbeki first from the ANC leadership then the presidency (Pearce 2005, "SACP Divided..." 2007).

This was officially over Mbeki's illegal interference in state investigations ("Full Zuma..." 2008). But it was apparently about much more. Mbeki was infamous for his "revisionist" AIDS policies (which unscientifically questioned the linkage between HIV and AIDS) that may have allowed hundreds of thousands of South Africans to die a premature death (all of which the SACP denounced publicly) (Brigland 2008). The whole AIDS situation in South Africa was and is tragic. Though wealthier than many other African nations, South Africa avoided addressing this serious issue for far too long:

> For over a decade [1991–2001], South Africa has been a country in denial. The result is that it now has more HIV-positive people than any other in the world. It is at last coming to terms with the appalling consequences of this plague, yet its government remains, in the words of a top official in the international war against AIDS, "the most difficult country that we have to deal with anywhere" ["The Cruelest Curse" 2001].

Mbeki made it much worse:

> One further reason, however, is the attitude of the government, and especially of the current president, Mr. Mbeki. Mr. Mandela's record on AIDS was not good; he found the topic embarrassing. Mr. Mbeki, however, has found it fascinating, so fascinating indeed that he has dabbled in bizarre theories not just about the causes of AIDS, but also about a supposed conspiracy involving the CIA and the big pharmaceutical companies to sell drugs by promoting the thesis that HIV causes AIDS.
>
> The president's reluctance to accept that HIV causes AIDS, coupled with the obduracy of the country's first black health minister, Nkosazana Zuma, has led to

a catalogue of blunders: a venture into a dangerous cul-de-sac in quest of a cheap miracle cure called Virodene; the rejection of several offers by drug companies to provide, at a discount, drugs that did work; the long refusal to make the anti-retroviral drug AZT available in public hospitals, though this was provenly successful as a cheap treatment for halving the chances of passing on HIV from mother to newborn child; and the refusal, until last September, to allow nevirapine, an even cheaper retroviral drug, to be used ["The Cruelest Curse" 2001, 1].

How have these seemingly bizarre attitudes affected the nation?

> Little is known for certain about how many people are now infected, and all forecasts involve some speculation. But the Ministry of Health reckons that 2.5m people are HIV-positive, and UNAIDS (the United Nations' AIDS body) puts the figure at 4.2m people—nearly a tenth of the population. A study for ING Barings last year predicted 8m infections by 2005. A study by Abt Associates, a Johannesburg consulting firm, forecast the number of deaths attributable to AIDS at 354,000–383,000 in 2005, rising to 545,000–635,000 in 2010. Average life expectancy is set to fall from 60 years to 40 by 2008.
>
> Scarcely any aspect of South African life will be untouched by an epidemic of this size. The cost in terms of personal misery is unimaginable. Some of the other consequences can, however, be guessed at.
>
> Since the young, and especially young women, are particularly vulnerable to AIDS, and since husbands and wives infect each other, South Africa will see a vast increase in the number of orphans: 2m perhaps by 2010, many themselves infected at birth. Traditionally in Africa, such children would be looked after by relations, but many South African families are already dysfunctional and, in any event, the numbers are likely to prove overwhelming ["The Cruelest Curse" 2001, 1].

Though Mbeki will be long remembered for this AIDS debacle, he was also known for his more autocratic style, not just towards other parties but even towards his allies the SACP and COSATU (Tutu 2006). This was not only resented but it made promoting quality public policy that much harder. The SACP tried to work with him and his administration but it became harder and harder. The next president would be better but only marginally.

In regards to Motlanthe, who was a placeholder between Mbeki and Zuma for the short time he was in office in 2008 and 2009 (and whom Zuma helped put there, though they would later become rivals), the SACP mostly opposed him like they did with Mbeki. Motlanthe continued Mbeki's wrong-headed AIDS policy, which the SACP still resisted (and which Motlanthe finally did reverse), a centrist public policy which again the SACP disagreed with, but he did have less of an autocratic style than Mbeki and thus this was less of an issue. Again, below I will detail the SACP's (and COSATU's) continuous push back against privatization, rationalization, and general liberalization of the economy mostly after Mandela. Even later, after Motlanthe was out of the presidency but was still a high-serving figure in the ANC, he stated that the SACP "needed political education" and the ANC did not need its communist allies ("Motlanthe Says…" 2012) As he was part of the more right-wing faction of the ANC, Motlanthe's words should not surprise the reader. Zuma, who replaced Motlanthe in 2009 as ANC leader and president, was much closer to the SACP, maybe more so than even Mandela.

As mentioned, Zuma was not only an SACP member for decades but was briefly in the Politburo, right before he left the party in 1990. It is unclear why he did this, but as noted, many members departed the SACP in the early 1990s, due to the widespread changes that resulted when the ban was lifted. As mentioned, Cronin relayed that some left due to fatigue, others gave up "the fight," and others left for different careers (Cronin AT Interview, 1995). This latter reason could fit Zuma, who moved his political career to the ANC itself (though was a member of both organizations like many SACP members). Regardless of him not being an official member after 1990, the SACP continued to back Zuma, and vice versa, for the next twenty years. This benefitted the SACP, as Zuma moved up the ANC leadership, eventually becoming head of the ANC, and also the president of South Africa ("Zuma Sworn In…" 2009).

Some on the right, and even a few ex-communists, have hinted that Zuma is still a member of the SACP (this is mostly to be dismissed), or at the least, is still a "communist" (which is possible, though as detailed throughout this book, that can mean many things, and thus very little). There is no doubt that Zuma was a communist and a leader of the SACP, but so was Mbeki, and that meant little decades later and once he was in power ("Who Is…" 1997; Gordin 2009). Still, Zuma himself does admit to being a "socialist" and wanting to "redistribute the wealth" (McGreal 2007, Wines 2007). Though he has also said he supports the current capitalist system and desires more foreign investment, all leaders of South Africa need to take and support such positions during this capitalist phase of the "national revolution" ("Zuma Calls for More Foreign Investment" 2010). This can be seen with the debate on the new centrist National Development Plan (NDP), but that is covered in the next section, along with the fall of the RDP and the fading of GEAR.

NDP

This section will examine South Africa's economic policies since 1994, which have been pushed by the ANC and partially accepted by the SACP.

Overall, for a "leftist" regime such as the ANC's, South Africa has been surprisingly open with its economy and has allowed multinational corporations back in (many left during apartheid) ("Who Is..." 1997). This is not to say elements within South African society, from COSATU to disgruntled youths to the SACP itself, have not loudly protested against these changes. This is especially true in regards to the Growth, Employment and Redistribution (GEAR) economic reforms and more recently the National Development Plan (NDP), both of which have supplemented the earlier and more leftist Reconstruction and Development Program (RDP). Still, the ANC has pushed ahead, and the SACP realizes this and has adapted once again.

The original economic plan for the new South Africa, the RDP, only marginally embraced overt economic liberalization; both the SACP and COSATU approved of this leftist stance. It was to be the mechanism that would economically transform South Africa into a more egalitarian society, though to be clear, it was not the socialist blueprint that the SACP eventually wants enacted. The first major outline of the RDP was called the *Base Document*, and it stated some of the primary goals of the RDP:

> The five key programmes of the RDP: 1. Meeting basic needs 2. Developing our human resources 3. Building the economy 4. Democratising the state and society 5. Implementing the RDP...
> The RDP is a programme to mobilise all our people and all our resources to finally get rid of apartheid and build a democratic, non racial and non sexist future.
> The RDP is a programme: to address the whole problem, not just part of it; based on the needs and energies of all of our people; to provide peace and security for all; to build the nation; to link reconstruction and development; to build and strengthen democracy [*Base Document* 1994, 1].

Jay Naidoo (then head of the RDP), followed by President Mandela, and later the *White Document* itself made it clear:

> The RDP is an integrated and coherent way in which government is aiming for sustainable economic growth while trying to meet the socio-economic needs of our people. the main features of the RDP relate to skills and human resource development, economic growth, meeting people's basic needs, and the democratization of institutions so that decision-making in government is a process of a partnership between itself and the major stakeholders of society [Cargill, 1997].
> My Government's commitment to create a people-centred society of liberty binds us to the pursuit of the goals of freedom from want, freedom from hunger, freedom from deprivation, freedom from ignorance, freedom from suppression and freedom from fear. These freedoms are fundamental to the guarantee of human dignity. They will therefore constitute part of the centrepiece of what this Government will seek to achieve, the focal point on which our attention will be

continuously focused. The things we have said constitute the true meaning, the justification and the purpose of the Reconstruction and Development Programme, without which it would lose all legitimacy [Mandela, 1994].

The Government's central goal for reconstruction and development is to meet the social and economic needs of the people and to create a strong, dynamic and balanced economy which will—create jobs that are sustainable, and increase the ability of the economy to absorb new job-seekers in both the formal and less formal sectors—alleviate the poverty, low wages and extreme inequalities in wages and wealth generated by the apartheid system, meet basic needs, and thus ensure that every South African has a decent living standard and economic security—address economic imbalances and structural problems in industry, trade, commerce, mining, agriculture, finance and labour markets—integrate into the world economy utilising the growing home base in a manner that sustains a viable and efficient domestic manufacturing capacity, and increases the country's potential to export manufactured products—address economic imbalances and uneven development within and between South Africa's regions—ensure that no one suffers discrimination in hiring, promotion or training on the basis of race or gender—develop the human resource capacity of all South Africans so the economy achieves high skills and wages—democratise the economy and empower the historically oppressed, particularly the workers and their organisations, by encouraging broader participation in decisions about the economy in both the private and public sector create productive employment opportunities at a living wage for all South Africans—develop a prosperous and balanced regional economy in southern Africa based on the principle of equity and mutual benefit [*White Paper* 1994, 1].

The *Base Document* was much more leftist than the *White Paper* or later yet, GEAR, as one can see:

Our central goal for reconstruction and development is to create a strong and balanced economy which will ... end poverty, create jobs and meet the basic needs of our people; address the structural problems of the economy; build the economy in South Africa and Southern Africa and integrate South Africa into the world economy; protect worker rights; develop the human resources of all our people; end all discrimination, e.g., that based on race, sex, disability, religion and language; make the economy democratic by involving all stake holders including trade unions and small business in an open and transparent process of economic decision making [*Base Document* 1994, 1].

Though quite leftist, it does state that "integration with the world economy" was a necessary means to those more egalitarian goals. This would be an issue for the SACP, but both GEAR and the NDP would go much more towards the right than this plan.

Still, the ANC even then promised that the RDP was not socialism or anything like it. As a matter of fact, the RDP itself consistently stressed not only a large role for the private sector, but its own mechanisms would be limited and "rationally" driven by a "business plan." As a *Forbes* series on the South African economy said so well, "The RDP is about a creating wealth and opportunity" and "Opposed to populist solutions which would have it rob the rich to pay the poor, and committed to fiscal discipline and a market-based economy the new government must resort to more effective management of existing resources in order to begin meeting its people's most basic needs. Meanwhile, it must hope that its moderate economic policies will encourage investment and growth which will create new opportunities" (*Forbes Economic Series* 1997).

This is indeed odd terminology for a strictly leftist plan, unless it never was one in the first place. As the *White Paper* later stated:

> [E]conomic policy must specifically address South Africa's problems on the basis of its strengths. The GNU [Government of National Unity] draws on the following basic strategy to achieve its objectives: financial and monetary discipline in order to finance the RDP, reprioritise public sector activity, and facilitate industrial restructuring and the establishment of fair and equitable user charges—the establishment of an economic environment conducive to economic growth—trade and industry policies designed to foster a greater outward orientation so as to sustain high employment levels and levels of participation in the economy—a modernisation of human resource programmes to meet the challenges of changing production processes—a reform of labour market institutions in order to facilitate effective and equitable collective bargaining and restructuring of employment patterns....
>
> A combination of factors therefore demonstrates the Government's commitment to reducing consumption expenditure. These include:—forcing the Government to reprioritise its expenditure rather than seeking new sources of finance—the redirection of consumption expenditure to capital expenditure through the RDP Fund—an additional decrease in consumption expenditure in the Public Service by not filling all vacancies created by natural turnover—a systematic change management programme linked to performance assessment required forward planning on all projects and programmes—the introduction of systematic business plans for all projects and programmes of the Government [*White Paper* 1994, 1].

Thus, as one can see, both rightist and leftist elements existed within the RDP, and this would later allow the ANC to use globalization to help in the development of South Africa, much to the irritation of its more leftist allies, both the SACP and COSATU.

The SACP and COSATU have indeed disagreed in the past on the issues within the RDP and its direction, but here they are mostly in agreement. Members of both these organizations helped conceive and develop the earlier and more leftist conceptions of the RDP. Then, both organizations saw a steady recasting of the RDP in a more rightist mold, conducive to foreign investment. Though the SACP has often been more circumspect in its criticisms of the ANC, both it and COSATU consistently complained that the RDP was either moving towards the right, or becoming unimportant altogether (Davis 1996).

The larger conglomerates and multinational corporations within South Africa not only approved of this rightward move of the RDP, but also readily pushed for it through their own contacts within the ANC, which have grown every year since 1994. The RDP has always promised to be "businesslike" and conducive to international business and investment. Again, as the *Forbes Series* stated, "[The RDP] is designed to encourage domestic and international investment as the means of creating new opportunities and wealth. The RDP's architects accept that investment will only flow if government demonstrates fiscal discipline and encourages development of an open economy" (*Forbes Economic Series* 1997). The business community warned that if the RDP did not live up to these promises, the relatively well-off economy of South Africa would dearly suffer. The ANC listened to these political and economic arguments and allowed the RDP to fade, to be replaced by GEAR; the SACP resisted this trend relatively ineffectively at first, though it was more effective later on.

By the late 1990s, the RDP was in serious trouble on a number of fronts. It was of course attacked for not meeting the expectations that it had raised since 1994; though the RDP had made real progress, it was not enough. Even without considering the issue of expectations, it was a fact that far too many poor South Africans were still untouched by the RDP, and sentiment was rising against the ANC because of this:

> The poverty in which a great number of South Africans live is reflected by research of the Small Business Development Corporation which reveals that 45 per cent of the country's citizens are either employed in the informal or subsistence sectors or are unemployed. The greatest source of resentment is the racial disparity in earning power, educational levels and health care. According to the 1991 census, 53 per cent of white people had completed their high school studies, but only 2.2 per cent of blacks. In the white group 10 per cent of working people were in managerial positions, but only 0.37 per cent of blacks. The pattern extends to every aspect of South African life. One of the greatest threats to stability in South Africa is the possibility that disillusionment of the poor will result in the belief that they have been abandoned by their new government [*Forbes Economic Series* 1997, 1].

This was all reflected by the polls:

> Conducted among 2 241 respondents countrywide during June and July [of 1996], the survey found that 45 percent of people were satisfied with current

political developments, compared to 76 percent in May 1994. Satisfaction with economic developments also dropped, but by a smaller margin—34 percent of respondents were positive during the recent survey compared to 51 percent from the 1994 survey. The number of respondents who expressed dissatisfaction with the political situation rose from 10 percent to 40 percent during the same period and dissatisfaction with the economic situation rose from 31 percent to 51 percent.... Reasons for a change in levels of satisfaction with the political situation may have included the NP's decision to leave the national unity government, the continuing conflict in KwaZulu-Natal and the Sarafina 2 "debacle." The fall in the value of the rand, difficulties experienced in implementing the RDP and the wide range of unfulfilled socioeconomic needs were factors influencing satisfaction with the economic situation... [O'Grady, 1997, 1].

One would think that this would force the ANC to radicalize the RDP, but just the opposite happened, even though the SACP did think a turn towards the left was what was needed.

The ANC began to reorganize the RDP as it also worked on the even more centrist GEAR. These RDP organizational reforms were justified because many saw the RDP Office as too powerful and stifling:

The biggest challenge facing the Government of National Unity (GNU) is ensuring the success of the RDP, with which it aims to change the lives of millions of people. Despite all the efforts that have been made to ensure the success of the RDP in the first year, critics point out serious flaws in the programme. One flaw which the Government has acknowledged, is that the implementation of the Programme has been slow. This is the result of delays caused in the process of identifying projects and ensuring the flow of financial backing for projects that have been approved. Critics also say that because of the new government system, there are few delivery mechanisms, which is why last year, nearly half of the funds allocated to the RDP were not spent. Most critics also stress that without economic growth generated by the private sector, the success of the RDP is in doubt. The programme will have to be fully backed by the private sector in order for deadlines to be met, since the Government does not have all the resources for such a massive task. According to the critics, the RDP has ignored the necessity of implementing a coherent population development strategy. An unsustainable population growth is expected to have a negative effect on the objectives of the RDP in the long-term. The critics say, moreover, that the Government should also do more to end the culture of civil disobedience, which leads to the non-payment of services, rates, taxes and mortgages. This type of action is believed to be slowing down the implementation of the RDP [Keyter 1995, 1].

So, while we hear about the millions of rands set aside for various projects, millions of people are still waiting to see reconstruction taking place in front of their own eyes. In fact, political freedom hasn't been translated into economic freedom. Yet certain organisations those which have many years of experience in grassroots development have long since perfected efficient delivery methods [MacRobert 1996, 1].

Instead of the RDP being "above" the many ministries, each ministry would now have a mini–RDP department within it, which would try to direct its ministry to concentrate on the RDP mission statement. This RDP department would also attempt to coordinate with the other RDP departments in other ministries to create a coherent national policy. No other than then–Deputy President Thabo Mbeki oversaw this change:

> Mbeki is to appoint a task force to oversee the re-allocation of the RDP's projects, programmes and staff to various line-ministries. His representative, Thami Ntenteni, said this emerged from a meeting between Mbeki and outgoing RDP Minister Jay Naidoo on Tuesday. The task force would have to work fast: "We expect to see some movement after the Easter weekend," he said. Ntenteni said that as the decision to close the RDP office, hand the fund over to the finance ministry and shift its responsibilities to departments was a presidential one, complaints about a lack of consultation were not relevant ["Confusion...," 1].

Though on paper this sounded like a good idea, in reality it was the beginning of the end for the RDP. This also meant that the last vestiges of the original early 1990s leftist economic plans for South Africa (which the SACP had heavily pushed for at the time) had been replaced by centrist and even right-of-center reforms (which much of the ANC had advocated since 1994).

After the RDP got demoted, the ANC then began concentrating on a new way to package its macroeconomic thinking with little input from the SACP (though it would later critique the results). The RDP's more leftist rhetoric and promises were toned down or eliminated, and probably rightfully so since they only created unfulfilled expectations. But the businesslike realism that had always been the foundation of the RDP not only remained but also become predominant, much to the chagrin of the SACP. As a matter of fact, GEAR is basically the RDP with less rhetoric and more clarity. An early critique of GEAR also summed it up well:

> The strategy's primary concern is to boost investor confidence by adopting the main tenets of neoliberalism.... The document claims that the achievement of sustained growth on a higher plane requires an outward oriented economy.... Built into the proposed framework is an extremely conservative mandate for the monetary authorities.... The document focuses on job creation as the main source of income redistribution.... Overall, the document's abandonment of the RDP is indicative of a panic response to the recent exchange rate instability and a lame surrender to policy dictates and pressures from international financial institutions and domestic conglomerates ["Govt's Economic Plans..." 1].

Many different economic players, domestic but especially international, saw GEAR as the best plan for South Africa; obviously the SACP did not agree, and neither did its numerous allies within COSATU.

What GEAR argued was that living standards in South Africa could only rise if economic growth through higher productivity, rationalization of the economy, and more international investment was achieved; this is relatively standard Western economic theory. Again, the RDP always argued that economic growth was important, if not an end unto itself. GEAR's macroeconomic policies focused on fiscal responsibility, rationalization of the economy, greater tax revenue through better collection and not higher taxes, more trade and bigger trade surpluses, and so on. It has been argued that GEAR was a milder and better-worded form of the standard International Monetary Fund austerity plan for so many developing nations. Though GEAR did not go as far as some of the more extreme IMF plans, recently the IMF itself has lessened its demands from poor nations, and thus GEAR and the IMF almost met in the middle. It is also true that some leftist issues (such as workers' rights) were still important in GEAR, if not as much as the SACP wanted.

Did these more centrist and right-of-center reforms pay off for South Africa? To some degree they did, but the SACP argues not nearly enough for the high social costs they incurred and that the results were not that good. The still very high unemployment rate may be the single largest negative factor in the South African economy:

> Jobs, however, have become the paramount issue [by 2001] for many South Africans. Officially, and on a strict measure, unemployment is not far off 25 percent. On a broader definition, it is 36 percent. Probably only 40 percent of the economically active population is employed in the formal, non-agricultural sectors of the economy. Moreover, since 1994 about 500,000 jobs have been lost. Meanwhile, the population is growing at over 2 percent a year, as is the labour market, though AIDS is already cutting the rate of growth of the working-age population ["Jobless and Joyless" 1].

It was not all bad, with many "black market" jobs helping on the margins:

> The situation is not as terrible as the figures suggest: many people work, and work productively, even if they do not have an officially recognised job, as the swarms of hawkers and pedlars at traffic lights attest. But far too many have no job worth speaking of, which is why over 3m people are actively looking for work. And as the economy has changed, jobs seem to have been lost in the formal sector and gained in the informal one. The dearth of decent work is one of the greatest disappointments of the new South Africa ["Jobless and Joyless" 1].

The rate would be close to 30 percent by the late 2000s ("South African Unemployment" 1; Creamer 2013). Also, international firms still feared that the ANC would only tighten the already burdensome job laws of the nation:

> One problem is the web of labour laws that enmesh employers and therefore encourage them—notably in the mining industry—to invest in machinery rather

than men, or not to invest at all. They act in two highly damaging ways. One is simply to add to the expense of employment: the cost of labour relative to capital has doubled since 1990. Another is to make it intensely difficult ever to get rid of workers, as Volkswagen has recently discovered: it was ordered last month to reinstate 1,300 employees sacked last year in an illegal strike ["Jobless and Joyless" 1].

But the ANC partially realized this and actually pushed pro-job, pro-growth policies, though the SACP often saw this as not only selling out but ineffective. Regardless, the ANC pushed towards the center on these issues:

> As it happens, the public-service minister, Geraldine Fraser-Moleketi, wants her own ministry to be partly exempt from the Basic Conditions of Employment Act. She also wants to "outsource" some of her department's activities, to the apparent disgust of the labour minister and other members of the cabinet. It is a government, after all, that rules in alliance with the union movement, COSATU. And yielding to COSATU on labour laws helps the ANC to get away with a macroeconomic policy that has brought growth per person of under 1 percent a year since 1995. The price is a labour policy that benefits those with jobs, notably COSATU's 1.8m members, not the 3m–5m with none.
>
> In fairness, the government has done lots of things right. It has reduced the national budget deficit from 8 percent in 1994 to a planned 1.9 percent this year and a forecast 1.7 percent for 2001–02. Inflation, too, has fallen, from 9 percent in 1994 to about 6 percent today. The disciplined fiscal and monetary policies responsible, coupled with measures to open up and liberalise the economy, have brought South Africa investment-grade status from the rating agencies, Moody's and Standard and Poor's, and its long-term foreign-currency debt rating has been upgraded by Fitch IBCA.
>
> The aim has been to promote "growth, employment and redistribution," GEAR. But growth has not even reached the modest rate of the 1970s (an annual average of 3.3 percent); jobs have disappeared; and any redistribution achieved has been combined with increasing inequality. Above all, the foreign investment that might have been expected to come to a country that was doing so many things right has not materialised ["Jobless and Joyless" 1].

This did indeed aid the prospects for foreign firms to invest in South Africa by the late 1990s:

> It is true that foreign direct investment has grown since 1994, and South Africa has been especially successful at attracting car companies. All Mercedes right-hand-drive C-class cars are now built not in Stuttgart but in East London, and all BMW 3-series models are built in Pretoria. Fiat and Volkswagen also produce cars for export, and Ford makes engines at its Port Elizabeth factory that it sends abroad.
>
> Moreover, the foreign companies that have come in are generally pleased with their investments, and many are expanding. But South Africa has not been able to attract enough new companies. Many of those that have been investing

recently—especially American companies such as Ford, GM and Eastman Kodak—had pulled out of South Africa in the latter days of apartheid. And by the standards of other countries, South Africa has lured relatively little foreign direct investment: $32 per head in 1994–99, compared with $106 for Brazil, $252 for Argentina, $333 for Chile ["Jobless and Joyless" 1].

Still, it was not all good news on the international economic front:

At the same time, money has been leaving South Africa: the $9.8 billion it invested abroad in 1994–99 exceeded the inward flow by about $1.6 billion. And its big companies, long confined by apartheid's isolation, are now anxious to seek stock-exchange listings abroad. The capital they need for expansion is far more expensive if raised in South Africa, which still has some exchange controls, than in Europe or North America. So in the past few years, Anglo American (mining), Billiton (mining), Old Mutual (insurance), South African Breweries and Dimension Data (a hugely successful information-technology company) have all sought primary listings elsewhere ["Jobless and Joyless" 1].

Regardless, centrist economic reforms had made South Africa more investment friendly:

The urge to seek a foreign listing will disappear when all exchange controls are abolished, which the government hopes will be within a few years. But will the jobs have arrived by then? Alec Erwin, the trade minister and one of the government's most determined optimists, argues that the economy has structurally changed; it is internationally competitive, and it now has a significant high-tech industry as well as all its old basic strength in minerals and raw materials. It should also be said that the government is open, committed to reforming the civil service and relatively uncorrupt by the standards of many countries. It has an excellent central bank, run by the capable Tito Mboweni, decent transport and a first-world legal system. It is also politically stable ["Jobless and Joyless" 1].

Though only making modest successes, the ANC saw the need to push on with GEAR, and later the NDP:

Yet it needs more. Perhaps the measure that would do most good would be to speed up the privatisation programme. Several big state enterprises—involving energy, steel, telecoms, the airports and the national airline—have been sold, or at least partially sold, and the sales have generally been handled well. However, privatisation is pursued grudgingly in South Africa. Nico Czypionka, chief economist at SG Securities, thinks the speedy sale of Eskom, the huge state electricity company, would alone bring in 80 billion–90 billion rand and thus go far towards paying off the government debt and freeing money for other spending. Even the proposed sale later this year of another 20 percent of Telkom, the telecoms outfit, should bring in 15 billion–20 billion rand, and may help to make it cheaper to use telephones and the Internet.

The government has not managed all sales well. It underestimated the market for mobile telephones, guessing it would be 600,000 by 2000, whereas it turned out to be nearly 8m. But its real mistake was to hold a "beauty contest" rather than an auction for the third operator's licence, perhaps thus missing out on as much as $200m; 18 months later, the lucky winner has still not been announced. Some also think the government could have secured much more than 6 billion rand for the 30 percent of Telkom already sold. But the cost of going slow on privatisation is not just revenue and efficiency forgone. It is also foreign investment forgone, and the chance to tell foreigners that South Africa welcomes them ["Jobless and Joyless" 1].

Thus, the economic situation was getting better for multinational corporations and their needs by the early 2000s.

But the ANC needed to balance these "market friendly" reforms with politically astute, more leftist ones to make sure the poor masses of South Africa would keep the ANC in power and not some more "leftist" party (which did not and does not exist at the national level). But recently there have been rumors of a desire for a new "workers' party" from the former leader of the ANC Youth League and the radical union NUMSA. The SACP also realized this and tried to convince the ANC to back off on some of this movement towards the right. On a few issues the ANC listened to its leftist partner, but by the early 2010s, the NDP was being developed, which was more of a push towards the right for South Africa. This time, unlike with GEAR, the SACP would approach the problem with somewhat more subtlety.

The NDP is seemingly *the* strategic economic plan for South Africa until 2030. It will initiate programs that not only finally start to lower the chronic unemployment but also alleviate poverty and promote equality. It not only takes over from both the RDP and GEAR but goes beyond the controversial Black Economic Empowerment (BEE) programs that have seemingly done little for the masses and are often seen as empowering a few "rich blacks" at best, and at the worst seen as fronts for "white money" ("BEE..." 2010, "Guard..." 2010, "Zuma Calls for Redefining BEE" 2010, Vena 2011, "Manuel..." 2011).

The National Planning Commission (NPC), dominated by the ANC but with other parties involved, has worked on the 483-page working draft of the NDP for years, trying to be inclusive of the many varied economic interests that South Africa has. The SACP is officially for many of the ideas behind it, it is mostly for the draft, but it still has serious reservations about the NPC, the process, and many of the NDP's details. It is not alone. The above mentioned radical and controversial former leader of the ANC Youth League denounced the NPC and its leader ("Malema..." 2011).

Regardless, the NPC was formed to create the NDP and to solve some of the more troublesome economic issues South Africa still faced more than a decade after apartheid ended. These issues included:

A politicised public service, rampant corruption, an ailing health care system and continued divisions in society are among the biggest problems facing South Africa, according to the National Planning Commission...

Although it acknowledges progress since 1994, the report concedes frankly the government's failure to address a number of problems and emphasises the trade-offs and concessions required from many political and economic interest groups before agreement can be reached on a development plan.

Other problems identified include substandard education, particularly for black children; infrastructural constraints; unsustainable, resource-intensive growth and distorted spatial development leading to economic marginalisation.

Examining the scourge of unemployment, the report argues that the highly segmented nature of South Africa's labour market affords protection to a core of well-organised sectors and public servants, whereas a larger group of low-paid formal and informal workers remains on the periphery...

The report recognises the many challenges facing the education system, including problems with curriculum design, language use and the efficacy of the government bureaucracy...

The report points to the significantly uneven investment and underinvestment in infrastructure in recent years across the logistics, information and communication technology and water and energy sectors. To address this, the report notes that higher levels of investment are needed—with an emphasis on bringing in more private money...

The report is strongly critical of the ailing health care system, saying it has been undermined by poor policy decisions, institutional failures and a massive disease burden from infectious diseases such as HIV/Aids, tuberculosis and pneumonia, as well as violence, road accidents and lifestyle diseases such as diabetes.

Mistakes included poor human resource management, too much centralisation of basic institutional functions, a badly implemented strategy to shift the patient burden to primary health care facilities and failure to manage the relationship with the private sector.

The commission also emphasises the need for a depoliticised public service. It says that a culture of "quick fixes" aimed at reforming visible examples of poor performance has resulted in greater instability in public institutions and that the interaction between the political and administrative elements of government is particularly problematic...

The document singles out corruption as one of the most "striking breakdowns in accountability" that undermines citizens' confidence in the democratic system. It points to research by the corruption-busting Special Investigating Unit indicating that overpayment and corruption in up to 25 percent of state procurement processes result in a loss of R30-billion a year [Donnelly 2011, 1].

On the surface, the SACP of course agreed that much more needed to be done, that poor governance was to blame for some of the issues, and that its partner the ANC was partially at fault. This is the reality that South Africa faced, and it was no deep secret for anyone.

The whole alliance had been careful to agree with much of this criticism, even though it was to blame for many of these factors after almost two decades in power, but the issues went deeper for the SACP. Though the SACP would agree that its ally, the ruling ANC, had been short-sighted at times, incorrect on some public policy, and unfortunately too corrupt and/or incompetent too often, it could not come out and say it as strongly as the NPC did. But though there was agreement on some points, the SACP had a major dilemma with this NPC diagnosis: it (and later the NDP itself) hinted at liberalization of the economy as one of many solutions, which the SACP (and COSATU) rejected. But the NPC was just the starting round of this fight for the SACP; the NDP was the real problem.

What did the NDP call for? A quick summary is presented below before some quotes from the document itself:

[T]he national development plan has now moved to centre stage after the ANC's 53rd elective conference in Mangaung this week [12/21/12]...

Planning Minister Trevor Manuel, chair of the national planning commission that authored the plan, said it had received an "exceedingly warm reception" at the conference...

Mineral Resources Minister Susan Shabangu and ANC policy head Enoch Godongwana said the conference would argue for broader state intervention in the economy and adopt the national development plan...

It is also speculated that Cyril Ramaphosa's appointment to deputy president of the ANC may give much needed impetus to the plan, because he is the deputy chairperson of the national planning commission....

The national development plan aims to achieve something that has thus far eluded the ruling party in post-apartheid South Africa: the elimination of poverty and reduction of inequality. It acknowledges important progress made since 1994, but identifies persistent problems such as crisis levels of unemployment, inequality and poverty.

The plan is often seen as moderate and less interventionist than the national growth path or the industrial policy action plan, but in the run-up to the conference, government and union representatives denied this, describing the three as complementary.

But the plan is not without controversy, especially on the labour front. It proposes that a tax incentive be offered to employers to reduce the initial cost of hiring entrants to the labour market and entry-level wages be agreed between employers and unions. The adoption of a more open approach to immigration to expand the supply of high-level skills is also suggested, and it calls for the simplification of dismissal procedures for non-performance.

The national development plan raises concern about the possible costs of nuclear power, is in favour of fracking if responsibly done, wants more emphasis on renewable energy, argues for a systems operator independent of Eskom to distribute electricity and wants to promote universal broadband access.

It has the objective of reducing the proportion of households with a monthly income of below R419 a person from 39 percent to zero by 2030. And the Gini coefficient, the most common measure of inequality, should also fall from 0.69 to 0.6. (The coefficient of the Central African Republic's is 0.61 and Brazil is 0.58.) [Steyn 2012, 1].

As with the NPC analysis, there is much common sense here, clear analysis of the issues South Africa faces, and both left- and right-of-center solutions suggested. The NDP itself went into more details:

> Our future—make it work.
> South Africa belongs to all its people and the future of our country is our collective future. Making it work is our collective responsibility. All South Africans seek a better future for themselves and their children. The National Development Plan is a plan for the country to eliminate poverty and reduce inequality by 2030 through uniting South Africans, unleashing the energies of its citizens, growing an inclusive economy, building capabilities, enhancing the capability of the state and leaders working together to solve complex problems. South Africa's transition from apartheid to a democratic state has been a success. In the past 18 years, we have built democratic institutions, transformed the public service, extended basic services, stabilised the economy and taken our rightful place in the family of nations. Despite these successes, too many people are trapped in poverty and we remain a highly unequal society. Too few South Africans work, the quality of school education for the majority is of poor quality and our state lacks capacity in critical areas. Despite significant progress, our country remains divided, with opportunity still shaped by the legacy of apartheid. In particular, young people and women are denied the opportunities to lead the lives that they desire...
> Drawing on our collective successes and failures as a nation, we need to do more to improve our future. On the present trajectory, South Africa will not achieve the objectives of eliminating poverty and reducing inequality. There is a burning need for faster progress, more action and better implementation. The future belongs to all of us and it is up to all South Africans to make it work...
> The approach of the plan revolves around citizens being active in development, a capable and developmental state able to intervene to correct our historical inequities, and strong leadership throughout society working together to solve our problems. The plan addresses the need to enhance the capabilities of our people so that they can live the lives that they desire; and to develop the capabilities of the country so that we can grow faster, draw more people into work and raise living standards for all, but particularly the poor. This is a plan for South Africa, requiring action, change and sacrifice from all sectors of society [*National Development Plan 2030* 4].

As one can see, it has a leftist, even statist, tone to it, which the SACP does indeed support. The problem is in the details. Critics see this as a lot of rhetoric but little fundamental economic change, and there is some real truth in this objection. This is not the place to deconstruct this almost 500-page document, but a brief overview will help show why the SACP is both right to support, but also criticize, this plan on its merits (let alone politically).

The NDP overview argues for many things that few in South Africa would object to: reducing crime and corruption, investing more in infrastructure and education, and aiming for growth to help lower poverty (*National Development Plan 2030* 8). But the devil is indeed in the details. It does not offer any radical solutions, which the SACP and parts of COSATU want at this point, and it suggests some "neo-liberal" solutions such as more economic rationalization and aiming for an export-centered economy (which makes sense considering the objective conditions of South Africa, but to build dependence on the world capitalist economy rubs SACP the wrong way) (*National Development Plan 2030* 10). It also suggests, like most economists throughout the world, that a more "flexible labour market" would be best to lower unemployment, which may be true, but as leftists argue elsewhere, this can be used to lower wages and limit workers' rights (*National Development Plan 2030* 9–10). It does argue for some leftist goals, such as sustainability, rural equality, and more equitable access to resources; the SACP obviously supports these initiatives (*National Development Plan 2030* 10). On a similar note, the NDP pushes for better education, health care, and social welfare programs; again, the SACP approves of this, but unlike the SACP, the NDP has no radical plans to bring these about, and thus the SACP is rightfully skeptical at their success (*National Development Plan 2030* 11). Finally, it calls for fighting crime locally, rooting out systematic corruption, and in general building viable communities throughout South Africa; all of which the SACP agrees with, but argues that without changing some of the fundamental societal issues that caused these problems (capitalism, racism, the rural/urban divide, etc.), changing them is nearly impossible (*National Development Plan 2030* 12).

The NDP is partially to fully supported by many of South Africa's political and economic actors:

> A number of chief executives and chairpersons of some of the largest companies in the country have committed to the national development plan in an open letter and Cas Coovadia, managing director of the Banking Association of South Africa, said the banking industry would be happy if the ANC adopted the plan as the "critical vision" for the country.
> Media reports have suggested the plan is not to the taste of parties such as the South African Communist Party (SACP) or trade union federation Cosatu. Earlier this year, Cosatu said it would not back the plan because it echoed incorrect comments about inflexible labour laws. But Jeremy Cronin, the party's deputy general secretary, denied that this was so for the SACP, noting that it had welcomed

the plan's broad vision without necessarily agreeing with every detail. Cronin also announced this week that he was not available to serve on the ANC's national executive committee [Steyn 2012, 1].

Numerous South African businesses and business associations have also backed it, partially because it is the political thing to do, but also it is the least "socialist plan" they can expect to get from the ANC and its leftist allies (Mokgabuti 2013). A think tank, the Institute for Security Studies, argued this:

> Certain union leaders and the Congress of South African Trade Unions (COSATU), a tripartite alliance partner, have attacked tenets of the National Development Plan (NDP), which was adopted by South Africa's cabinet in 2012. Some have gone as far as suggesting that it should be completely scrapped. This despite the fact that the NDP arguably provides a clear and pragmatic roadmap for addressing South Africa's pressing problems such as poverty, unemployment and inequality. Scrapping the NDP may be a case of "throwing the baby out with the bathwater," considering the absence of solid alternative suggestions from the plan's critics in the labour unions on addressing challenges such as corruption [Tamukamoyo 2013, 1].

But for every supporter, there are minor and major critics of the NDP.

The SACP's Cronin, as we have seen for a few chapters, is still a powerful (and intellectual) voice within the SACP and a "moderate," so his somewhat supportive words should not surprise the reader (though his recent dropping out from the ANC Executive Committee after being on it for two decades could be telling for the future) (Mkokeli 1). He argued:

> "There's a cherry-picking reading in certain quarters of the plan," Cronin told the *Mail & Guardian*. "It clearly recognises the role of the private sector, but so does the industrial policy action plan and the new growth path. There is a great deal of convergence between all three documents," he said, although they also differ in their scope, objectives, time frames and status....
>
> Cronin has noted that the new growth path and industrial policy action plan are essentially government policy documents and the emphasis is therefore likely to be more on what the government has to do, but he said the development plan was not necessarily less state interventionist. "It has many non neoliberal features," he said. For example, it reiterates the need for a virtuous cycle of growth and development and reinforces the linkages between sustainable inclusive growth and social development interventions [Steyn 2012, 1].

Cronin was putting on a good face for both political and economical reasons. He was right that the NDP, by definition, puts the state in the center of solving many of South Africa's worst issues, which the SACP supports. And he admitted that on some of the details of how to solve said problems, he did not agree with its "neo-liberal" approaches, though he added that many of its methods are leftist and helpful. Still, he added elsewhere:

South Africa's National Development Plan (NDP) was fatally flawed and impossible to implement, Deputy Public Works Minister Jeremy Cronin told National Planning Commissioner and former mining luminary Bobby Godsell in a public debate at the weekend.

"It's fatally flawed as an implementation plan," said Cronin of the 484-page document, which seeks to triple, in real terms, the 2010 size of the South African economy by 2030, lower unemployment to 6 percent and reduce inequality on the Gini coefficient from 0.7 percent in 2009 to 0.6 percent in the next 17 years.

The deputy general-secretary of the South African Communist Party (SACP) and African National Congress National Executive Committee member was disdainful of the negligible inequality reduction being targeted.

"This target, on a critical issue, is pathetic, let's admit it," said Cronin, who also criticised the 26-person National Planning Commission (NPC) for being made up of 25 part-timers, some with day jobs that bore little resemblance to their commission roles...

"It actually envisages a shrinkage of the manufacturing sector, from 12 percent of gross domestic product in 2010 down to 9.6 percent in 2030," Cronin said, adding that a broad vision had to be built around South Africa's reindustrialisation, infrastructure provision and skills development [Creamer 2013, 1].

As one can see, Cronin (and thus the SACP) attacked the NPC for lacking expertise (as others have), but more to the point, saw the NDP as "fatally flawed" for being "unrealistic" in its goals and finally taking a "neo-liberal" approach by embracing deindustrialization and emphasizing service jobs (Creamer 2013; Hlongwane 2013).

Though many Western nations, including the U.S., have promoted similar neo-liberal economic rationalization policies for the last four decades, they have had mixed results. For the less skilled, it has been financially disastrous as factories left America; for other, higher economic strata, the results have been more complex and mixed. The SACP, being a classical Leninist party on industrial policy, sees manufacturing, heavy industry, and the like as not only good for the working class (decent- to good-paying jobs) but also good for South Africa (industrialization is seen as a key development benchmark for Leninists, though such a metric in the 21st century seems somewhat antiquated). Cronin and the SACP are not alone in seeing the NDP as problematic at best.

COSATU (and its many unions) also had serious reservations about the NDP. As one summary put it, "The militant National Union of Metalworkers of South Africa (NUMSA) also rejected the 'right-wing' plan. The South African Communist Party (SACP) received it coldly too" (Hlongwane 2013). As COSATU itself stated:

THE National Development Plan (NDP) fails to take forward a radical economic shift; rather it threatens to reverse "progressive advances" made by the

African National Congress (ANC)-led government over the past few years, the Congress of South African Trade Unions (Cosatu) said on Friday.

In a statement on Thursday, Cosatu spokesman Patrick Craven said the NDP failed to fundamentally transform the structure of the South African economy; it failed to take forward the promotion of a new growth path to industrialise the economy; it failed to place job creation at the centre of the country's economic policy; and failed to make redistribution and the combating of inequality and poverty a pillar of economic development...

"The NDP does none of these things and, in particular, its jobs plan is problematic and unsustainable, based on creating low-quality precarious jobs outside the core productive sectors of the economy.... Cosatu will reject its proposal for a social accord, which envisages undermining worker rights, reduction of wages, particularly for young people, and other proposals which are totally unacceptable to the labour movement," Mr. Craven said...

"The main message from the meeting was the need to unite the alliance, working together in a campaign to implement the second phase of the transition ... to achieve a fundamental transformation of our economy and put us on a new growth path to an economy based primarily on manufacturing industry, and the creation of decent, sustainable jobs," Mr. Craven said...

"Cosatu remains fully in support of a planned economy and a strong interventionist state. We have always rejected the view that the market economy can provide solutions to the country's triple crisis of unemployment, poverty and inequality.... Developing countries like South Africa will never escape from the growth path we inherited from the days of colonialism and apartheid, and nor will it create large numbers of decent, sustainable jobs which we desperately need, without a radical economic shift, a developmental state and a plan for a new growth path, which is effectively and speedily implemented" [Marrian 2013, 1].

The SACP basically agreed with COSATU on all these points. NUMSA, one of the more powerful and radical unions in COSATU, stated in April of 2013:

Over the past few weeks, the leadership of the National Union of Metalworkers of South Africa (Numsa) has been vilified for announcing the union's reservations about the national development plan (NDP). We have been characterised as "spoilers," and our leaders are described as "populists" and "demagogues" who suffer from "an infantile disorder." In this throwing of mud and trading of swearwords, little has been said about the substantive issues that Numsa has raised, in particular the unlikelihood of the policies of the NDP to deal effectively with the often mentioned challenges of poverty, unemployment and inequality.

More worrying is how, in the aftermath of the adoption of the NDP at the ANC's 53rd national congress in Mangaung late last year, there is a refusal to look critically at the NDP, although it is a known fact that in the run-up to the ANC's policy conference in July 2012 some of the party's discussion documents raised serious and vexing questions about South Africa's proposed long-term socioeconomic development plan.

> More astonishing is how, after Mangaung, the NDP became holy writ,
> immune to critical evaluation, despite the ANC national conference resolution
> describing the plan as "a living and dynamic document" [Gina 2013, 1].

As is evident, NUMSA is not satisfied with the NPC or its document, the NDP. And it is correct to point out that the ANC itself debated the NDP a great deal before adopting it at their national congress in late 2012. Once again, the SACP sees wisdom in the unions' positions. But the SACP needs to be at least supportive of a plan that the ANC helped create and then ratified.

The SACP is taking a guarded approach towards the NDP since the ANC had already ratified it at its 2012 national congress and as we have seen, the SACP is usually the supportive ally. Plus, President Zuma has made veiled threats that one is either for or against the NDP, and the ANC is for it. He stated, "You may have views [on the national development plan], but you must respect the views expressed by ANC delegates in Mangaung [12th ANC Congress]. You must choose your words [when criticizing], particularly if you are one of us." In response, the SACP stated, "[S]outh African Communist Party provincial secretary Themba Mthembu said the party supported the NDP" (Letsoalo 2013). The SACP understands which way the wind is blowing on the NDP.

Plus, the NDP is not that different from GEAR, in the sense that it is too right-of-center on many issues for the SACP (and others such as NUMSA), but both GEAR and the NDP dealt with the reality that South Africa is still a capitalist society and the current public policy has to reflect that (if not giving lip service to a more leftist future). In addition, both still had relatively extensive welfare programs for the poor; if anything, the NDP aims to lessen poverty and inequality in a more blatant (if not highly realistic) way than GEAR did. Still, decades into the "revolution," the SACP (and South Africa's poor masses) expected more progress in their move to some form of real socialism. Thus, the motto that the SACP and COSATU often have at their rallies, "Build Socialism Now!," seems a tad more hollow each year.

Conclusion

I think it is likely that for the next decade the alliance between the ANC and SACP will be at most strained, but it is unlikely to be threatened in any significant way. Though the two parties have real differences that may only become more pronounced as time passes, they still both realize that they need each other far too much to threaten the alliance.[65] As the SACP's Hani stated soon before his death, "We feel [the SACP's] presence in this broad alliance has actually strengthened the alliance.... We actually radicalised the ANC. There is clearly a role for the SACP.... This is also the time where we should consolidate this alliance.... We can only become influential if everybody can see we are really independent..." (Hani 12). Though much of this is more clichéd than anything else, Hani was right to argue that the SACP must appear independent or lose all legitimacy.

The easiest way the party can do this is by being critical of its ally: in the spring of 1991, the party even debated if the ANC was "too bourgeois" to take power after apartheid (Lodge 1983, 175). Hani stated rather baldly, "Let's accept the fact there'll always be a struggle within the ANC ... for the predominance of ideas of various classes within the ANC..." (Hani 13). The SACP obviously decided long ago that the ANC was reliable enough as an ally, but the SACP must stay critical of all of its partners. Still, the current political environment is far too dangerous for either party to think of breaking free and fighting the alliance's many common enemies alone.

The "old" National Party may be long gone, and even the New National Party (NNP) is officially gone since the mid–2000s (bizarrely merging with the ANC), but neither were friends of the ANC, SACP, or their policies (National Party Manifesto, 1995; "Ex-Apartheid Party...").[66] Though the ANC may have moved to the center from its more leftist position during the long struggle as an illegal party, it is still far too leftist for the NP and later NNP and its mostly white followers. Because the ANC is often perceived as a "black" party, the NNP was able to recruit many "Coloureds"[67] and Indians who saw "black domination" as something to be greatly feared. This strategy was so successful that with the help of the Coloured vote the NNP was able to win the Western Cape Province in the 1994 elections (November 1995 Election Results). The NNP, however, was not the only political opponent that wished the ANC and SACP to stay united for the time being.

The alliance is in constant fear of widespread ethnic conflict. Both the ANC and SACP are officially "nonracial" (Meer 235).[68] This means that they have no desire to take sides on any of the many ethnic conflicts that now bedevil South Africa and have done so for a long time. The most important conflict of the 1990s involved the Zulu people led by then minister of arts and sciences Buthelezi and his Inkatha Freedom Party (IFP).[69] The Zulu people have been a distinct ethnic group for at least 150 years,[70] and many of them seemed to have little desire to stay within the South African union after 1994 (Neuhaus Chapter 10). The IFP, the political voice of the Zulus, had walked out of Parliament and constitutional committees more than once in the 1990s to disrupt the ANC's plan to create a relatively centralized state.[71] The IFP had the NP and the right-wing (and mostly white) Freedom Front (FF) as allies on this federal issue, for all three wanted full cultural (and maybe political) freedom for their respective ethnic groups; the irony of the NNP and FF wanting this needs no elaboration (*Freedom Front Manifesto*, 1995; *National Party Manifesto*, 1995). The ANC and SACP both see the need for political decentralization, while maintaining some economic centralization (*ANC Manifesto*, 1995).[72] Regardless, the IFP, NP/NNP, and the FF are all irrelevant now at the national level, and even by the early 2000s were not serious players. Thus, while the alliance faced a serious threat from the IFP in the mid–1990s, there was at least one other threat that may have kept the alliance united back then.

Both the right-wing Afrikaners and such black nationalists as the Pan Africanist Congress (PAC) vehemently oppose the alliance. Though such groupings were and still are small and mostly powerless at this point,[73] if economic conditions do not improve in the long run, such radical organizations may attract more followers. This is especially true of the extremist Afrikaners whose organizations have been slowly gaining support again as many whites lose jobs and become disgusted with ANC scandals.[74] Black nationalists have further to go to become a force in South Africa, but with high unemployment and extremely high underemployment for blacks, there is indeed some fertile ground for such extremist groups (Stedman 191). With all these forces aligned against the alliance, both partners have good reason to stay together for the duration.

As they maintain the alliance, they will continue to play their current roles. The ANC will continue to lead the "Democratic National Revolution," that is, the formal and informal aspects of this stage of the transition now going on in the new South Africa. For now, the SACP does not have a problem with this, and it fully supports this role for the ANC both politically and ideologically. The SACP is currently satisfied to play the role of the leftist, critical voice in the alliance, and to contribute its excellent organizational skills to the ANC. As it stated in 1992, "The SACP's basic role is to be the leading political force of the South African working class.... [But] the ultimate aim of the party is the building of a communist society..." ("The Way Forward..." 44). The SACP understands that during this period of South African history, both capitalist and multiclass government are needed. However, the SACP is a communist party and has never concealed its intention to build socialism in South Africa.

This means that the alliance will dissolve sooner or later; which it will be is still unclear. Ultimately, unless the ANC either absorbs the SACP[75] or the SACP takes over the ANC, neither of which is likely or possible, the two will have to part ways at some point. As Mandela pointed out at the 9th SACP Congress, the two parties "do have different agendas" (9th Congress AT, 1995). Lodge stated, "If the SACP is to remain true to its principles, it may be forced into becoming a party of opposition in a post–Apartheid South Africa" (Lodge 1983, 172). He said in another work, "But in the longer term, many believe that a split is inevitable" (Keller 1992). Van Heerden thought, "The African Nation Congress (ANC) is set to develop a completely new relationship with its long term ally, the South African Communist Party (SACP). A parting of the ways may be the eventual result" (van Heerden 5). And as Mandela himself said:

> Our alliance is therefore not a marriage of convenience. Neither is it a commun-
> ion of similar organisations, which only differ in name. We talk of an alliance
> precisely because we are two independent organisations with political platforms
> and long-term goals that do not necessarily converge. But there in the theatre of
> practical work, we continue to learn that there is more that unites us than
> divides us: in brief, a people-centred and people-driven programme of demo-
> cratic transformation. To realise this requires unity in action [Mandela 1995].

This is an optimistic way of looking at a situation that ultimately has no real solution. In some ways, the question is not if but *when* this split will occur. It will probably depend on the very different bases of support the SACP and ANC have.

The SACP's program Path to Power was quite clear on this point. "The crisis of racial tyranny cannot be resolved, except by the revolutionary trans-formation of our country" ("Path to Power" 72). It added, "There is contra-diction between the multi-class leadership role of the ANC, and the working class vanguard role of the [Communist] Party" ("Path to Power" 112). Under the current ANC regime, such a "revolutionary transformation" cannot take place. The document added that the goal of the SACP was "the establishment of a Socialist South Africa, laying the foundations of a classless, communist society" ("Path to Power" 72). As Goodman commented, "The SACP and ANC are presently partners in a delicate alliance. With the ANC advocating social democracy, and the SACP calling for socialism, movement leaders acknowledge that splits will inevitably develop between the historic allies" (Goodman 12).

Since 1991, it has become clear that calling the ANC's policies "social democracy" is somewhat overstating its position on the political spectrum. Though officially the ANC does still hold some social democratic ideas, what has actually been done in the new South Africa is far more centrist (and even at times right of center) than left of center, let alone socialist.[76] The ANC's centrist policy agenda stems from its multiclass makeup and the balancing act that it has been forced into once taking power. It must placate the capitalist conglomerates, the white middle class, *and* the poor black masses.

The SACP has always been a far leftist party and can stay aligned with a centrist party like the ANC for only so long. Nel explained the general communist formula for developing countries: "Within the context of the national democratic state, the communist power involved should then execute the second phase of the revolution. This stage would involve the establishment of a socialist system" (Nel 41). This establishment must come sooner or later, if the SACP stays consistent with its ideology and goals.

As the SACP itself has consistently maintained, it sees the socialist transformation of South Africa as inevitable (Slovo 1991 8, *Political Report* 1). Whether this is true or not is not the point; the SACP, and most of its members, certainly believe it to be so. And if they do believe it, the SACP will have to turn on its ultimately capitalist ANC ally one day; there is just no way around it. It is true that if the ANC moved far to the left, this conflict could be avoided, but is this likely? SACP leader Cronin did imply in his interview that though this is not probable, he feels it is a possibility to "convert" the ANC through hard work and persuasion on the part of the party. Cronin also said that the SACP would never give up its communist ideology and become a social democratic party, but if it did make this move to the center, the alliance could continue (Cronin Interview AT, 1995). But since neither party is likely to make these rather drastic transformations, it is safe to assume that a break will occur. The question once again, therefore, is when?

What event could cause such a drastic break between decades-long allies? For now, two scenarios suggest themselves. In one, a severe nationwide strike that the ANC "breaks" in a crude and violent manner could certainly push the SACP to side with the workers somehow against the ANC (if nothing else, the ANC would surely lose COSATU as an ally in such a scenario). In another, the ANC could be forced by a significant electoral defeat to "ditch" its sometimes embarrassing communist ally to gain coalition partners to set up a new government. Neither of these events is likely to occur soon,[77] but when the break comes, it will be severe.

CHAPTER 3

The Collapse of Communism
The End of the Beginning

Introduction

The international dimension is central to an understanding the unique role of the SACP in South Africa. As noted in earlier chapters, the SACP owed its very survival, in part, to its international connections, notably the now defunct Comintern (and its various fronts) and the collapsed Soviet Union. One must understand the role of these international factors to appreciate the larger context in which the SACP operated as it adapted to its new environment within South Africa.

The SACP's communist ties date back to the creation of the mother party itself in the 1920s, which was the Communist Party of the Soviet Union (CPSU). Formed out of the merger of various South African leftist organizations in 1921, the SACP (the CPSA until 1950) was created for the specific reason of joining the newly formed international communist organization, the Soviet Comintern. This willingness to be tied to the Comintern would be regretted decades later, since, by that connection, communist parties throughout the world would be groomed to be become loyal appendages of the CPSU, which were often also seen as expendable (Johns 234). Be that as it may, at the time, the communists in South Africa perceived such globe-spanning ties as essential. As the SACP itself stated in 1921, "The Party will derive great strength and inspiration from its connection with the world communist international, at present led by the Russian Communist Party" (Lerumo 119).

In 1969 J.B. Marks, a Communist Party member and later Secretary-General of the ANC, characterized the connection between international communism and the SACP this way:

The [international] armed struggle enjoys the fullest support of our Party.... We South African revolutionaries are deeply conscious of the international significance of our struggle.... Above all [the East Bloc nations] have rendered and are rendering valuable practical support to our freedom fighters: money, food, clothing, medicines, assistance in military training and—most precious of all—arms [Lerumo 175–177].

Henry Pike, an admitted right-wing partisan in South Africa, also had his own view of the connection:

Orders originate in the Kremlin, are relayed to the CPSA and then filtered into and through the various other groups considered by Moscow to be of lesser significance, but of great immediate puppet value [read: ANC]. Moscow's minion in all the double-dealing is the CPSA, and every decision is calculated to bring this organization closer to the final goal of ruling South Africa under the Kremlin's directions. If this goal is ever realized, every other organization, including the ANC, regardless of how important it may consider itself, will bow to the CPSA-Moscow axis accordingly [Pike 502].

Finally, the late Joe Slovo, long-time leader of the SACP, stated:

Our external policies were dominated by blind adherence to the decisions of the Soviet Communist Party; a practice which took root during a period when all affiliates of the CPSU-dominated Comintern were obliged to follow its decisions [Slovo 1994, 8].

Whatever the tone of these statements, they do bear witness to the fact that the SACP, since the late 1920s, has been closely aligned with some form of "international communism," be it the Comintern or the Soviet Union, or, since 1991, a loose federation of surviving leftist organizations.[1]

International communism, at most a shifting network of local communist parties, was greatly affected by changes that occurred within the Soviet Union throughout the decades (1920s–1990s). With the Soviet Union at its core and with its various international organizations tying together disparate local communist parties and associations (unions, "fronts," etc.), this configuration is unique in modern history. Though there have been several attempts to emulate the communist model (the al Qaeda network could be cited here), there has been no other similar developed world system of political parties.

While that system was sometimes difficult to pin down, the fact remains that international communism (be it called the Third International, the Comintern, Cominform, or later the Foreign Department of the CPSU) created networks of differing degrees of cohesion among various Marxist-Leninist communist parties throughout the world.[2] Soviet and SACP expert Colin Legum agreed: "The Cominform ... dictated policy to the SACP and other affiliated parties" (Legum 106). Such networks affected communist parties in different ways and degrees. For the SACP, such international networks were a crucial factor in the formation of both the domestic and foreign policy. Both the interwar period and the Cold War were significant eras for every communist party, since the global tug-of-war between the West and the Soviet Union could greatly affect local conditions, often with no direct relation to local events or party actions. This lack of connection between Soviet needs and local conditions, combined with the strong connection between the Soviet Union and these local communist parties, created many and serious tensions.

Because of this situation, the SACP learned to become a highly adaptive organization from the very beginning. Starting in 1928, going through the twists and turns of the 1930s and 1940s, and finally the existential challenges of the late 1980s and early 1990s, the SACP has been continually forced by both domestic and international pressures to change, survive, and finally thrive. Though we shall briefly review the previous periods of adaptation, this chapter concentrates on the late 1980s and early 1990s, when the SACP was once again compelled to adapt or wither (or even die). But this time it was indeed different, for though no one knew it then, this would be the last time the SACP would ever have to jump through Soviet-created hoops. First the Soviet East Bloc would fall, and then the Soviet Union itself disintegrated, all while the SACP had to analyze and accommodate both these external shocks and various extraordinary domestic changes, such as the lifting of the ban on the group and the collapse of apartheid. Also this time, at least with respect to the external shocks, the SACP would have to go it alone, both materially and ideologically, since the Soviets themselves were the problem. The SACP would survive this, their greatest challenge, but it would also stake out new territory. All of this would leave the SACP in a "New South Africa" (non-racial and led by the ANC) and a "New World Order" (dominated by the neo-liberal policies of the West).

What follows, then, is a summary attempt to follow the various twists and turns of the Soviet/SACP relationship, be it through international communist structures or otherwise. I will also discuss the tremendous events of the late 1980s and early 1990s, both abroad and in South Africa, and how they affected the SACP.

The Early Years: Ultra-Leftism

In the 1920s and 1930s, the Moscow-based Comintern was the coordinating body for international communism. This organization, though a legitimate if not revolutionary internationalist organization at first, would soon become a sad and destructive tool of Soviet foreign policy. The organization also lost whatever credibility it had as it began to present itself as virtually infallible to its members, especially when it made glaring errors, such as the Chinese Massacre of 1928 (where the Comintern directed the local communists to disastrously align with the local nationalists) or the utterly disastrous Nazi-Soviet treaty a decade later (which almost led to the destruction of the Soviet Union itself). Most communist parties, though, generally accepted the Comintern's leadership position, though with occasional resistance (Ellis and Sechaba 19).

The SACP, at least after 1928, was of one of the more compliant parties. "The CPSA [SACP] never questioned the ultimate authority of the Comintern"; such blind loyalty would be betrayed by the Comintern's use of stock formulas and opportunism to formulate policies (Johns 207, 1975, 230). Also, as Legum pointed out, these international connections were tight but dangerous:

> Throughout its 56-year history, the SACP has faithfully adhered to the Moscow line even though, at times, this ideological loyalty has led to splits in the party...
> The SACP has always hewn the Moscow line—those who didn't were either expelled or, in the case of two members, liquidated in Moscow [Legum 104, 106].

Regardless of these liabilities, the SACP was loyal to the Comintern and its successors for decades.

As mentioned above, the SACP was formed out of a collection of leftist and socialist political organizations in 1921 (*South African Communists Speak, 1915–1980* 62; Ellis and Sechaba 13). Using a rudimentary form of the classic communist "cell" structure, it grew slowly for the next few years, recruiting mostly white workers and intellectuals. After backing the racist Rand Mine Strike of 1922 (though with reservations), the party started to slowly redefine itself. At this point on the international dimension, the SACP was still relatively isolated from Soviet influence. As a matter of fact, Johns stated, "The CPSA gave little thought to the affairs of the Comintern [before 1928]," but after that date, "The Bolshevization of the party shook the Communist Party of South Africa to its roots" (Johns 1975, 200, 204). For the next few years, the SACP would not only be drawn into the foreign policy of the Soviet Union but also the deadly internal politics of the Joseph Stalin–dominated CPSU. As Stalin began his murderous reign in his own party, he would affect almost all the other communist parties, including the SACP, with bizarre accusations that would soon become deadly mass purges.

By the mid–1930s, the SACP would become intimately connected to the international aspects of Stalinism. "The Sixth Congress of the Comintern in 1928 marked the end of the CPSA's autonomy from Moscow and the beginning of absolute discipline to central authority which was demanded by Stalin" (Campbell 33). As the SACP entered 1930s, it also entered a new "ultraleft" period in its history. The Soviet Union began to face a new and more threatening enemy by the 1930s than just the amorphous threat of "imperialism" or "international capital." Fascism, in a number of different forms in various nations, started to seize state power. Italian Fascism and German Nazism were the two main manifestations of this movement. Both the domestic situation and foreign policy of Nazi Germany would affect the Soviet Union, and eventually the SACP.

The German Communists, who had split from the moderate Social Democrats in the early 1920s, were fighting on two fronts. One was against the leftist Social Democrats and another was against the more obvious enemy, the rightist Nazis. The attack on such would-be allies as the Social Democrats was itself directed from Moscow. Stalin had been conducting purges for years, both on the far "left" (Trotskyites, anarchists) and relative "right" (Right Bolsheviks, Mensheviks, Social Revolutionaries, and other left-of-center groups such as Social Democrats). If anything, the German Communists were more vigorous in their attacks on their leftist brethren, all of this supported and even promoted by Stalin and the Comintern ("The Communist Party [KPD]" 1). This internal conflict spilled into South Africa soon enough.

This antirightist Soviet policy facilitated a purging of the SACP in the 1930s. The SACP had just accommodated itself to working with "native" organizations, such as the ANC (Ludi 8). This Comintern directive was actually the beginning of an "anti-rightist campaign," started in Moscow at Comintern headquarters but enacted by local agents in South Africa (Forman 80–81). Just as some of the founders of the SACP were condemned as rightist "racists" at the 1928 meeting for not being "pro-native" enough,[3] the same line was extended to other leftist organizations in South Africa.

The primary enemy in South Africa was still the government, but other enemies were also cited: rightist elements within the SACP,[4] other leftist groups, centrist parties, and so on (Roux 1964, 97). After 1930, "ultra-leftism" increased within the SACP under the leadership of Douglas Wolton[5]; all "reformist" groups were vilified (Ellis and Sechaba 19; Roux vii). "A harshly intolerant, ultra-left period ensued in the leadership, which cost the Party untold damage in membership and influence" (Lerumo 72). Much later, the SACP admitted "excesses" were done during this period. "The manner in which this 'Bolshevikization' was applied was often dogmatic and intolerant" (*Red Flag in South Africa* 20). But it took almost sixty years for the SACP to be able to admit these issues.

In 1934, the communist leader M.M. Kotane condemned this leftist period, "Our Party members (especially the whites) are ideologically not South Africans, they are foreigners who know nothing about and are not interested in the country in which they are living in at present" (Lerumo 133). This is in obvious reference to foreign (often Russian) Comintern agents. Slovo had also criticized this period, though in 1994 he stated, "We went through a period during which we absorbed what was described as 'Leninism' without realising that much of it was wrapping paper for Stalinism" (Slovo 1994, 7). These are clear statements against the foreign Comintern agents that had pushed ultra-leftism in the SACP, but criticism of the Soviets them-selves was either minimum or absent until after the collapse of communism in the early 1990s.

This South African ultra-leftism fit the pattern happening throughout Europe, where communist parties condemned the rest of the left (and many of their own members) as "traitors" and "pawns of capital." This damaged the SACP, both in terms of morale and organizational strength. Again, the SACP admitted this all, though decades later: "This sectarianism had greatly weak-ened the international working class movement" (*Red Flag in South Africa* 25). During this period, the party not only lost the members it purged, but many others quit out of fear or disgust with the new policies. Still, this ultraleft policy of the Comintern would soon be ended.

The ultraleft policy was reversed when the Soviet Union discovered how much of a threat fascism truly was. By the mid–1930s, after more than a decade of being in power in Italy, and after solidifying power in Germany, interna-tional fascism was gaining real global influence. The luxury of being able to attack potential allies such as the Social Democrats and other leftist organi-zations was gone and Stalin and his supporters in the Comintern finally real-ized fascism was the real threat.

Thus, the Comintern started the "Popular Front" policy at the Seventh World Congress of the Comintern, where George Dimitrov (a Bulgarian Communist) called for "united fronts" where local communists were to align with any and all progressive and leftist organizations to fight fascism (Lerumo 73; *Red Flag in South Africa* 25). On the surface, this did make sense: other leftist organizations were flawed in the eyes of the communists, but during such desperate times, the entire left had to unite against the common foe of violent right-wing fascism (Lerumo 75–76). Still, for the SACP's rank and file (and even members of the leadership), this severe reversal was difficult. Attacking fascism of course made sense, but aligning with other leftists who had just been the "enemy" mere weeks before was the difficult part.

The SACP did follow the Popular Front strategy. Internally, this meant the end of ultra-leftism and the dreaded purges associated with it. The beginning of the Popular Front strategy "marked a crushing defeat for dogmatic, ultraleft tendencies in the Communist movement" (Lerumo 1971, 74).[6] This meant that the SACP did end one of its worst Stalinist periods. It attempted to mend old wounds between itself and various other progressive organizations in South Africa. Though fascism per se was not an immediate threat in South Africa, many Afrikaner social and political organizations agreed with the racial and foreign policy position that the fascists held. "Hitler's *herrenvolk* ideology found fertile soil among certain sections of the white racists of South Africa" (Lerumo 75).

The SACP correctly identified these trends as protofascist and called for a "front" against them. This policy was neither a clear-cut success nor failure, since the SACP was still weak from its own internal purges of the early 1930s; the party was not a significant force in South Africa at this point. Still, regardless of the ineffectiveness of its attempts to follow Comintern policy, the fact that the SACP did follow "the party line" is significant. This was especially true considering that Moscow would soon initiate another policy twist.

The War Years: Twists and Turns

The initial Comintern position was that World War II was basically a war between imperialists and therefore the only winner was international capital and the only loser was the working class the world over; this harkens back to leftist lines of thought before World War I. "It was the [SACP's] duty to both oppose the war and to resist the nationalists" (Lerumo 78). The SACP line was that if oppression was to be fought, such a battle was to start in South Africa, not Europe. As the SACP stated, "We have declared that this is an unjust war in which we have no interest except our desire to end it" (*South African Communists Speak 1915–1980*, 137). There was an implication that the "democratic powers" (England, France, and the United States) were to be favored to a degree since they too opposed international fascism, the primary enemy. This line, though, would soon be exchanged for yet another.

The Soviet Union, though maintaining the conflict was an "imperialist's war," still put out feelers to the West to form some sort of alliance against the would-be Axis powers. But between the appeasement policy of the democratic powers towards Hitler and the cold shoulder that the democratic powers gave to the Soviet Union in general,[7] the Soviets began secretly to also put out feelers to Nazi Germany. This would soon lead to one of the greatest shocks in the history of international communism.

The Soviet Union, the then undisputed leader of world communism, signed a non-aggression pact with the Nazis in 1939. Though this surprised the world, this opportunistic move did make sense in some ways: though Nazism was the enemy, a treaty with Germany was needed to buy time because the Western powers had done nothing so far (and it did buy two years for the Soviets).[8] Still, this meant a new twist in international policy: the Popular Front strategy of aligning all of the left against fascism was put on hold (Campbell 36). Since the Soviet Union and Nazi Germany were officially at "peace," the Comintern removed the antifascist element in the Popular Front policy, thus gutting the various Popular Fronts, including the one in South Africa.

The SACP was again caught off guard by the ever-changing policies of the Comintern, which by now had become a tool of Soviet foreign policy. The SACP now condemned the democratic powers for various "international crimes," while cutting down on antifascist rhetoric (Ellis and Sechaba 22). This also meant that it once again started to distance itself from its new leftist allies in the Popular Front. Though the leadership could follow the complex logic of these twists and turns, they had reservations about the wisdom of so many policy about-faces, especially this one. The rank and file of the SACP had it even worse: they had no idea why or how the fascists were no longer the enemy. These twists did not end here. The Soviet Union would regret its just-formed pact with Nazi Germany on June 22, 1941, with the start of Operation Barbarossa, the massive German invasion of the Soviet Union ("World War II: Operation Barbarossa" 1).

As the Germans rolled deep into Soviet territory, the Soviet Union was facing an existential threat. Obviously, the non-aggression pact had been grossly violated and the Soviet Union was desperate. The Comintern, in one of its last major directives, once again called for another Popular Front to fight an all-out war against the fascist Axis (the primary members being Nazi Germany, Imperial Japan, and Fascist Italy). This time, not only were communists to align with progressive forces in their countries, they were also to support almost any form of home government as long as it opposed international fascism. In other words, this form of Popular Front was the rawest form of Comintern opportunism: communists throughout the world were to support even reactionary regimes as long as that regime was against the Axis powers. This meant that the SACP was to actually support the racist regime in South Africa, because as with all British Commonwealth countries, it supported England against the Axis.[9]

In 1941 the SACP stated, "Soviet Russia has been attacked by the fascist Axis without the slightest justifiable reason.... The Communist Party of South Africa calls upon the working-class and all democratic and freedom-loving people to give their unqualified and wholehearted support to the Soviet Union in its struggle against the Nazi aggressors" (*South African Communists Speak 1915–1980* 162). For the whole war, the SACP basically gave up the class struggle, at least at the national level, to aid in the war against international fascism. In 1943, "it is time for all South Africans, whatever their class, their color or race, to come together" (Lerumo 136). This multiclass strategy, which was yet another reversal in policy, would once again adversely affect the SACP.

The SACP was now in the unenviable position of having to support a local regime that was supporting the Allies but was also anticommunist *and* racist.[10] The SACP had not dropped the ball on the major issue in South Africa, race, since the mid–1920s. The SACP, like the other organizations it was aligned with, had been fighting the social and institutional racism without reserve for decades. To reverse (or at the least, tone down) such an antiracist position was undoubtedly painful and difficult, both organizationally and personally.

Still, the SACP prided itself on being one of the most loyal parties in the Comintern. Thus the SACP once again obeyed orders, changed its stance, and attacked international fascism at almost any cost locally. "The oppressed people of the country, declared the Party, could not be indifferent while the socialist Soviet Union ... was locked in a titanic struggle for survival" (Lerumo 79). Such a change in policy was difficult and politically costly for the SACP.[11] Many members became confused and disenchanted, and some even quit. Structurally, the party was hurt by such confusion, weakening the national organization. Even the SACP now admits that these constant shifts in key policies during the war period adversely affected the organization (*Red Flag in South Africa* 29).

The Comintern itself was dissolved by Stalin in 1943 as a "good will gesture" to the Allied powers. The capitalist Allies naturally resented the existence of an organization that was nominally designed to promote worldwide socialist revolution against capitalism. Even the SACP knew this, stating in 1944 that the Comintern was seen as a subversive organization by the "right" of the Allied powers, so its dissolution would aid the alliance and the fight against Nazi Germany. The official reason given in 1943 by the Presidium of the Executive Committee of the Communist International, though, was as follows, "[The Comintern] has become a hindrance to the further strengthening of the national working class parties" (*South African Communists Speak 1915–1980* 178). This statement, ironically, is probably the truest statement to ever come out of the Comintern for decades, since most experts now agree that the Comintern sabotaged domestic socialist revolutions again and again for the sake of Soviet foreign policy (it might be added that Trotskyites had argued this since the late 1920s). At least indirectly, this was also true of the SACP and its own mission of building socialism in South Africa.

The dissolution of the Comintern did not affect the communist parties of the world as much as one would think. It would soon be replaced by other organizations, all of them tied to the USSR. There is no denying that by losing the name of the organization there was a real psychological effect on the various communist parties of the world. There would also never be the same degree of centralization as there was under the Comintern, though at times there would be *greater* control over specific parties.

Eventually the Axis was defeated, and once again the Soviet Union directed the various communist parties to fight capitalist, reactionary, and/or colonial regimes. By the 1950s, the primary Soviet foreign policy was to oppose "imperialism," that is, the United States and its allies.[12] This antagonism would soon become the Cold War by the late 1940s. This was the end of the major twists and turns in policy for international communism and the SACP, at least until the late 1980s.[13] Still, the SACP was shell-shocked after all of this: both organizationally and ideologically, the party was at its limit. After so many purges and twists in policy, many rank-and-file members quit the party out of weariness and/or disgust.

The Cold War: Lengthy Stability

The newly elected racist nationalist regime of 1948 also began an anti-communist campaign with little restraint: the SACP was soon banned. The Soviets then ordered the SACP to create fronts to defeat the nationalists. As Philip Nel explained, "During the 1950s the SACP played a large role in setting up the Congress Alliance ... as well as the formulation of the Freedom Charter and other anti–Apartheid activities" (Nel 12). With that foundation, the policy for the next thirty years would be laid.

There are some signs at this point that the SACP leadership started to have doubts about Soviet policy. The SACP finally did make some careful criticisms about Stalin, "the Great Genius of Mankind," when Khrushchev partially revealed Stalin's numerous and dire crimes in the mid–1950s. As early as 1956, after the 20th Party Congress of the CPSU, the SACP did make some extremely guarded comments:

> It is difficult and painful for the Soviet people and their leaders ... to re-evaluate objectively and critically the role of the late Josef [*sic*] Stalin. For Stalin rendered services of incalculable value to the cause to which he devoted his life.... But at the same time, it became essential to correct the false picture that, in later years, was built of Stalin as in infallible miracle-worker.... Stalin, inevitably, made mistakes [*South African Communists Speak 1915–1980* 242].

Though this statement sounds far too reserved to most Western ears, for the SACP it was a tremendous admission. Though the Eurocommunists did indeed have their faith shaken in the "Motherland of Socialism" by these revelations, if anything, the SACP renewed its commitment to international communism, and the CPSU, at this point (Revel 1).

This was mostly due to the SACP's renewed need for material support as domestic repression increased and the armed struggle began in the early 1960s. Publicly, the SACP would stay a loyal Stalinist party for the next forty years: "The South African Communist Party has throughout its history closely, at times almost totally, aligned with the brand of Marxism-Leninism applied by the government of the Soviet Union" (Ellis and Sechaba 9). They took on the CPSU's line in regards to Stalinism: though Stalin himself committed "excesses," the Soviet system and its foreign policy were essentially and "scientifically" correct.

For the next thirty years the Soviets and the SACP had a surprisingly stable relationship, especially considering the twists and turns it had gone through in the previous decades. The Soviets (the "Second World") basically fought "Western imperialism" (the "First World") on the side of the developing world (the "Third World"). The SACP denounced imperialism while still seeing it in a relatively subtle way:

> Like all social and economic processes dominated by capitalism, the current phase of imperialist restructuring is highly contradictory in character. It is, partly, driven by innovative and progressive technical advances that greatly expand the potential integration and capacity of human societies. But it is also driven by the insatiable pursuit of private profit. It is marked by deepening inequality within countries, between countries, between classes, and by the exploitation and deepening of gender oppression. It often afflicts the young, and marginalises the disabled. It is accelerating the destruction of our environment, and it is associated with unpredictable and often volatile economic instability [*SACP 10th Congress* 24].

As detailed before, the Soviets supplied arms, training, and guidance to communist parties and their allies throughout the world, including the SACP and the ANC. This policy would produce results, as many "Marxist" regimes were set up in the developing world, but these would often only be drains on Soviet resources.[14] Concerning South Africa, the situation was different. The Soviets did see it as a real prize for both its resources and its geopolitical location, but their surrogate the SACP and its allies never did succeed in overthrowing the regime in a traditional sense. By the 1990s, when the ANC and SACP finally started to make real gains, the Soviet Union itself, ironically, was starting to collapse.

Soviet Policy: The African Frontier

The SACP fought the nationalist regime from the mid–1960s to the mid–1980s in much the same way communist parties throughout the world fought their "native regimes": they combined military insurgency (MK) with political subversion (ANC). The SACP entered the mid–1980s following the same basic platform it had adopted in the early 1960s: maintain and strengthen its alliance with the ANC, use MK to exert pressure on the apartheid regime, and plan for the day when the ANC would take power.

The Soviets agreed with this plan, and as Peter Albright made clear, the Soviet Union wanted "to promote the emergence of radical black governments in Rhodesia, Namibia, and South Africa.... Moscow had adopted a simple strategy, specifically, it has sought, whether acting alone or with Cuba and/or the GDR [East Germany], to win recognition for itself as the prime supporter of 'anti-imperialism' in South Africa" (Albright 17). As a matter of fact, the Soviet Union had a great interest in all of southern Africa. As Albright added, "The 1970s witnessed a major increase in the involvement of the Communist States in Southern Africa" (Albright 3).

This would fit the Soviets' overall strategy for the "Third World" (developing world). As Rubenstein stated in *Moscow's Third World Strategy*:

> Over the years since the mid–1950s, the objectives of the Soviet Union in the Third World have been to undermine the ability of the United States to threaten the Soviet Union, to divert U.S. resources and attention away from Europe, and to keep the United States on the defensive, constantly concerned over shifting vulnerable areas and thus unable to mount a stiff or sustained challenge anywhere. Moscow regards the rivalry as protracted in nature; it accepts the inevitability of setbacks, but persists [Rubinstein 32].

And as Laqueur added:

> The existence of communist parties in the Third World gives the Soviet Union certain advantages, but it also creates major problems.... But the Soviet Union cannot wash its hands of world communism which, with all the difficulties that have risen, is still a source of strength to the Soviet Union in many respects [Laqueur 5].

As Laqueur also noted, "a confluence of nationalism and communism" had begun in these nations (Laqueur 4). The communists had always opposed Western imperialism, and now that there were more and more newly independent nations, this fit their strategy. The United States, though, was at a natural disadvantage because it often still supported its European allies and their "Third World" colonies, at least at the start of the Cold War (Vietnam being the best example, with the U.S. backing of French colonialism) and/or right-wing authoritarian regimes throughout Latin America, Africa, and Asia. Thus, "the Soviet Union has been more active diplomatically in the Third World than any other nation" (Laqueur 23). Historian C.F. De Villiers claimed the Soviets had a plan for postcolonial Africa:

> The Russians came to Africa soon after the close of the colonial period, seeking to fill the vacuum created by the withdrawal of colonial influence.... The official Russian attitude to the continent since 1955 has been: support all African nationalist movements, remove all suspicion amongst black leaders of communist aspirations for control of Africa and represent the socialist camp as being in the vanguard in the independence struggle of the Black African [De Villiers 74].

The Soviets often aided national liberation organizations, such as the MPLA in Angola, FRELIMO in Mozambique SWAPO in Namibia, and of course the ANC/SACP/MK alliance in South Africa (Albright 6–7).[15] There was even a division of labor among the former East Bloc nations, with the Soviets as arms dealer, the Cubans as personnel suppliers, and the East Germans providing intelligence and security training (Albright 12).

The Soviets had numerous and important strategic interests in Africa, especially South Africa with its political potential and natural resources. "There is a palpable Soviet fascination with the future of South Africa itself" (Laqueur 193). Bardis stated:

> The USSR, which has always been imperialistic, became even more expansionist in Southern Africa after the collapse of Portuguese rule and the decline of British influence in that region.... Extending its influence to South Africa would definitely generate many advantages for the USSR.... Unfortunately, the entire West, including the United States, has been rather passive in its attitude toward Soviet expansionism.... Countless facts prove conclusively that the Soviet Union is seriously interested in South Africa [Bardis 115].

Campbell and Albright, both scholars of international communism, and Urnov of the CPSU International Department, agreed with this assessment:

> Southern Africa has been the scene of increased Soviet interest and activity in the 1970s.
> Soviet leaders have an interest in impeding Western access to raw materials and minerals in South Africa.
> Why are we in southern Africa? Your question implies that we do not have legitimate interests here; however, we do [Campbell 150; 151; 153].

Albright generally agreed with this position, but presents a Soviet Union with a rather confused foreign policy.

Albright did agree that the Soviets wanted to dominate southern Africa's resources, but were fearful of the U.S. and were lacking in resources to act decisively. As Albright stated:

> Soviet leaders, have ... had an interest in impeding Western access to the raw materials and minerals of Southern Africa and disrupting Western use of sea lanes around the southern end of the continent.... [But] Soviet leaders have seemed to believe that the USSR has an interest in avoiding an escalation of racial conflict and guerrilla wars of the area into a nuclear confrontation with the United States.... [And] there has been a gap between ... the interests that Moscow has perceived in regard to Southern Africa and the capabilities at hand to fulfill them [Albright 16].

This may make sense, but it shows that the Soviets hardly had the situation under control. If the Soviet's interests in the region were "legitimate" or not is hardly relevant. What is important is the fact that the Soviets did see South Africa as an entry point into all of Africa and used the SACP to gain that access.

In South Africa, the Soviets had to rely on the SACP, ANC, and MK because "the USSR has maintained a mostly unofficial presence in South Africa" (Legum 103).[16] De Villiers added, "The clearest characteristic of the evolvement of Russian offensive interests in Sub-Saharan Africa is perhaps that it is not a primarily military offensive" (De Villiers 84). Others agreed with this assessment. "The USSR has no diplomatic representatives in South Africa and thus the Soviet Union's tools of statecraft are severely limited and clandestine operatives are of manifest importance" (Campbell 128). Also, as Campbell pointed out, "There has always been a strong ideological content in Soviet policy, first towards the SACP, and later towards the ANC.... The USSR's motivations in Southern Africa are ... political rather than economic" (Campbell 160, 161).

Laqueur agreed in part, noting how the use of local communist parties, such as the SACP, "does create opportunities for infiltration and gaining influence," but stressed the economic aspect more: "Soviet policy toward Africa at the present time is heavily concentrated on the Horn of Africa and the southern part of the continent. The strategic location of these areas, and the mineral wealth of Southern Africa, are no doubt major factors attracting Soviet interest" (Laqueur 5, 187, 189). Pike put it more bluntly:

> Communism's interest in South Africa concerns the Cape sea route, the geological treasures, especially gold, and finally it is a small stepping stone to reach that biggest bastion of the hated free-enterprise capitalism, the United State of America [Pike 550].

This statement does show that both relatively unbiased but also right-wing authors agree on why the Soviets were interested in South Africa.

Laqueur also added, "The Soviet Union has not been a generous aid donor in the past"; he estimated that the USSR gave sub–Saharan Africa $1.2 billion to the West's $5.7 billion from 1954 to 1979 (Laqueur 195). Henze agreed that "Russian enthusiasm for socialism in Africa has not been matched by economic support for it" (Henze 47). Though the absolute dollar of such aid is very much less for the Soviets than for the West, it must be noted that the Soviet economy was much smaller than the combined economies of the Western nations (or even of the U.S.) and thus as a percentage of its GDP, Soviet aid was still significant. It was also crucial, if not huge, for the SACP and the ANC during the long decades of underground existence.

Laqueur at least partially agreed, adding that "Soviet economic assistance to African countries is an important instrument of policy, even if it is a limited instrument.... The Soviet Union ... is simply not in the position to provide aid to Africa on a vast scale." Regardless of other types of aid, "The Soviet Union far outstrips the United States as an arms supplier to the African continent.... Soviet military advisers have assumed increasing importance in Africa in recent years." Most of the Soviet aid went to Ethiopia, Angola, and a few others, with 4,000 Soviet advisors on the continent (plus the 23,000 Cubans in Angola, and another 17,000 Cubans in Ethiopia) (Laqueur 195, 199). It was not just material aid that appealed to African regimes and "freedom fighters." "For many [African elites] Soviet formulas for capturing and retaining power have had great appeal" (Henze 52).

Bardis agreed with this analysis of Soviet policy. "Within South Africa, the Soviet Union is especially successful in promoting agitation and violence through the South African Communist Party (SACP) and the African National Congress (ANC)" (Bardis 116). Vanneman added how

> Soviet policy toward South Africa stresses support for the insurgent ANC, which has been publicly allied with the SACP for decades. The SACP is the Kremlin's

key instrument in South Africa and is the classic, small, elite intellectual vanguard party.... The ANC is also enmeshed in a complex network of pro–Soviet front organizations [Vanneman 13].

Nel agreed with this, saying, "The peculiar Soviet view of international affairs made Soviet support of national liberation in South Africa inevitable.... The Soviet Union therefore did not only believe it was right to support the African National Congress (ANC) and the South African Communist Party (SACP), but also that in doing so Moscow was aligning itself with history" (Nel 4–5). CPSU General Secretary Leonid Brezhnev himself stated in 1981, "The CPSU will consistently continue the policy of promoting cooperation between the USSR and the newly-freed countries and consolidating the alliance of world socialism and the national liberation movement" (Laqueur 189). Laqueur commented, "Soviet planners evidently hope that, with time, a large bloc of anti–Western, Marxist states with close ties to the USSR can be created" (Laqueur 189).

Laqueur later did add, "Soviet officials and analysts are able to muster only guarded optimism when contemplating the prospects for Marxist socialism on the [African] continent" (Laqueur 191).[17] Gleb Starushenko, of the former USSR Academy of Sciences, agreed with this. "[The Soviet leaders] believe the restructuring of South African society along socialist lines is a matter for the future," he noted. Dr. Victor Goncharev, of the former Soviet Institute of African Studies, saw socialism in South Africa in no less than one hundred years (Legum 112, 115). It is unclear if the SACP knew how pessimistic their own Soviet patrons were, but the South African communists had little choice but to fight on.

Other scholars on the subject concur. Peter Vanneman stated, "After the unrest in the mid–1980s, Moscow was less sanguine about an imminent revolution and began pursuing other avenues of influence. It also directed the SACP to concentrate more on political tactics" (Vanneman 13). The SACP proceeded to do so, with the secret talks with the nationalists beginning at that point.[18] Nel added:

The Brezhnev regime became increasingly disillusioned with the potential of the Third World to maintain a steady non-capitalist development... [By the 1980s,] Soviet observers argued that South Africa was now practically invulnerable.... Informed observers are thus agreed that Soviet policy towards South Africa is characterized by a fundamental circumspection [Nel 46].

Later in 1991, Slava Tetekhin of the CPSU stated, "It is clear now that the transition to socialism is not an easy thing. It will take much time" (Tetekhin 18). What "much time" meant is not elaborated in the article, but surely the SACP was getting the hint that the winds were shifting.

This Soviet pessimism translated into lukewarm support of the armed struggle in South Africa:

> The USSR—along with Czechoslovakia, Bulgaria and the German Democratic Republic (East Germany)—currently provides 90 percent of all military aid to the ANC.... It also clear that the USSR was never so convinced of the ANC's ability to attack the existing system in the RSA [South Africa] that it lent its wholehearted support to such a move.... The USSR has never attempted to encourage the ANC to intensify its armed struggle drastically [Nel 54–55].

The Soviets did not see the ANC as politically "deep enough" and it had a reputation for being too brutal. Still, "The ANC [via the SACP] remains the only established medium through which the USSR may exercise any kind of influence on South African politics" (Nel 55, 58). Such conservatism on the part of the Soviets was not uncommon during the Cold War, but no one suspected that it would eventually lead to a major policy reversal by the late 1980s.

Regardless of the Soviets' estimations of success for the SACP, the Soviet scholar Andrei Urnov pointed out that South Africa was still strategically important to America, and therefore also to the USSR. "The imperialist powers quite consciously pursued a policy of strengthening the South African regime both economically and militarily" (Urnov 226, 307).[19] So the Soviets felt compelled to back African leftist parties for geopolitical reasons, no matter what the chance of success were. Henze agreed, stating, "The Soviets' primary aim is to use South Africa to weaken and divide the United States" (Henze 50). By the 1970s, the Soviets started to turn their focus to Rhodesia and South Africa (Henze 44). As Laqueur added, "No secret is made of the fact that the communist foothold in Africa south of the Zambezi will ultimately result in depriving [Western] 'imperialism' of ... strategic materials found in the southern part of Africa" (Laqueur 13).

Therefore, with this all in mind, Bardis' citation from a U.S. State Department report of 1986 made sense. "In addition to working for South Africa's diplomatic isolation, the USSR seeks to exploit internal discord in that country" (Bardis 119). But as Laqueur pointed out, "The Soviet Union has made significant gains in Africa since the early 1970s.... Despite these gains in Africa, however, the Soviet Union has continued to suffer ... serious setbacks in its African policy" (Laqueur 187). Therefore, within the Cold War context, by definition South Africa became important for the Soviet Union. This globally antagonistic position of the Cold War, though, would soon be jettisoned by the new and reformist Gorbachev regime in the Soviet Union.

Before Mikhail Gorbachev's rise to power in the Soviet Union in the mid–1980s, the SACP had already demonstrated its solidarity with various leftist, socialist, and communist organizations during this long period of relative stability. One example was the 1977 Lisbon World Conference against Apartheid. As the admittedly partisan Pike explained, "Personalities of both the CPSA and the ANC were represented in this collection of Marxist clowns and political puppets.... The collaboration between CPSA and other communist parties and revolutionary movements was well reflected in this meeting" (Pike 507). The SACP saw the need, both materially and ideologically, to associate with and bolster other left-wing movements throughout the world. Just as the SACP received material aid for decades from the East Bloc, they offered advice and solidarity to many other communist parties and leftist fronts in many nations. This would all change by the late 1980s, as the SACP's ideological world began to collapse.

The Collapse of Communism: A New Era

The SACP faced a number of ideological and policy shifts during the period between the late 1940s and 1980s, but none of them was nearly as severe as when, beginning in 1989, "communism collapsed." This collapse, though, did not happen suddenly: the East Bloc had been showing strains for at least a decade, with explosive outbreaks of rebellion at different times. Plus, it would take three more years until the Soviet Union itself imploded. The Soviets had gained domination over Eastern Europe after World War II and when China went "Red" in 1949. But this "communist bloc" soon become fractured (the Yugoslav Break and the Sino-Soviet Split) and even Stalinism was denounced publicly by 1956. But after that, from the late 1960s until the early 1980s, Soviet policy was basically consistent and international communism was relatively stable (if not only semimonolithic, since it had lost to some degree Yugoslavia, Albania, North Korea, and, of course, China).

But such ideological coherence would soon come to an end. This began with the Polish solidarity movement of the early 1980s, increased by 1989 as various East Bloc nations jettisoned communism, and climaxed in 1991 with the collapse of the Soviet Union itself. A detailed explanation of the collapse of communism is beyond the scope of this discussion; suffice to say for now that economic mismanagement, political corruption, and general moral bankruptcy all contributed to the implosion (McCauley 69; Sonnenfeldt 71, 82, 91; Gorbachev 1987a, 108; Buston 135).

The collapse itself greatly affected the remnants of international communism, including the SACP, but here I will concentrate on the period just before the total collapse in the late 1980s. During this precollapse period, the SACP was again forced to perform the ideological gymnastics that it had mastered long ago. These twists and turns, if not as complex as those of the World War II period, were in some ways far more important: they led to the unprecedented defection of the SACP from what was left of international communism.

In 1985 Mikhail Gorbachev was made the new (and soon to be last) General Secretary of the CPSU and therefore the new leader of the Soviet Union. After the disappointingly mild reforms of Yuri Andropov[20] and the political limbo of Konstantin Chernenko, the Soviet Politburo was finally ready for the more radical and reformist ideas of Gorbachev (McCauley 13–14). Even the conservative leaders of the Soviet Union understood that the "system," seventy years old, was rotting at the core, though to what extent was debated fiercely. Neither they nor Gorbachev were clear on where the reforms should go, nor how far.

Meanwhile, back in South Africa in 1985, the Nationalist regime had just concluded a round of significant constitutional reforms. These reforms even resulted in a tricameral constitution, which finally included Indians and Coloureds, but still shockingly and mostly excluded the black majority (Urnov 223). Not surprisingly, the majority of South Africans rejected these shallow and ineffective changes (Halloran 24). In reaction to these developments, the SACP and ANC promoted the policy of ungovernability in the squalid townships. This was a relatively spontaneous uprising amongst township dwellers against the nationalist regime and its education policies, its general repression, and even the lack of utilities in the townships. It was organized at some point by the ANC and others, but initially there seems to have been no one instigator. Still, the ANC did effectively fan the flames once it began. Ungovernability became a real threat to the regime after a few months. As Nel commented:

> In 1985 the world, including the Soviet Union, was under the impression that it would only be a matter of months before the South African government fell and was replaced by a government that would probably be dominated by the African National Congress (ANC) and the South African Communist Party (SACP) [Nel 8].

Still, this impression quickly changed:

> By 1986 international expectations of the imminent collapse of the South African state proved to be ill-founded, as this state ruthlessly repressed real and imagined threats to its security.... Soviet commentary [in 1986] also became more cautious and sober [Nel 23].

Thus, on the surface ungovernability did fail, at least if its intention was to directly overthrow the regime. This uprising, though, did greatly contribute to the general pressure for regime change and eventually led to the lifting in 1990 the bans on ANC and SACP, and finally the 1994 elections.

In any case, the SACP maintained a close and important relationship with the Soviet Union throughout all of these changes in the 1980s. It still recognized the material, ideological, and even moral leadership of the Soviet Union, and the Soviets still saw the SACP as an important ally in southern Africa. And at first Gorbachev did back the ANC and SACP and their struggle, writing supportive articles and giving their leaders medals. But even as Gorbachev acted the good ally, he was preparing to cut a deal in southern Africa, one that would match the many regional agreements Gorbachev was pursuing (Nel 21–22).

The initial round of reforms in the Soviet Union initiated by Gorbachev had little direct effect on the SACP, either materially or ideologically. These Soviet reforms called for ending corruption, some form of competition between socialist enterprises, and a war on "decadence" (Sonnenfeldt 26; Gorbachev 1987a, 6; Gorbachev 1987b, 112, 164). The SACP, naturally, saw no problem with such innocuous (and hardly original) reforms. The next round of reforms, starting in March 1986, included the famous glasnost (openness) and perestroika (restructuring), which were much more significant for the Soviet Union, international communism, and the SACP.

Glasnost proposed less censorship, more ties to the West, and general political openness. Perestroika proposed some forms of political competition, initially within the CPSU, but later between "independent parties" (Gorbachev 1987a, 1–16; Gorbachev 1987b, 112). Gorbachev had to fight and defeat various conservative political enemies within the Politburo and ruling elite of the Soviet Union to enact these changes (Doder 299). As these reforms started to shake the very foundations of the East Bloc, and especially the Soviet Union, they began to affect even faraway South Africa and the SACP.

These reforms did have a significant effect on the SACP, since they threatened to undermine common assumptions and perceptions that all communist parties had held literally for decades. The Stalinists in the SACP, whose initial reaction was to reject both glasnost and perestroika, were still deeply embedded. As late as 1992, after the fall of the USSR, "South African Communists were among the most loyal devotees of Stalin and Stalinism" (Ellis and Sechaba 9). Of these Stalinists, Harry Gwala was one of the more extreme, and he rejected Gorbachev's more liberalizing reforms.

Still, the ideas of glasnost and perestroika were not totally alien to the SACP, since international communism had been introduced to them with the advent of Eurocommunism in the 1970s. Eurocommunism, as proposed by the Spanish and Italian Communist parties (and later partially adopted by the French party), offered a revision of some basic communist (that is, Stalinist) assumptions about political freedoms and pluralism by calling for communist parties to forsake the more rigid aspects of Stalinism while continuing to seek socialist goals. The Eurocommunists also called for a distancing from the CPSU and the Soviet Union (Beilenson).

Such moves were a serious blow for both the unity of international communism and the foreign policy of the Soviet Union. As the Spanish and Italian parties fully adopted this program, the French party continued to hold out (Beilenson; Manning 32–33). Still, such major "defections" from the Soviet hard line ultimately proved to be as dangerous to international communism as many hard-liners within the USSR had predicted. The rest of the international communist network, though hardly accepting of all the tenets of Eurocommunism, did mull it over. Various communist journals and papers debated the pros and cons of reform and Soviet policy, including the SACP's own journal, *The African Communist*. Though the SACP did reject Eurocommunism at the time, it adopted most of its program years later.

Still, by definition, Eurocommunism was a European issue at its core. Since most of the communist parties that made up international communism operated in less developed nations, such debates must have seemed to them remote and even alien at times. Ideas about integrating into the domestic political system, as Eurocommunism proposed, seemed ridiculous to communist parties that were at best persecuted and at worst banned (such as the SACP). To debate whether socialist industrial complexes should compete against each other or not (i.e., Yugoslavia) was not exactly relevant for the rank-and-file parties hiding in the brush or jungles of the developing world and still preparing to overthrow their countries' regimes.

Still, the leaders of these parties could not afford to ignore the changes in Europe. Like many other communist parties, the SACP rejected the basic tenets of Eurocommunism at that time, ten or more years before the mid–1980s. "The Party had been unstinting in its criticism of Communist Parties which had broken decisively with the Soviet model of Communism" (Ellis and Sechaba 182). In the final analysis, though, Eurocommunism was not the most important issue for the SACP in 1970s or even the 1980s. The party faced tremendous obstacles and opportunities within South Africa during this period, such as the Soweto uprising and its aftermath; the party needed to focus on the problems at hand. It was not long, however, before the reforms initiated in the Soviet Union in the mid–1980s hit closer to home.

The Soviet Union had been the heart and soul of communism for over seventy years and now it was significantly changing. These events could not be overlooked by parties that turned to the CPSU as their ideological guiding light. So when Gorbachev proposed a degree of political space for noncommunist actors within the Soviet Union, first in the media and then in the political system itself, communist parties such as the SACP took notice. The Gorbachev reforms, for some, proved to be quite disquieting. As analyst Dirk Kunert commented, "Glasnost has left the intelligentsia militariat of the Third World in a twilight zone of utopianism, populism, and Leninist revolutionism" (Kunert 1).

Though there were individuals within the SACP such as Gwala who outright rejected the Gorbachevian reforms, officially, the leadership (i.e., Joe Slovo and Chris Hani) accepted glasnost and perestroika as useful tools to renew and strengthen communism.[21] This was a new twist in the ideological history of the SACP: from more or less blind acceptance of the tenets of Stalinism to jumping on the bandwagon of Gorbachevian reform. Put somewhat more critically, "In Pavlovian fashion, [SACP leaders] have responded to external stimuli, echoing glasnost directives" (Kunert 3). One of these "directives" in 1987, issued indirectly through a Soviet *Pravda* article, urged the ANC/SACP alliance to be more flexible and amicable towards negotiations with the Nationalists. The alliance soon did just that, though for its own local reasons too (Vanneman 15).

The SACP even started to invite "liberal" members of the CPSU to publish in its journal. One such scholar stated, "Socialism is not the property of the Soviet Union, or the East or the West.... The fundamental lesson is that pseudo-socialism cannot be reformed but needs to be completely overhauled.... Eastern Europe never produced socialism. It was pseudo-socialism that existed there" (Jobarteh 91). This is strong language for a CPSU member and must have come as a shock to loyal SACP members. Another scholar from the Soviet Afro-Asian Solidarity Committee, Slava Tetekhin, was somewhat less critical and commented a little later:

> Lenin's view of the Russia of the future was distorted by his successors.. The nationalisation of industry was a decision forced upon the Bolsheviks through acts of sabotage by big business. But the nationalisation process in Stalin's model did not give the means of production to the people.... It alienated the means of production from the immediate producers. At the same time working people were cut off from real political power.... Stalin's purges took the lives of

thousands of the most capable people.... Power was increasingly held by the bureaucracy.... [But] socialism began to prove its historical potential [Tetekhin 15].

Another SACP member, Explo Kofi, tried to explain that the Stalinist abuses were more due to historical and international "factors," and not "personalities," as Slovo supposedly claimed (Kofi 48). Not only does this piece soft-pedal Leninism at the expense of Stalinism, but it also is unfair to Slovo. Slovo never really addressed the personality of Stalin, but at times did make Stalinism sound more like a mistake than anything else.

In any case, these statements became the perfect transition tool for the CPSU and the parties that still followed their lead, like the SACP.[22] Though the CPSU was finally and fully condemning its own Stalinism (albeit thirty-five years late), it still could not attack the Stalinism of the very system that it still operated in the Soviet Union. But this is what liberal communists like Gorbachev (and of course Slovo) needed: a condemnation of the "bad old days" in conjunction with maintenance of the current system. This way they could begin to change the system without losing too much support within their communist parties. Eventually this balancing act would fail for Gorbachev, and an antireform coup was attempted in 1991.

Though what Gorbachev was proposing would eventually help lead to the collapse of communism (decades of abuse, corruption, and international pressure still mattered), at the time such reforms seemed necessary and well measured. The immense problems that the East Bloc faced and of which the SACP was aware (but usually ignored in party pronouncements and articles) were not just going to go away. The SACP did have the ideological courage to accept reform within the established communist societies of the East Bloc.[23] Still, "as the new decade began, the SACP was somewhat disquieted by the pace of glasnost and perestroika," and "although the SACP has adhered to Moscow's ideological line as strictly as any communist party outside the Soviet bloc, both it and the ANC have reason to be suspicious of the Kremlin.... The USSR has a long record of sacrificing local communists to the interests of the Soviet state" (Vanneman 23, 31). The SACP did move on and it even started to hint that such political freedoms may have a place in the ANC-led regime that both the ANC and SACP hoped would one day exist (Ellis and Sechaba 10).

Another aspect of Soviet reforms affected the SACP more directly: the Soviet Union, after more than forty years of fighting "Western imperialism" throughout the world, declared that "international peace" was necessary. Even as early as 1980, Vasily Solodovikov, the Soviet ambassador to Zambia, stated,

"There is a political way [to peace]. We, as socialists, think that a political solution in South Africa is possible, but it's up to the people" (Nel 60). In 1986, the Soviets hinted about a peaceful settlement for South Africa in a paper by Gleb Starushenko of the Soviet Africa Institute (Nel 24). But 1987 would be the year for historical changes in Soviet foreign policy. Nel commented on the pivotal 27th Congress of the CPSU held in March of 1987, "Mikhail Gorbachev and a new team of foreign policy makers for the first time suggested that all regional conflicts should be resolved by means of diplomacy and negotiation" (Nel 23).

These ideas translated quickly into foreign policy. In December 1987 the ANC held an international conference in Arusha, Tanzania, and Soviet delegates talked of peace settlements for southern Africa. In August 1988 Boris Asoyan, head of the Soviet Ministry of Foreign Affairs, stated, "All race groups must come together [in South Africa]" (Nel 60). Though the SACP shared a policy of "non-racialism" with the ANC, to propose that blacks cut a nonviolent deal with their violent white oppressors, before they were in a position of strength, was definitely a new turn in Soviet policy.

The momentum for regional peace settlements increased on all fronts.

> The Soviet Union had introduced a fundamental revision of foreign policy doctrines by late 1987 [Barrell 65].
>
> The Soviet government committed itself to withdraw its forces or refrain from seeking the overthrow of the existing order.... The Soviet Union would lend its weight to negotiating a solution to local problems [Ellis and Sechaba 182].

By the summer of 1987, the situation had gotten worse for the ANC and SACP vis-à-vis the Soviets. In June of 1987 Victor Goncharov, Deputy Director of the Africa Institute, commented that the South African revolution was, at a minimum, decades off. Then in August, Gorbachev himself stated, "Apartheid will finally come to its end. But we do not believe in the thesis 'the worse, the better' ... What we need now is new ideas, a fresh approach and joint attempts" (Nel 28–29). This was a condemnation of the policy of ungovernability, which the alliance was still pushing at the time, though it hinted at the eventual peace talks of the early 1990s that did happen in South Africa. Nel summed it well from the alliance's perspective:

> Moscow wants to avoid such [bad] impressions at all costs, especially at a time when the USSR is really trying to improve its relations with the U.S. and other nations.... In [Gorbachev's] speech he publicly declared that the Soviet Union now accepts, at the highest level, the principle that a domestic political solution should be promoted in South Africa; that the interests of the whites will be respected by the Soviet Union; and that the USSR, together with other countries,

is prepared to support innovative strategies geared toward a political solution [Nel 30].

Was this a betrayal of the SACP by its Soviet patron? At the time, it may have seemed so to some. But the alliance, at least the more liberal elements, generally accepted this turn. Slovo carefully explained the changes in 1989:

> The way I choose to understand Mikhail Gorbachev's proposition that there are human values which take priority over class values is that the assertion of certain values is in the mutual interests of otherwise contending classes. But the values remain class-related.... The undifferentiated formula that we must seek a political settlement for every internal struggle can become a slogan which has the effect of preventing or holding back the ultimate peaceful resolution of an internal conflict.... The universalised concept of national reconciliation tends wrongly to denude conflict of its class and social base.... Of course where a conflict (whatever the original cause) demands a negotiated, even compromise, agreement, there is no question of a "fight to the death" ... We will readily support peaceful coexistence [Slovo 1989, 87–88].

As it turned out, the reversal of much of traditional Soviet foreign policy seemed to have hurt Soviet interests worldwide more than the local communist parties.

There is also the fact that the Soviets themselves were somewhat split on this issue as it applied to South Africa. Nel saw two main Soviet camps: the diplomats and the strategists. The diplomats wanted a fair settlement for all parties involved in the local conflict. This faction included the Soviet Ministry of Foreign Affairs, various liberal academics, the Africa Institute, and the Institute for the U.S. and Canada. They saw a need to work with the West to bring this about. The strategists also wanted a settlement but favored the local national liberation parties, such as the ANC. This faction consisted of the Soviet Committee for Solidarity with the Peoples of Asia and Africa, Vasily Solodonikov (former Africa Institute director), and the International Department of the Central Committee of the CPSU (Vladimir Shubin and Andrei Urnov). They were much less favorable toward working with the West and still saw violent revolution as an option (Nel 75–76). Eventually, the diplomats would win out, which made the Soviets appear more opportunistic than ever.

Gorbachev, who was certainly closer to the diplomat faction, saw the need to put international peace *above* local conflict, especially in certain "Third World" settings such as South Africa, but also in Cambodia and Nicaragua. In effect, this represented a historic change: "The traditional class interests of Soviet foreign policy should be understated for the sake of more universal interests" (Nel 82). Anatoly Adamishin, USSR Deputy Foreign Minister, had already voiced a desire to avoid bloodshed in South Africa (Legum 115). Coming from its Soviet patron, the leader of "World Revolution," this was a shock for the SACP. Vanneman added, "Moscow is even meeting secretly with South African officials [in 1990], an act of duplicity from the ANC's perspective" (Vanneman 23). But was the SACP seeing it that way also? From the evidence the answer was "not quite yet." However, the SACP was beginning to have serious doubts about its "Elder Brother in World Socialism," for this was obviously a major break from past Soviet foreign policy and it did affect the SACP directly.

Why did the Soviets make this drastic change? The Gorbachev clique argued at the time that the "new" Soviet Union did indeed believe in "peace on earth" and there were probably some academics who did as well. But most analysts agreed with Nel when he said, "Fundamental changes in Soviet thinking about international relations were forced on the USSR through events over which the Soviet Union had little or no control" (Nel 87). In other words, between a collapsing economy, the beginning of the loss of the East Bloc, and general unrest at home, the Soviets could ill afford to continue to fund wars of national liberation throughout the developing world.[24]

Things got harder for the alliance partners in South Africa. Not only were the Soviets cutting their losses in South Africa, they started to pressure the ANC to do the same:

> ANC spokesmen also acknowledge that Moscow is trying, not so much by pressure as by persuasion, to bring ANC policy and strategy in line with the new Soviet evaluation of the dynamics of change in South Africa.... One such spokesman hinted that the ANC is currently being advised by the Soviet Union ... that it should be prepared to start negotiating with the South African government [Nel 34].

And the SACP was forced to get into the act:

> The SACP, especially through someone like Joe Slovo, its Secretary General and until recently the Chief of Staff of Umkhonto We Sizwe, has played an important and constructive role in selling the new Soviet approach to the ANC. Since the second half of 1986 Slovo has, in a number of interviews, speeches and articles, played a significantly more moderate view on questions such as socialism, white interests, and the role of negotiations [Nel 35].

And though left-wing elements in both the ANC and SACP resisted this trend, soon enough Slovo, Hani, and Mandela (still in prison) did buy into this new, more conciliatory position pushed by the Soviets.

Right-wing critics of the USSR, like Vanneman, had a different, more maniacal, view of Gorbachev's "grand peace strategy." Vanneman stated:

> Mikhail Gorbachev's long range policy ... is two pronged: Multifaceted diplomacy combined with a carefully orchestrated, low intensity campaign of sabotage and subversion.... Moscow was unprepared for the unrest in South Africa's townships in 1984–1985 with young radicals calling for spontaneously for revolutionary activity without guidance from Moscow [and] emphasizing political alliances with opponents of the regime, reminiscent of the popular front strategy of Stalin [Vanneman 14].

Though this sounds plausible, there is no real evidence to back it up. On closer inspection, Gorbachev comes out innocent: the Soviets did not have many choices by the late 1980s. We now know that if anything, the USSR was worse off both economically and socially than was generally suspected at the time and therefore the Soviets had few choices. Regardless, Soviet foreign policy literally disappeared soon after this statement was made, when the Soviet Union itself imploded in 1991.

These twists and turns were not that different from the rather opportunist foreign policy of the Soviet's for the past seventy years. As Laqueur stated:

> [T]he Soviet Union may frequently have to choose between support (even if only rhetorical) for the communist party and friendship with a regime that wants to combine collaboration with the Soviet Union with the repression of communism at home.... The Soviet leadership in 1964 even recommended to Third World communist parties ... that they dissolve voluntarily and join "progressive" official parties [Laqueur 5–6].

To a certain extent, this was true even for South Africa. Though the Soviets never asked the SACP to "dissolve" and merge with the ANC, they certainly did push both the SACP and ANC into a tight union. Later, the Soviets pushed the alliance to the bargaining table with the Nationalists.

Gorbachev made it clear that regional peace was now a goal of the Soviet Union and was willing to compromise on a number of issues to gain this goal. John Saul pointed out, "An economically-strapped Soviet Union now [1990] seeks first and foremost, to escape from costly overseas entanglements, and it seeks ... to curry favour with the capitalist centres of finance and technology" (Saul 1990, 37). As Kunert added, "Entire left-wing contingents are suddenly plunged into a deep crisis. They are lashing out against the USSR for consorting with 'U.S. imperialism'" (Kunert 144). It is true that the Soviets had never gained a great deal directly from its adventures in the developing world. By the late 1980s the USSR was so economically desperate it readily jettisoned such liabilities to gain favor with the West and save much needed resources. As Laqueur pointed out:

The Soviet Union may frequently have to choose between support (even if only rhetorical) for the Communist Party and friendship with the regime that wants to combine collaboration with the Soviet Union with the repression of communism at home [Laqueur 5].

Ellis and Sechaba agreed:

For the ANC and SACP, the New York Accords [for Southern Africa] were a bitter pill indeed.... The hardest blow to bear was that the Soviet Union had given up its commitment to the armed struggle and to revolution in South Africa. In fact, it was forming a steadily closer relationship with the [nationalist] Pretorian regime [Ellis and Sechaba 192, 193].

Finally, as Vanneman put it, "The USSR has a long record of sacrificing local Communists to the interest of the Soviet state" (Vanneman 31). The Soviet Union did not go quite that far in South Africa.[25] This retreat from revolution was shocking to diehard revolutionaries throughout the developing world, especially for the SACP. This new policy also reduced the global role of the Soviets (which was somewhat the point).

Was this Soviet reversal a genuine policy decision or just a complex rationale for the necessary consolidation of resources and general "retreat" from the developing world? John Saul saw the latter explanation as more likely:

Surely the primary function of such jejune formulation must be that of putting the best face possible on the bald fact of the Soviet Union's own global retreat. It represents one kind of ideological fallout from the Eastern Bloc's economic collapse [Saul 1990, 36].

This would result in making the Soviet Union less influential in all of southern Africa. Obviously, these predictions, if anything, did not go far enough.

Finally, not only did the Soviet Union disappear but its collapse reduced the role of the new Russia in Africa. This was due primarily to economic factors and meant a total cutoff of supplies, training, and morale support for the SACP, "In South Africa, certainly, the collapse [of communism] has had important resonance within the mass movement" (Saul 49). This was an understatement. Though money and arms from the USSR had been declining for years, after 1991 the SACP was caught off from its source of guidance and material of seven decades.[26] These regional policy reversals were nothing compared to what was about to happen for the whole communist world.

In 1989 the European communist world was rocked to its foundation and would disappear within three years. It was obvious that the East Bloc would be drastically reshaped by these social and political changes, but very few predicted that this was the beginning of the end of communism in Eastern

Europe, let alone the collapse of the Soviet Union itself (Keylor Chapter 16). As these events were happening, the SACP watched them diligently. But as a critic of the SACP added, "[The USSR] ... was in a state of collapse ... but [the SACP] remained faithful Stalinists to the end, outlasting Gorbachev on that reactionary tradition" (Mokonyane 130). This is actually incorrect. As outlined earlier, the SACP was prompted by these events to change both its ideology and structure.

The SACP already had serious reservations about some of the changes occurring in the East Bloc. Still, it tried to keep a positive attitude:

> No matter what setbacks and disappointments experienced in the socialist countries, the Marxists' philosophical outlook and interpretation of history have not altered.... The condition of the world today, therefore, by no means indicates that capitalism has won.... The achievements of the socialist countries, for confidence that the socialist perspective is realistic and realisable.... The SACP has called for the strengthening of relations between communist parties internationally ["Capitalism vs. Socialism" 14–18].

Such rallying cries were admirable, but events unraveled so fast in the next couple of years that such slogans would not be enough.

The SACP agreed with Gorbachev, when he stated, "Socialism will take many forms, depending on the context" ("The Crisis in the Socialist World" 21). But the SACP drew the line when it sensed, quite correctly, that more than relatively safe "top-down reforms" were afoot. There began a debate within the SACP on what changes were truly necessary and whether emulating the Soviet Union mechanically was the best idea (Ellis and Sechaba 5).[27] A trickle of articles in the SACP's *The African Communist* started to call for reform *and* caution. The party started to hint that though some of the demands for change were genuine, to a great extent the Western media was exaggerating, distorting, and generally exploiting the situation in the East Bloc for its own selfish and ultimately capitalist purposes.[28] Still, the SACP was somewhat lost at this point (Adam 33).

Initially, the SACP accepted the Gorbachev reforms, if not without reservations. Though critics of the SACP saw the acceptance of such reforms as more automatic, "It was almost a reflex action for the SACP to welcome any new approach coming from Moscow" (Ellis and Sechaba 182) The SACP accepted the need for modifications to the regimes of the East Bloc. Slovo himself started to critique the Soviet system. In October 1988, "Slovo honestly admit[ed] that SACP was part of a worshipping personality cult" (Adam 27). But as Adam further explained, "By blaming human error rather than fundamental Leninist tenets, Slovo fails to recognize the intrinsic causes of Stalinist tyranny" (Adam 27). The SACP also commented on East Germany, a state with which the SACP had had a long relationship, "Nor does it serve any purpose to deny that the GDR has problems ... and then there is the problems of the bureaucracy which seems to plague all the socialist countries" ("The Class Struggle..." 20).

For the SACP such statements were a radical departure from past policy. The SACP was actually being *critical* of the East Bloc, the archetype for its own future Socialist South Africa. "Sovietism's hideous developments, which were accompanied by applause and their ringing endorsements, were now rationalized away as accidental" (Kunert 3). Kunert is overstating the case, but the SACP was indeed reserved in its critique. The SACP accepted Soviet directives as it had for decades, but this time the Soviets themselves were undermining some basic doctrines of Stalinist (and even Leninist) communism. These Soviet critiques included such formally sacred concepts as the "dictatorship of the proletariat" (at least the Leninist interpretation) and the natural supremacy of a bureaucratic command economy. The SACP could and did accept glasnost and perestroika; what it could not accept was the beginning of the end of international communism.

Thus a new direction in policy was pushed upon the SACP. Within a year of their introduction, the SACP was forced to accept Gorbachev's reforms. Now in the early 1990s, the SACP was forced by the situation to make another change in policy: the SACP started openly to condemn some of the reforms and "capitulations" that the ruling (but ever-weakening) communist parties of the East Bloc were enacting, especially the CPSU. In other words, the SACP went from mild but basically unconditional support of East Bloc reforms to a critical view of such things. The most common complaint of the SACP was that those parties were being "overly critical" of communism's history, achievements, and doctrine.

The SACP began to speak of the "identity crisis now besetting some socialist countries" ("The Class Struggle" 16). The SACP even found a CPSU official, Vladimir Bushkin, to state in the SACP's own journal that the "self-criticism" within the Soviet Union, though occasionally useful, had gone too far (Bushin 19). The SACP admitted that reform might be needed, but outright condemnation of communist "achievements" was unacceptable. Taking one example, the SACP felt it necessary to add, "The achievements of the [communist German Democratic Republic's] citizens in the spheres of culture and sport are legendary. Living standards in the GDR are the highest in the socialist world" ("The Class Struggle..." 19).[29]

At this point, the SACP started to make difficult decisions and admissions. The SACP stated in 1990:

> The seriousness of the crisis which has overtaken the international communist movement cannot be overstated.... The collapse of the communist-dominated governments of Eastern Europe, the gathering complications frustrating the implementation of the policies of Perestroika and glasnost in the Soviet Union, the Tiananmen Square Massacre in Peking last June, the formal abandonment of many of the policies of Marxism-Leninism by a number of communist parties— all these factors have greatly altered the balance of forces in the world.... Today this system is in a state of disarray.... Communist power in many countries has been broken by popular insurrection ["The Class Struggle..." 13–14].

This was an amazing and open admission for a party that supported the very system that was "broken by popular insurrection." The SACP started to admit to itself and the public that the Soviet system was indeed rotten at the core, while of course still maintaining that the ideology of Marxism-Leninism was correct. Case in point: in the very same article the SACP praised the Soviet Union for slowing imperialism, providing inspiration, and supporting the "Third World struggle" ("The Class Struggle..." 14).

This is not to say that the SACP had broken with the Soviets entirely; this did not happen for another year. As the SACP put it in late 1990:

> Perhaps the South African liberation movement ... has taken the support of the socialist countries too much for granted in the past.... Anyway, socialism has not failed regardless of East Bloc.... We believe that what is going on in the international communist movement today is not a process of demolition but of cleansing.... Nothing that has happened in Eastern Europe or elsewhere makes us believe that [our] perspective needs to be altered ["The Class Struggle" 17–19].

The SACP was already cutting its losses by distancing itself from the rapidly collapsing East Bloc, while still reiterating their support for Marxism-Leninism and socialism in general. This became a common theme for the next few years.

After whole communist regimes collapsed in Eastern Europe and Gorbachev's position in the Soviet Union become weaker by the month, the SACP started openly to question its faith in the dissolving Soviet system. The SACP Central Committee stated in 1991, "The SACP has never tried to run away from the reality of the major crisis for socialism represented by the events in eastern Europe and the Soviet Union over the last two and a half years" ("Internationally: Aluta Continua" 4). A year later it added, "Internationally, the deep crisis of the world socialist system, has had, and will continue to have, a negative impact on our struggle" ("The Way Forward..." 43). This is an understatement, to say the least. Ellis and Sechaba claimed that by 1991, the Soviets had already shifted their loyalties to the negotiations that the ANC was having with the Nationalists and away from some nationalist/socialist insurrection (Ellis and Sechaba 4). The SACP Central Committee added:

Here in South Africa it is crucial that socialists begin to cast off any inferiority complexes that the last few years on the international scene might have produced.... Yes, there has been a severe crisis in international socialism. Yes, we will not run away from the reality. But how brilliant is the capitalist alternative? [But] we say no to the political tyranny of a bureaucratic, anti-democratic socialist model ["Internationally: Aluta Continua" 4].

Of course the "bureaucratic, anti-democratic socialist model" that the SACP is clearly condemning was the Soviet Union.

In the past, the SACP may never have opposed the East Bloc on key ideological issues, but once the East Bloc lost some and/or all of its communist veneer, it also lost its legitimacy in the eyes of the SACP (and other communist parties throughout the world). As a matter of fact, it become more and more obvious to the SACP that the outer core of international communism, that is, Eastern Europe, was no longer communist and thus *had* to be repudiated by all remaining "true" communist parties, which included the SACP. The Soviet Union was still a special case: communism still existed but was on the verge of collapsing. The SACP seemed to realize this, but as long as Gorbachev was in power, the Soviet Union still had some legitimacy. This state of affairs, though, would not last. This was the beginning of the end of the ideological gymnastics that the SACP would have to perform to reconcile itself with the "Motherland of Socialism," the once powerful Soviet Union.

Many communists in South Africa were shocked by these events. As Mike Davidow explained in the *African Communist*:

If someone would have told me five, ten years ago, that ... the CPSU would no longer be the ruling party [of the USSR]; I would simply have laughed.... Lenin was pointed to as the "source of repression." The Bolsheviks were described as "fanatics," "bloodthirsty" and "cruel" ... [And Soviet socialism] is characterized as "oriental feudal despotism," "barracks socialism," anything but socialism.... Anti-sovietism and anti-communism have appeared in the USSR, sophisticated and from inside [Davidow 30].

Davidow felt that though the USSR did indeed make errors, they were due more to the poor objective conditions than anything else. "[The critics of communism] cherish the naive illusion of a Scandinavian solution.... [But Soviet] perestroika is aimed at raising socialism to a new and higher state, more human, and more democratic.... But a quiet 'counter-revolution' endangers this programme." He felt, like so many other supporters of the old Soviet system, that this criticism had gone too far. He complained, "There has been a five-year long recital in the minutest detail of every Soviet ill or misdeed." He went on to explain how "the failure to link socialism with the scientific, technological revolution set back the USSR at least 15–20 years." In other words, it would seem that a lack of scientific and technological know-how caused much of communism's problems, not human errors or even just plain tyranny. He concluded that the "new" Soviet media blindly worships "democracy" without considering its drawbacks (Davidow 31–35). This view was quite representative of many communists just before the Soviet system fully collapsed.

In 1991, the first coup in Soviet history happened, but this time the "revolution" was not led by the people calling for democracy, freedom, and more ties to the West as they did in the East Bloc, but by conservative members of the CPSU, the KGB, and the Soviet military ("Collapse of Communism" 224). The coup plotters had a simple plan: seize Moscow, force Gorbachev to step down, and install an antireform, neo–Stalinist regime. Though the coup went well initially, within days it began fall apart in a number of ways.[30] This is not the place to go into the details of either the coup or its collapse, but the results of both contributed to the destruction of the Soviet Union.

The person who "defeated" the coup plotters was Boris Yeltsin, not Gorbachev (who was basically under house arrest for most of it). Yeltsin represented a group of former CPSU members who also called for reform of the Soviet Union but did not see any place for communism in its future. Though it would take time before Yeltsin became the president of the new noncommunist Russian Federation, he would become the informal but legitimate leader as soon as the coup was put down (Conquest).[31]

The rise of Yeltsin and his procapitalist "liberal" faction within the former Soviet Union and the disintegration of the CPSU were too much for the SACP. "The slavish support for the Soviet Union made the SACP one the last foreign parties that understood Eastern Europe ... the SACP exiles suddenly found themselves searching for new international allies against their will" (Adam 33). There was also the fact that, "the Soviet model of socialism, the [SACP's] guiding light for seventy years, has been found wanting" (Ellis and Sechaba 5).

Indeed, the SACP now openly condemned the ideology, policy, and actions of the "Soviet" government for the first time in its history. It attacked both Yeltsin for his "traitorous" procapitalist ideology, but it also condemned Gorbachev, who had "dissolved" the CPSU after the coup. The SACP at first kept these condemnations to itself, but it was soon forced by the magnitude of the events to publish such attacks. The SACP, facing a historical crossroads, finally made the decision to become fully and indefinitely independent from any international body. It justified this move in a number of ways.

One SACP member, Mkhula, writing for the party, stated how Gorbachev had openly "betrayed" the CPSU and international communism. He argued that Gorbachev, possibly because he had been "influenced" by poor advisers,[32] had allowed the coup to develop and then gave up on the CPSU. He commented:

> I cannot recall a case where the captain of the political ship not only abandoned it during the first troubles, but before doing it sealed the wheel-house and all the storage rooms and fuel tanks, while his friend switched off all communications, including the intercom [Mkhula 64].

He went on to condemn both Gorbachev and Yeltsin for disbanding the CPSU and seizing its property: "Needless to say, the actions of both Gorbachev and Yeltsin were entirely illegal" (Mkhula 64). Though he never claimed that Gorbachev was involved in the coup, he did argue that his reforms allowed it to happen. "Most of the coup leaders were members of the CPSU Central Committee.... If these people committed a crime against the state, they also committed it against the party to which they belonged.... All of [the coup plotters] had been hand-picked by Gorbachev just months before the coup" (Mkhula 64).

Mkhula did argue that the coup had support from elites and the general public for a number of reasons. He claimed correctly that 32 of the 72 regional party secretaries were in on the coup and that as much as 40 percent of the population saw the coup in a positive light. He cited Alexander Prokhanov, who saw only five limited "strata" rejecting the coup: the (Russian) White House, dissidents and youth, perestroika supporters, women's groups, and professional politicians (Mkhula 66–67). The vast majority of the population, workers and "peasants," were either supportive of or apathetic towards the coup. Therefore, he concluded that the real culprits were Yeltsin and his supporters. "There is no doubt that Yeltsin and his lieutenants were seizing the moment to take power into their hands, at the expense of Gorbachev and the union structures" (Mkhula 67).

Mkhula explained that at least one survey showed that "socialism" in the USSR was not well supported: 25 percent rejected the old system and 41 percent rejected Gorbachev's reformed socialism. He went on to state that 15 percent to 25 percent of the "people" supported Yeltsin and his new regime (Mkhula 67). Since he did not cite his source for the survey data, we have no way of knowing if these numbers are correct. Still, if they are even remotely accurate, they are a ringing condemnation of Soviet socialism (and its various reformed permutations) by the very people who lived under it; for the SACP this must have been jarring. Mkhula concluded his piece by not just blaming Gorbachev but also the CPSU for being so out of touch with its members and for not purging both the coup plotters and the Yeltsin faction sooner (Mkhula 67).

This was no lone critique by a SACP member. Soon enough the leadership of the SACP would overtly attack its decades-old patron. Slovo himself came out and stated in 1992:

> The corpse [the West] is trying to bury is not true socialism. It was weakened and succumbed through self-inflicted wounds.... Gorbachev himself has completely lost his way.... He is colluding in the chorus of vilification against Lenin, the greatest Soviet and world revolutionary which [*sic*] this century produced [Slovo 1992, 22].

Slovo and the SACP finally joined many Western leftists by saying that "communism" was not dead, because it never truly existed in the Soviet Union. This was the SACP cutting its losses, nothing more nor less, since the documentary record was quite clear that the SACP had always believed that the Soviet Union was not only truly communistic but also communism's role model. Still, I do not doubt the sincerity of Slovo and his faction once they changed their line on the Soviets.

These colossal events forced the final, and in some ways most significant, ideological gymnastic act by the SACP. The SACP was finally forced to literally condemn its ally, its patron, its "guiding light," the Soviet Union. Such an act, even during the period of Gorbachev's reforms a mere five years before, would have been unthinkable, let alone during the long stable decades of Soviet rule. As Kunert stated so well, "[The SACP leaders] find themselves confronted with a horrifying *fait accompli*. The terrifying vision of an organisational and ideological vacuum opening up has come to haunt them" (Kunert 6). The SACP remained committed to communism, but not to what was left of the Soviet Union.

Though it must have been odd for the SACP leadership to argue communist theory without reference to its patron the CPSU, it did so. As Joe Slovo stated in 1992:

> The vision of socialism is alive and well.... True, there are certain negative aspects of our past which we need to wipe clean. But on the balance we can carry our name with pride...
>
> We remained absolutely convinced that, despite some horrors of Stalinism, it is socialism and only socialism which can, in the end, assure every individual and humanity as a whole of freedom in the true sense [Slovo 1992, 18, 22].

As discussed above, the SACP was still convinced that some form of socialism was the future for South Africa. What that form would be was still debated, but some type of radicalized social democracy seemed to be the

SACP's view of the future. This last switch in policy, from supporting Gorbachev's communist reforms to condemning him and his reforms, was most significant, for it was the first sign of a truly independent SACP. As L.H. Gann commented:

> The collapse of the Communist order in Eastern Europe forced the South African Communist Party to rethink some of its ideological assumptions.... Exposed to the sudden shock of Eastern European realities, the SACP of late has taken a more ambiguous position than hitherto with regard to the future of the South African economy [Gann 95].

As Slava Tetekhin, a high-ranking CPSU member, stated, "The initial shock was caused not so much by the collapse of socialism in Eastern Europe, as by the collapse of our image of socialism" (Tetekhin 16). The SACP struggled with this "shock" for most of the 1990s.

The SACP, like the CPSU before it, did drop the very important "dictatorship of the proletariat" thesis, the belief of a command economy, and even the need for a violent revolution for the ANC to come to power.[33] Communist leader Chris Hani gave a tentative critique of the SACP/CPSU relationship soon after the CPSU's collapse:

> There's no doubt at all the very formation of the South African Communist Party owes a lot to the victory of socialism in the Soviet Union.... Theoretically, we owe a lot to the Soviet Union.... We were very close to the Communist Party of the Soviet Union and other socialist countries.... We are aware of the dominant role played by the CPSU in the whole international communist movement,.... [But] I think generally we all agreed as South African communists that [agreeing always] was not the right thing to do.... I think there was a position of over-dependence [Soviet] supply [Hani 9–10].

Even as he attacked the "over-dependence" in the relationship, he still had to praise the CPSU. Still, as the SACP itself put it:

> The old-style, highly centralized economic planning had worked outstandingly in the early phases of socialist construction ... but there were serious weaknesses, too much centralised planning, a undemocratic bureaucracy, and above all the heavy handed hand of Stalinism had led the Soviet Union into stagnation [*Red Flag in South Africa* 61].

Slovo even added, "We accept that the market is an effective watchdog over economic efficiency and viability, and that its absence in socialist economies contributed [to] their ruination.... We reject old-style statism and commandist bureaucratic control" (Slovo 1992, 27–28). Hani also agreed with this, stating that the East Bloc fell because "the market forces were completely ignored" (Hani 7). This is almost too much to believe: one of the most Stalinist and far left parties in the world actually arguing that the lack of market economics caused the downfall of the East Bloc. One must admire the SACP's audacity and honesty in making this genuine reversal.

When the SACP considered leaving its communist title behind as noted above, it was clear that major changes were afoot. The South African Communist Party, at its 8th Congress, put to vote the idea of changing its name to the "Social Democratic Party of South Africa," as the Italian Communist Party had recently done. Though this proposal was rejected, the fact that it was discussed surprised quite a few "diehards" in the party.[34] Overall, the SACP did not collapse nor even give up communism, as had many regimes and parties in the past decade. As Hani put it so well soon before his murder, "The crisis of socialism cannot spell the end of history.... So as long as that contradiction of social production and private appropriation remains, there'll always be a case for socialism" (Hani 6).

Conclusion

By the early 1990s the SACP, one of the most loyal Stalinist parties during the long Cold War, was forced to remake itself by both domestic and international forces. In this chapter, we looked at the international factors that affected this communist party. Though all parties must consider global events in their calculations, the SACP was intimately linked to international powers, and these linkages transformed the SACP, for better or worse, in the late 1980s and 1990s.

The SACP, though basically a "Stalinist" party for much of its history, has been surprisingly flexible in its seventy-five years of existence. It often needed to be dynamic, to keep up with the many twists and turns of the official Soviet line for communist parties. The Comintern, and then later other Soviet bodies, used foreign communist parties in Byzantine plots before and during the Cold War. The SACP needed to fight the imperialists, then the social democrats, then the fascists, and finally the Western democracies, all at the order of the Soviets.

This is not to argue that the SACP had no domestic policy of its own. Just the opposite, actually: the SACP had to constantly juggle these foreign directives while pursuing its own needs and goals in South Africa. One of these was to create an eventual socialist South Africa. But a more immediate one was to infiltrate, aid, and direct its ally, the ANC. At times, the SACP succeeded in greatly influencing the upper ruling bodies of the ANC. Even today, when the ANC is quite independent of the SACP, it still has real influence. This was all quite difficult while trying to be a "loyal" communist party within the international communist movement.

It would be unfair to portray the ties to the Soviets as merely a liability. The Soviets provided invaluable assistance, both in material and more intangible goods, for decades. Before the armed struggle, the Soviet Union provided some funding but mostly advice and moral support, and in general was a guiding light for such small communist parties as the SACP. It cannot be overstated how impressive the Soviet Union (the first communist country) must have been for a struggling, persecuted party like the SACP, especially after World War II when Soviet prestige was so high.

Nor should the Soviet material support be dismissed. Though never huge by absolute standards (or as much as right-wing critics would argue), it was still crucial for the struggle in South Africa in a number of ways. It did allow a small party like the SACP to publish pamphlets, books, and the like, which most communist parties saw as necessary for the struggle. It also allowed for the SACP to get through the lean years of the 1950s, when it was first banned but had not yet integrated fully with the ANC. Finally, the arms and training that the East Bloc provided were also very important to the struggle. Though MK never proved to be a true military threat to the nationalist regime, it did create a useful "siege mentality" amongst the white population. This in turn led to such 1980s policies as ungovernability, which ultimately forced the regime to come to the negotiation table.

Still, by the end, the Soviets had become a liability to the SACP. Gorbachev's initial reforms in the mid–1980s did not greatly affect South Africa or the SACP. The SACP even carefully welcomed them and started to incorporate them into its party and platform. But the party soon became wary of what was happening in the East Bloc. Between the literal collapse of some of the weaker (and cruder) East Bloc regimes[35] and Gorbachev going too far in his condemnations of Stalinism, the SACP started to reconsider its support of the USSR. As Slovo stated relatively early, "The days of Marxism by edict from a single source are gone" (Slovo 1989, 92). Such a statement would never have been uttered previously.

Then two events struck the SACP at its very core. The first, and less important, was the declaration of "world peace" by Gorbachev and the Soviet Union. By putting regional settlements above the local class struggle, Gorbachev argued that ultimately "human rights" were being served (an alien and bourgeois concept for most communist parties, including the SACP).[36] For the local parties involved in that local class struggle, this looked like an abandonment of the world revolution. For the SACP, it was also a shock, but Slovo tried to put on his best, though qualified, face when asked about "peace." He stated, "Socialism and peace are inseparable correlates. Socialism inevitably needs peace to develop" (Monteiro 30). But regardless of this and other supportive comments from the SACP, this new Soviet policy meant much less funding, aid, and moral support; this was a great blow to the SACP. It paled in comparison to the next one.

Unlike the other shocks to the SACP, this one rocked the party to its core. Gorbachev had been conducting his top-down Soviet reforms for years and they were starting to catch up to him and his party. Though most of the changes were improvements by most standards (i.e., more openness, democracy, and freedom), they had cracked the rotten Stalinist system open and created a serious power vacuum. This vacuum was first filled by a cabal of KGB, military, and dissident CPSU members when they conducted the short-lived and ill-fated 1991 coup. Though they were readily overthrown within days, it was by Boris Yeltsin and his liberal allies, not by the already defeated Gorbachev. The CPSU was shattered and demoralized, and was soon easily disbanded by Yeltsin by decree after decades of totalitarian rule ("Russia Moves to Relaunch CPSU"). This was the end of European Stalinist communism.[37]

The SACP was naturally shocked by these historic events. Though it had already cut its losses by distancing itself from "excessive self-criticism," it was not prepared for the total collapse of communism in the East Bloc. At first and briefly, it was just taken aback but it recovered surprisingly and impressively well. It soon began to condemn the coup plotters, Yeltsin, and Gorbachev for betraying communism, both within the Soviet Union and throughout the world. This partially referred to the ending of material support to other communist parties, but it mostly meant the total lack of responsibility the CPSU showed by just allowing itself to implode. The world would no longer have a "communist guiding light," and though the SACP now claims this was for the best, at the time they were rightfully bitter about this new state of affairs ("Russia Moves to Relaunch CPSU").[38]

The SACP did recover from these external shocks and this whole period aided it, if not painfully, to reform itself. Before the collapse of its longtime patron, the reforms of the SACP were half-hearted. But after the situation forced it to become independent and free thinking, the SACP was able to capitalize on this new situation and improve itself. As we shall see in the next chapter, the "New SACP" is now better equipped to face the ever changing and challenging environment that the new South Africa imposes on it.

CHAPTER 4

The New South Africa
The SACP and the Future

Introduction

Our discussion thus far has shown that though the SACP has faced both domestic and international shocks, it has adapted well to its new environment. It used the domestic changes (the fall of apartheid) to transform itself from a small, semiconspiratorial organization to a mass-based, leftist political party. The international shock (i.e., the collapse of communism) forced the SACP to make a number of ideological changes with which it had toyed with for a decade. These include the acceptance of democracy both within the party and society, a rejection of violence as political tool, and a final repudiation of Stalinism (as well as a move away from aspects of traditional Marxism-Leninism). All of this aided the party in developing its symbiotic relationship with the ANC, a relationship which has enabled it not only to survive but also thrive in the new South Africa.

Though the SACP has done surprisingly well since the ban was lifted in 1990, can this communist party continue to both draw new members and increase in political influence? More to the point, can it really build socialism in the new South Africa? Ever since the 1994 All Race Elections the question has remained open for scholars, politicians, and the South African public. Clearly, the SACP has indeed gained a relatively secure position in the political position for the foreseeable future. By staying "within" the ANC, the SACP has maintained its powerful, if not somewhat veiled, position within both the ANC and the government.

In the 1994 election, the SACP gained a number of positions. As outlined above, the SACP now holds a number of cabinet positions, posts in the provinces, and scores of parliamentary seats (though all under the ANC name).

In the next few local and national elections, the ANC gained even more strength at the grassroots level and at the ballot box (though as of this writing it has slightly slipped in the polls) and the SACP, as usual, gained a great deal at the polls by riding on the ANC coattails. Electoral politics, though, are not the only place where the SACP has gained in recent years.

As economic frustrations rise among the very poor of South Africa, the leftist role that the SACP plays within the ANC becomes that much more important (*Advance to Power*). The SACP has usually been seen as the "leftist voice" of the ANC and this has never been more true than today. As the ANC attempts to implement seemingly reasonable policies such as the privatization of some industries,[1] the SACP gains a chance to flex its political muscle and oppose such centrist (and even right-of-center) positions. Though the party has always been careful to criticize its ANC ally in the most qualified terms, the SACP can still grab headlines by opposing unpopular ANC programs. This has been the case of the National Development Plan (NDP) for the last few years.

In such situations, the ANC is at a natural disadvantage for a number of reasons. Since the ANC is a multiclass party, it has the responsibility of representing more than just the narrow interests of the working class and/or poor, unlike the SACP which does see itself as the defender of one class, the proletariat (*Advance to Power*; SACP, *The South African Road to Socialism* 1; *Political Report* 1). The ANC is the party in power in a pluralistic democracy, so it must also placate many entrenched and new interest groups that constantly demand attention. These can range from the Afrikaner farmers to factory owners to coastal fishers to township dwellers. The SACP, not officially in power, has the luxury of being able to ignore such contending interests (or at least pretending to do so) when it formulates its policies and demands, stressing the needs of the working class.

This does not mean the SACP always, or even frequently, gets its way within the ANC or the government; actually, just the opposite is true and the SACP realizes this. Though it does hold some key positions within the upper strata of the ANC and the state and also commands respect at the rank-and-file level, overall the ANC has its own agenda and often enacts it against the will of the SACP (9th Congress AT, 1995; Letsoalo 2013). The SACP accepts this subordinate position for a number of ideological and practical reasons as explained in earlier chapters, but does exploit it when it can. It uses its "underdog" position to further push its leftist agenda for its working-class constituents.

Still, this situation is hardly politically optimal for the SACP. First, though being an underdog does indeed have its advantages, the facts are still clear: many of the SACP's most favored programs have stalled or been put off. The late Joe Slovo's Housing Ministry has yet to produce nearly enough houses ("Housing" 1). The Reconstruction and Development Programme (RDP) also stalled and its main office disbanded, due to political infighting, bureaucratic snafus, and a general distaste for it by all the other parties and much of the nonblack population ("Forbes Economic Series"). Finally, any form of nationalization seems out of question at this point; the only debates here are how much state property will be privatized ("No to Mindless Privatisation"; Letsoalo 2013). In such a situation, the SACP always has the danger of appearing marginalized within the political arena.

Thus, the SACP must carefully watch its public persona and preserve its appearance of being balanced and reasonable. On the one hand, it wishes to appear to be the underdog within the alliance and the government, fighting for the rights and needs of the masses. On the other hand, it must be seen to fulfill some of its promises to its working-class constituents. Finally, given the logic of its position, the SACP will need to part ways with the ANC sooner or later. When it does, will its public policy program be up to the task of offering workable solutions to South Africa's numerous and pressing problems?

Problems and Solutions

All the problems that South Africa faces cannot even be listed here, let alone detailed. A few key ones, such as education, housing, and the like are salient enough to test the respective left-of-center and leftist positions of the ANC and SACP, respectively. For such a test, there is little need for speculation on the ANC's position since it has been in power since 1994. For the SACP, much of the substance of this comparison will need to be extracted from its policy pronouncements and comments on current ANC policy, since the party has only worked directly on the housing (Slovo) and transportation (Cronin) issues.

The SACP has made it apparently and repeatedly clear that it is a *communist* party with a socialist program for the new South Africa. This means, at the least, at some unclear time in the (far) future the SACP will push for and/or create what it calls the "Second Stage" of the revolution. As outlined before, this stage will be a "socialist" one. What "socialist" exactly means is somewhat unclear in its details, but ultimately it will involve: (a) a radical curtailment of capitalist production; (b) the nationalization of some or many industries; and (c) a massive transfer of wealth from the rich to the poor within South Africa. The SACP hopes to create a socialist society, albeit a democratic one (unlike the old Stalinist East Bloc) due to its current reforms (9th Congress AT, 1995). This vision of the future will be contrasted with what the ANC has done and plans to do on these public policy issues.

Education is one of the most important policy issues in South Africa and it is not hard to see why. The facet of this problem that stands out most clearly is race. To put it simply: nonwhite South Africans get much less education and at a lower standard than do whites (Murphy 367–74; *Education* 1). The ANC faced these numbers when it took office:

> By 1992, per capita annual expenditure on primary education ranged from US$916 for whites. US$689 for Asians, US$575 for colored (mixed-race) people, and US$219 for black South Africans [*The Write Stuff* 1].

These numbers have indeed improved since 1994, but the differential is still great (*A Policy Framework for Education and Training*, 1994; *The Write Stuff* 1; *Education* 1). Such terms as "white education" are officially nonexistent in the new South Africa since education is no longer officially segregated by race. But the reality of the situation is still often racially based due to a number of factors.

As Americans have long realized, ending de jure school segregation is only the first of many steps that need to be taken in order to offer de facto equal education to students of all races. It has been many decades since America began to desegregate and as the numbers show, racial segregation still exists in American education. This is due to such factors as "white flight" from the cities, a decentralized system of school funding and administration, and informal but very real racial barriers to race mixing in some areas (especially in the American South but in other regions also) ("American Schools..." 1). All of these factors have little to do with laws that declare equal opportunity for all and far more with the practical problem of balancing societal freedom and the need to do significant social reengineering. South Africa faces a similar dilemma to America's but with much bigger gaps in education equality and grossly less funding.

If the ANC just massively desegregated all the schools and used some form of student shuffling to get black students to white schools and vice versa, it would surely face considerable public outcry ("Whites Bar Blacks..." 1). Almost certainly, the white communities (and especially the Afrikaner ones) would not allow their children to be "bused" to black schools; most would probably just pull their children from these schools, which is what partially happened in the American South in the 1950s and 1960s, during the start of Desegregation and even more so when bussing was enacted in the U.S. Non-white parents likely would also be nervous about sending their children outside of the relative safety of their own segregated communities.[2] Thus, no group would be happy with a quick and improvised "solution" to the education problem.

Another, simpler (though far more vexing) dilemma is the dreadful national economic situation within which the ANC must work. This problem is a constant with all the public policy issues that will be examined. Though South Africa is actually doing better economically than it did in the last years of the Nationalist regime, that is saying very little.[3] But it must be noted that South Africa has some excellent economic indicators when compared to the rest of Africa. Still, this does not mean that there are now enough available resources to go around to raise the standard of living of nonwhites to traditional white levels.

Though whites (especially in urban areas) do indeed have a relatively high standard of living, the rest of the population has had less access to such necessities as running water, electricity, and the like. This means that the necessary infrastructure for a modern school system does not yet exist ("State of the Economy" 1; "The World Factbook..." 1). Though the white working class is relatively well trained, much of the nonwhite population is a step (or two) below this elite stratum. With the unemployment rate as high as 29 percent and underemployment at 45 percent (though these numbers could be overstated due to the large informal economy in South Africa), it is clear that transforming the schools in this context will be difficult at best ("The World Factbook..." 1; "South African Unemployment" 1).

Before 1994, the nationalists often spent five times more on white students as black ones (Murphy 367–74). The educational infrastructure was also racially divided, with many of the whites going to well constructed, modern schools and blacks often sent to one-room buildings or worse in rural areas.[4] Though Coloureds and Indians did receive more funding per student than blacks, overall that, too, was quite inferior to the amounts spent on whites for education. See the numbers below:

> By 1992, per capita annual expenditure on primary education ranged from US$916 for whites. US$689 for Asians, US$575 for colored (mixed-race) people, and US$219 for black South Africans. Starved of funds and resources black schools and the quality of education they provided went into sharp decline. A huge shortage of educators and facilities means that in some schools student-

teacher ratios are as high as 120:1. In most cases, those students fortunate enough to complete the final year have never touched a computer. By the end of 1994, there were 1.8 million children in the six to 18 age group who were not enrolled at any school, and Bengu estimates that more than 60 000 classrooms are needed countrywide to accommodate children this year [*The Write Stuff*, 1].

The good news is that the ANC has begun to reverse this racial discrimination in educational funding. The bad news is that there is just too little money in the budget to do this fully, even decades later.

The numbers show that with respect to the budget, education was and is getting a decent portion of money out of a relatively small amount ("Commentary on the 1996/97 Budget" 1; *Education* 1). The simple fact is that South Africa cannot yet provide "white education" to everyone. As a matter of fact, if no money was given to whites and the savings were fully distributed, it would not be nearly enough. Funds could be diverted from other parts of the budget,[5] but this is hard to do: other ministries, special interests, and the like all resist such moves, as they do in any nation. Finally, any radical reforms by the ANC would be branded unfair and even "communist," and that in of itself would be damaging to the now centrist ANC.

So what can the ANC do? So far, it has eradicated all de jure racial restrictions in education but since then has moved slowly by just raising the budget and increasing training for teachers (*Education* 1).[6] Still, funding has increased, blacks have been let into local white schools, and the situation has improved (Crowe; *Education* 1). But little else has been done or can be done. Even the history curriculum was often still racist in the years after 1994, spending a great deal of time on the "discovery" of South Africa in 1652 by the Dutch and the Afrikaner Great Trek (van den Berg; Kitshoff 313–37). Black nationalist organizations such as PAC and AZAPO strongly condemned the ANC for this. But the ANC has corrected most of these problems since then and it is no longer a serious issue.

The SACP officially supports the go-slow education policy adopted by the ANC. It could do nothing else: the SACP must always, at least, appear supportive of its close ally. Moreover, the SACP does support a generally cautious public policy since it agrees that the situation is tricky and a careful balancing act must be maintained, both politically and financially. It should be noted that not unlike its ANC allies, the SACP has even been condemned by various leftists such as the Trotskyites, anarchists, radical trade unions, and the like for taking this stand on education (and other public policy issues). But except for the large trade unions, which in most cases still support the ANC, none of these groups have any real influence on policy.[7] As the SACP stated in 2009:

The ANC has committed itself to providing free education. But we also need to improve the quality of education by eliminating infrastructural backlogs, ensuring that teachers teach and learners learn, school governing bodies are effective, schools are safe, education departments are supportive, and community participation is enhanced. The SACP will campaign for changes in our curriculums: what is taught in our schools must enhance the dignity of our children, instills values of social solidarity, and produces students who understand our history and our challenges! Build Local People's Education Committees! ["Vote ANC!" 1]

Thus, for now, the SACP will continue to back the cautious ANC policy on education, but this is not likely to be the case indefinitely.

Still, the SACP does have reservations about current educational policy. It has again taken on the familiar role of being the leftist critic of alliance policies (though it declares it is far more than this, and in many cases that has been true). Though the SACP's critiques are carefully made, it has issued statements that can be interpreted only as negative about what the ANC has done with education. The SACP has problems with curriculum, but more about its economic slant than its historical distortions ("Blade..." 1). Many private schools and all colleges naturally still follow an implicitly capitalist educational model. This applies to both how they are run and what they teach. These institutions still charge high fees, which often exclude the poorer students of South Africa (though scholarships have greatly increased from a very low base).[8] But this is far more than just a question about school fees.

The SACP argues that all education, and especially higher education, is basically a socialization tool for creating obedient and useful workers for a capitalist society. According to the SACP, this has been the role of mass education for the last two hundred years throughout the world and it is no different in South Africa. Though the SACP, like all communist parties, is sometimes ambivalent about the kind of workers it does want, overall the party line has stressed "empowerment" for all workers ("Vote ANC!" 1). This means instilling some sort of anticapitalist sentiment in South Africa's children. With the centrist ANC in power, this will not happen in the near future.[9]

But if the SACP is to ever move South Africa to the socialist Second Stage of the revolution, it will need the youth on its side. Recently, it has even reactivated the Communist Youth League (CYL) with mixed results (*The South African Road to Socialism*, 20). South Africa, like so many developing nations, is a "young nation" with a majority of its population under eighteen ("The World Factbook..." 1). In the long run, only political mobilization and "political education" can ensure this happens. The SACP would be the first to deny that it wants to create any "Stalinist propaganda centers" in the schools, but it is also true that a socialist educational system would indeed teach its students in a very different way. Not only would a more pro-socialist slant be introduced to the curriculum (stressing, at the least, social democracy domestically and strong anti-imperialism on foreign issues), but the pedagogical methods would have to be changed too.

In 1996, the use of corporal punishment in education was banned. This is a larger change than one might suspect. Most South African schools relied heavily on corporal punishment before 1996, especially the much envied "Model C Schools."[10] Thus, this was a real victory for the ANC and SACP. Although it is not commonly known (nor was it usually enforced), Stalin actually outlawed corporal punishment in the Soviet Union (Teitelbaum 1945). Though this might seem the height of irony since millions of people were murdered by the Soviet regime, ideologically it was the logical position that the nominally "progressive" CPSU could take on educational discipline. All communist parties believe that the "New Man"[11] must be created through a careful and all-encompassing educational program. For a number of complex historical reasons, the CPSU adopted the position that physical coercion in the schools would psychologically damage the children. The SACP still believes in creating the improved "New Person" in South Africa and thus backed this ban.[12]

The massive educational changes that South Africa needs can only be accomplished by reforming much of the education system. If the SACP follows the same path as the early Soviets, and if it can fully enact its own ideology of workers' empowerment, another major reform would be to bring vocational training to the black masses. Though South Africa's *technikoms* (technical schools) are relatively good, they were bastions of white power for decades. These have been opened fully to all races, but many more would have to be created to even come close to fulfilling the needs of millions of black youth seeking practical job skills. The ANC has given lip service to this sort of reform, but again has moved slowly because under current conditions, there is no money for such massive educational restructuring ("Education" 1). The SACP may agree with this now, but if and when it takes power, it will have to break from such conservative policies or betray some of its core beliefs. This is also true with respect to the other major public policy issue that we shall examine, the housing crisis in South Africa.

On the housing issue, the SACP has been clearer about what it wanted and what it was willing to do to get more and better housing for the masses. Unlike education, where the SACP had no direct influence on policy in the 1990s, after 1994 the SACP had one of its most famous leaders head the very ministry that oversaw housing in the new South Africa. When Joe Slovo was appointed Housing Minister soon after the 1994 elections, no one was very surprised. He had been at the center of all the negotiations between the ANC and the nationalist regime (van Heerden). If anything, some on the left thought such a relatively minor post for such a major figure was unjust, but the housing position was indeed carefully chosen. Though neither Slovo nor the SACP had any specific expertise on the housing question, the appointment was an excellent choice for political reasons. The ANC needed a credible leftist to handle a situation which they surely knew would never be resolved fast enough to meet popular expectations; Slovo fit the bill to a T.

Though education is a crucial issue, housing may be one of the most politically charged in South Africa ("Housing" 1). Not only is housing a sensitive issue since it involves where and how people live (especially during apartheid), but the housing shortage in South Africa is also immense. As late as 2011, it was estimated that only 56 percent of the population had fully adequate housing (Le Roux 1). This shortage has contributed to many of the other problems that the country faces: crime, health issues, community problems, and so on. There is nowhere near enough housing, even poor housing, for the millions of impoverished people who now live in the rural areas and in the squalid urban "townships" such as the huge and infamous Soweto ("The World Factbook..." 1; "Housing" 1; Le Roux 1). The ANC needed both a practical and politically feasible plan for this problem. On both these counts the ANC, and its ally the SACP, have already partially failed.

The original housing plan itself was not practical, for it promised far too much: more than a million homes were to be built during the first five years of the Reconstruction and Development Programme (RDP) ("Reconstruction and Development Programme" 1). After two years, only about 50,000 units were created, and though many more would be built in the next decade, many of those have been criticized for being poorly made (Le Roux 1). Still, by 2011, three million homes had been built and 13 million more people had been given shelter ("Housing" 1). But the second number is telling: those 13 million need real homes at some point and many more still need better shelter in rural areas. But a quantitative shortage of new housing is not the only problem with the plan; the method of funding also has been a disappointment.

Now that the ANC has been in power for two decades, the reality of the situation is highly disappointing on housing. As it turned out, the RDP helped start housing projects but ultimately the housing was paid for by its occupants. The ANC government wanted to help poorer families through generous subsidies, but for most of the homeless, rural poor, and township residents, such subsidies are worthless. Since these people have little or no assets, they do not qualify for these subsidies in the first place. It should also be noted that squatting has became so common that the poor, ironically, have no "rent" to need help paying ("Reconstruction and Development Programme" 1; Le Roux 1). With a government strapped for funding, as outlined above, the ANC (or any other party) could do little more without radical reforms, which are not currently politically feasible.

Why is this? Just building more homes than already planned is not currently economically feasible, and though the ANC might have sought some sort of international funding for housing, there is just no donor or investor who has an interest in investing the many billions of dollars that would be required to even make a dent in the housing problem. The ANC, in theory, could redistribute current housing stock, as it sometimes implied it might before the 1994 elections,[13] but such a move would be the beginning of the end of domestic peace in South Africa. Not only would the Afrikaners fight to the end to hold onto their rural estates and urban homes, but also even the more liberal whites would reject such a move.[14] Any such housing redistribution could potentially bring counterrevolution to South Africa. Obviously, neither the ANC nor the SACP would want such a course of events to occur. Thus such radical solutions are off the table for the ANC, SACP, or any other party. So where does this leave the alliance?

This means, in effect, that housing has become one of the earliest of the public policy failures of the ANC-led government. Though most people blame the ANC, the SACP cannot disassociate itself from this situation. While it is true that the SACP, as an organization, cannot be directly blamed since it has no official seats in the government, it was still intimately involved. As noted, SACP leader Slovo headed the Housing Ministry for almost a year. He brought with him to this post, for better or for worse, the prestige and reputation of the SACP, with which his name was synonymous. But does this mean that, in the final analysis, the SACP policy for housing failed?

In most ways, it does not. First, this failed housing policy was far more the ANC's child than the SACP's, regardless of who headed the ministry. This is not shifting the blame; it is just the truth. The ANC, not the SACP, raised expectations with poorly chosen words and promises impossible to fulfill. The ANC is the one that moved toward the center on many issues, including housing reform, much more quickly than anyone (including the SACP) had anticipated. The ANC moved away from radical solutions for housing and other issues very early on. Finally, the SACP, in spite of its close relationship with the ANC, is not in power and therefore we have yet to see what a "true" SACP policy on housing would be like.

The SACP has been careful not to attack the stated ANC policy on housing; if anything, it has been even quieter on this issue than education since it, too, can be blamed. The SACP's general socialist ideology, which has been modified very little when it comes to pubic policy issues, does give us some insight into what the SACP sees as necessary to solve the housing crisis. The most controversial option for any socialist regime is general redistribution. As a matter of fact, almost by definition all communist parties openly advocate radical redistribution of resources, including housing. While such a reform would be politically difficult to achieve in any country, given the present circumstances it would disastrous in South Africa.

It is true that if (or when) the SACP does take power in the future, conditions could be so different that such a radical transformation of the housing situation might become possible, but that is merely speculation. The SACP has viable policy options that the ANC could have adopted but which the ANC chose not to enact (for good or bad). One of them is a massive, government-funded building program, funded by debt if need be. This would have hardly been a dreaded "socialist revolution" and could have been put into effect, but the ANC decided against it mostly for financial reasons: the cost would have been high and the plan thus politically difficult to enact. Still, more money could have been spent on housing even within the bounds of the current budget. But why was this not the case?

Early on in its rule, the ANC decided that it wished to keep the confidence of both domestic and international capital (Gumede 146). On some levels, this was probably a wise decision considering how much South Africa needed financial stability after years of economic decline under the nationalists. Plus, many right-wing skeptics predicted the opposite of the ANC, that once it took power it would squander the relatively good economy of South Africa; obviously the ANC wanted to avoid that political trap. To do this, the ANC had to submit a relatively small and prudent state budget. To placate white elites, it brought in an Afrikaner finance minister to add even more legitimacy to its economic plan. To its credit, the ANC did surprise everyone involved with how "reasonable" their budget was, but there were real costs, both social and political, in taking this austere route. Such prudent economic policies precluded any massive social spending, including on housing (*Draft Strategy and Tactics Document* 1).

The SACP, being sophisticated in its macroeconomic analysis, realized all of this too and desired, under the right conditions, South Africa to receive more potential international investment. It has shown little desire to start "adventurist" socialist public policy programs and risk losing this international support (*Draft Strategy and Tactics Document* 1).[15] So in both the short and long term, the SACP has made it clear that for a number of reasons it not only supports the relatively conservative economic policies of the ANC but also realizes their merits. Eventually, though, the SACP promises "true socialism" for South Africa. Even before that, the SACP has made clear, a form of social democratic welfare state would still be better than the mostly centrist policies of the last two decades.

There is also the fact that there are in fact two SACP's: the one SACP acting as a "good" modern party pushing a social democratic agenda within the ANC, and the other, a communist SACP that wants to build traditional socialism. Obviously, the parties of the center and the right of South Africa feel much more comfortable with the former SACP, and so do the Western powers such as Britain and America which have numerous economic and geopolitical interests in South Africa. This does not mean that the South African Communist Party has disappeared. As stated many times, it is still a devoted Marxist-Leninist party and remains committed to building socialism in South Africa.

Prelude to the 9th Congress

A few of the relatively recent SACP congresses have proven important for the future of South Africa: the 7th, 8th, and 9th. Later ones, starting in the late 1990s, would prove less crucial, but still important. The 7th was held in Havana, Cuba, in 1989 and was important for two main reasons. First, it was the last "illegal" or covert congress.[16] Even more important, this is the congress which drafted the new party platform, "Path to Power," the first major revision since the early 1960s. It was also the first relatively open congress: more than 1,200 suggestions were made from the floor (Ozinsky 26). This would be the party's first step away from its Stalinist past.

Though the 7th Congress was held in the late 1980s, the party had little inkling that international communism was about to collapse. Even they admitted this: "Who, in the first quarter of 1989, would have said that in just two and a half years the 20 million strong ruling CPSU would be dissolved in the Soviet Union?" ("Our Eighth Congress" 2). This lack of awareness is reflected in its continued strong support of international communism. "The congress reaffirmed the internationalist position of the SACP.... Delegates expressed their appreciation for the unstinting and principled support and solidarity of the socialist countries" ("For a Democratic Victory..." 12). Also, in 1998 it stated clearly:

> From its launch in 1921, the Communist Party in South Africa has committed itself to an internationalist perspective. We have always sought to understand the interconnectedness of our own struggle with socialist, working class, democratic and liberation struggles around the world. We have also seen the propagation of the values of internationalism within our country as a core Communist Party task. The SACP is, today, convinced that internationalism is more relevant than ever before [*SACP 10th Congress* 19].

On the domestic front, the situation was more stable. Mandela, by then the moral and de facto leader of the ANC, once again reiterated his support for the alliance:

> I salute the South African Communist Party.... I salute General Secretary Joe Slovo, one of our finest patriots. We are heartened by the fact that the alliance between ourselves and the party remains as strong as it always was [Johnson 1990a, 16].

With this foundation, which the party had relied on for decades, it could start to reform itself internally.

Though it did not see the collapse of communism coming, Gorbachev's reforms within the Soviet Union had made an impression on the SACP. The party spoke of constitutional theory, the end of the guerrilla war, and hinted at a more democratic South Africa, thus moving away from the more Stalinist and violent language the party had used in the past (Johnson 1990b, 20). As the party put it, "The leadership has sought to develop a proper balance between centralism and democracy.... The SACP should remain a working class party composed primarily of professional revolutionaries" ("For a Democratic Victory..." 10). This last part is interesting, for soon after this the party deliberately moved away from the Leninist-vanguard model to that of a mass-based party. Still, even at this point the party was already changing. Slovo himself stated:

> The commandist and bureaucratic approaches which took root during Stalin's time affected communist parties throughout the world, including our own. We cannot disclaim our share of the responsibility for the spread of the personality cult and a mechanical embrace of Soviet domestic and foreign policies, some of which discredited the cause of socialism. We kept silent for too long after the 1956 Khrushchev revelations.... It would, of course, be naive to imagine that a movement can, at a stroke, shed all the mental baggage it has carried from the past. And our 7th Congress emphasized the need for on-going vigilance. It noted some isolated reversions to the past, including attempts to engage in intrigue and

factional activity in fraternal organisations, sectarian attitudes towards some non-party colleagues, and sloganised dismissals of views which do not completely accord with ours.... The implications for socialism of the Stalinist distortions have not yet been evenly understood throughout our ranks. We need to continue the search for a better balance between advancing party policy as a collective and the toleration of on-going debate and even constructive dissent [Slovo 1989, 1].

These reforms were significant, but were hardly a total rejection of its Marxist-Leninist past; such a transformation has yet to happen even today.

The 7th Congress also reaffirmed the Leninist theory of Colonialism of a Special Type. The party still called for an armed uprising to bring this new democracy to South Africa, though this was to take place within the huge urban areas, instead of emphasizing the role of a strictly military-style revolution, which had been the policy for thirty years. "The programme definitely broke away from any position that puts prime emphasis on a bush-war" (*The Red Flag* 60). The party stated:

An insurrection is an act of revolutionary force. But, it is not always an armed uprising. An all-round civil uprising could lead to an insurrection even when the armed factor is absent or secondary.... There is no conflict between this insurrectionary perspective and the possibility of a negotiate transfer of power [Johnson 1990b, 18–19].

It was also hinted that there could be a negotiated settlement, but that it was unlikely. Again, the party stated, "There is no conflict between this insurrectionary perspective and the possibility of a negotiated transfer of power" (*The Red Flag* 60). The party even reversed its decades-old condemnation of one of its own, the legendary (but vilified) S. P. Bunting. He was made "Hero of the South African Revolution" and the party added, "He was unjustly expelled from the party.... The reasons given for his expulsion were flimsy to the point of being ridiculous" ("The Case of S.P. Bunting" 19).

Taking this same revisionist path, the SACP also boldly critiqued the "regional settlements" that the Soviet Union was then pushing. Though it admitted that there was a place for negotiations vis-à-vis regional conflicts, an insurrection in South Africa was still seen as a necessary tool (Nel 21–22; Monteiro 30).[17] As detailed earlier, these geopolitical changes were unsettling to the SACP; in the long run, however, this was probably for the best. It prepared the party for even greater changes in the years ahead, both on the domestic and international fronts. This slow evolution, from a Stalinist party to something more resembling a Western-style parliamentary party, would continue at the 8th Congress.

The most outstanding feature of the 8th Congress of 1991 was that it was the first one held legally in South Africa after more than forty years. That fact also made it the largest congress yet held at that point, with 414 delegates representing more than twenty thousand members ("Our Eighth Congress" 1). The size of the gathering was also testimony to one of the more important adaptations the SACP had adopted after its ban was lifted in 1990: the move to mass party status. The party probably had less than three thousand members total during the 7th Congress, a mere two years prior. Now there were many more, though this was not without its problems, "More than 90 percent of our 20,000 members are totally new to the party.... Therefore, a major effort at organisational and ideological consolidation will have to be undertaken" ("Our Eighth Congress" 1). For one, the party was not used to being this large. "The party continues to suffer from the over-extension of it proportion of whom are full-time in the ANC and in COSATU unions" ("Our Eighth Congress" 1). Of course, by the time of the 9th Congress four years later, there would be over seventy thousand members and even more structural problems ("Consolidating Our Strategic Unity..." 1).

The party also cemented into place its decision to remain a Marxist-Leninist party, even though by late 1991 it was becoming clear that communism was gone in all of Eastern Europe. The Soviet coup had come and gone just a few months before, ending both the Communist Party of the Soviet Union and the Soviet Union itself. This dramatic shock almost pushed the SACP into a social-democratic mold, as it did with other parties such as the Communist Party of Italy. Still, the 8th Congress vetoed any official move to social democracy (Nzimande 42). "The concept of democratic socialism was firmly rejected at our party's 8th Congress" (Lodge 1987, 176). Still as noted before, the SACP has since adopted many social-democratic–like policies, if not a name change nor a total abandonment of Leninism. So while the 7th and 8th Congresses did initiate reforms, they also both reaffirmed the SACP's commitment to Marxism-Leninism; the 9th would indeed commit the SACP to some fundamental reforms.

All this is not to imply that the 9th Congress was a replay of the 8th on the issue of social democracy. As a matter of fact, unlike the earlier congress, the term "social democracy" was just not brought up by the 9th Congress (9th Congress AT, 1995).[18] The SACP also officially and publicly recommitted itself to both the title and mission of "Marxism-Leninism." This was where things got interesting, for though the "liberals" of the party did not bring up changing the party name again, it was not because they were too weak; just the opposite was true. By the time of the 9th Congress, the liberals had exploited an external situation to gain ascendancy in the party through a number of behind-the-scenes political maneuvers. If anything, they did not formally declare their position openly because they did not wish to squander their hard-earned political capital on semantic battles.[19]

This liberal group, led by the already ailing Slovo and the up-and-coming Cronin,[20] had been "defeated" at the 8th Congress when they pushed the social democracy issue too openly and strongly. However, they not only learned from their mistakes but were also aided by what was happening in South Africa at the time. From 1991 to 1995, South Africa changed from a one-party racist state to a multiparty nonracial democracy, led by the SACP's closest ally, the ANC. Until the crucial April 1994 elections, there were negotiations between all the main South African political actors, but especially between the nationalists and the ANC. One of the most influential ANC delegates during these talks was none other than the "liberal communist" Slovo. He was the one that suggested the crucial compromise of the "Sunset Clauses" that permitted the 1994 elections to take place (van Heerden 5). Though he was resented by the far left for "selling out" to the Afrikaner Nationalists, these maneuvers were successful and brought enormous prestige to himself and his faction within both the ANC and the SACP (van Heerden 1993; ARM AT 1995).

Slovo and his allies, unlike the weakening "conservative Stalinists" in the SACP such as Harry Gwala, saw which way the wind was blowing both within South Africa and the ANC. The early 1990s was a time to compromise and adapt, not a time to dig in one's heels. The whole nation was changing, faster than it had ever done in the last forty years, and liberals within the SACP saw this and used it to change the SACP. Slovo informally dominated parts of the ANC/NP negotiations and then used the prestige he gained from that to get his way within the SACP.

The SACP, under this new, more liberal leadership, moved forward on its reforms. One of the ways it did this has already been discussed: if South Africa was to be a full democracy, then the SACP needed to move from its more cell-based, conspiratorial structure to a more mass-based party. The liberals knew that at the 9th Congress, even if they did not get a more formal declaration of change, important ideological changes also had to be affirmed. The 9th Congress would either be a final consolidation of liberal power within the SACP or a setback for their agenda to one degree or another. Though it would never be publicly described as that, the Congress was in fact a watershed for SACP reform.

The *9th Congress: Draft Strategy and Tactics Document*, issued by the party executive right before the Congress, recognized that international communism was in serious disarray, that South Africa was at a crossroads, and that the party had a important role to play at this juncture. The document started out by stating, "The most dramatic international event of the last several years has, of course, been the collapse of the Soviet Union ... this marked the end of the Cold War ... [and] has major consequences for the countries and peoples of the underdeveloped South" (*9th Congress Draft Strategy* 1). It goes on to state that a "long wave of contraction" started, with a "crisis of production," and changes in the 1980s such as the information revolution, the production of synthetics, and general globalization forced the communist nations to their knees (*9th Congress Draft Strategy* 1). The document went on to comment:

> While some socialist countries still remain, there is no longer a fully fledged second bloc capable of providing an alternative [to international capitalism].... In one sense, then, the post–Cold World is unipolar ... but, on the economic front, the collapse of the Soviet Bloc occurred at a time of declining U.S. hegemony and growing economic competition between the U.S., Europe and Japan ... the "New World Order" ... has largely proved to be a disorder.... Global capitalism ... has proved singularly incapable of turning this victory into anything resembling a stablised, let alone just, world order [*9th Congress Draft Strategy* 2–4].

Though this chaos could, in theory, be utilized to the developing nation's advantage, overall it just meant that there was no longer a socialist bloc on which to rely.[21]

But what was the SACP to do in the face of this unprecedented challenge? It stated quite clearly:

> Within the SACP, since at least 1989, there has been an open and ongoing discussion about the menacing and implications of these global developments.... Or, more specially, we have debated the implications of the crisis and collapse of the Soviet Bloc.... We have refused the path of unprincipled abandonment of our communist values, our communist organisation, and our commitment to a communist future. But we have also refused to be stuck in a dogmatic stupor.... We have not, as an ANC-led liberation movement, collectively thought through the implications of the new world situation for our national democratic revolution. This is not an SACP criticism of the ANC, it is a criticism for which we assume at least partial responsibility [*9th Congress Draft Strategy* 4].

In other words, the SACP was going to remain communist but needed to seriously reevaluate its position; as it turns out, it did so. The SACP also stated:

> All of this adds up to considerable insecurity as we approach the new millennium.... The imperialist-dominated "New World Order" holds out no solutions and no meaningful hope for the great majority of the world's population [*Strategic Perspectives* 1].

After outlining how the South African situation was indeed part of a much larger international context, the SACP then went on to discuss more specific issues concerning its future domestic plans.

It even went so far as to argue that the "National Democratic Revolution" (NDR) and the much prized Reconstruction and Development Programme (RDP) would become shells of their true potential if the new international situation was not fully addressed:

> We are attempting to consolidate a national democratic revolution in a global context and on a national terrain still dominated by capitalism. It is on this terrain, and not in some separate space, some liberated zone, that we to contest with our class opponent for the advance, deepening and defense of democracy, and for the decisive move towards socialism [*9th Congress Draft Strategy* 9].

The party was even more candid elsewhere:

> We need to understand very firmly that unless we analyze the new global situation honestly and locate our own struggle within it, our commitment to an NDR will be little more than the recycling of "worthy but unrealisable" ideals. Unless we understand clearly the new realities, policies like the Reconstruction and Development Programme (RDP) will remain an "ideal" that is constantly undermined by appeals to "realism" in the new global situation.... Even more seriously, the lack of an overall strategic vision can quickly lead to a pragmatism without principle, and to moral laxity within our movement [*Strategic Perspectives* 1].

The economic mistakes of other developing nations was high on the SACP's list, such as adhering to International Monetary Fund (IMF) structural adjustment programs (SAPs), authoritarian capitalism, being a dupe of U.S. influence, and reckless export plans (*9th Congress Draft Strategy* 4; "Reconstruction and Development Programme" 1).

Though the SACP was critical of the lack of South African economic progress, it did admit that "the ending of formal racist minority rule, while not the final victory of the National Democratic Revolution, lays the basis for the rapid advance and consolidation of the national democratic transformation process.... The main content of the new phase of the NDR is to carry forward the democratization process ... it is also the most direct route towards socialism in our country." This would involve "carrying the logic and assumptions of democracy ... into all other spheres of society—the economic, social, cultural, and in regard to gender relations" (*9th Congress Draft Strategy* 7, 8). In relation to another problem the party was trying to tackle, sexism, it stated:

> There can be no consolidation of democracy, still less an effective advance to socialism, unless we also, simultaneously, overcome patriarchy and actively transform gender relations.... This critical dimension is, unfortunately, often forgotten or marginalised. Patriarchy ... has persisted in socialist societies. Patriarchy has

to be consciously addressed and dismantled, it will not simply wither away [*9th Congress Draft Strategy* 10].

The document then proceeded to give specific public policy suggestions to rectify this situation: more land and utilities, fight against the power of traditional leaders, aid women in traditional roles, fight sexism at work, cut food prices, provide more public service, and fight for reproductive rights (*9th Congress Draft Strategy* 11).

The SACP not only concerned itself with such issues as gender empowerment, it also tackled some of the most troublesome theoretical problems that modern communist parties face, including when and how socialism is to be built. Once again, the party framed the whole question within the Two Stage Theory of Revolution:

> We use the slogan "socialism is the future, build it now" to assert our deep conviction that socialism is the only just, rational and sustainable future ... [and] that this future has to be struggled for here and now.... The NDR is not a detour but the most direct route to socialism.... [And] as socialists we are not riding on the back of the national liberation struggle.... [A]s the SACP we are struggling, here and now, for transformations ... which lay the basis for future socialist transformation ... [but] for "Far Left" formations, no significant advances can be made until socialism is achieved, and socialism, by definition, [will] "automatically resolve" all problems of working people. Within such a perspective, socialism becomes a wholly utopian construct ... this outlook serves only to marginalise socialism [*9th Congress Draft Strategy* 14].

In effect, the SACP took the position that to want socialism *now* was just utopian. This harkens all the way back to Karl Marx himself, who also denounced various socialists of his time as unrealistic, premature, and indeed utopian. The SACP continued in this vein, stating, "The socialist transition may well be of long duration. The transition may also be marked by contradictions, stagnation and major reverses" (*9th Congress Draft Strategy* 14–15). With socialism built in the far future, what does the SACP envision?

"For the SACP, socialism stands for the radical deepening and extension of democracy into all spheres of the society" (*9th Congress Draft Strategy* 15). Such safe (but noncommittal) statements are somewhat meaningless, except maybe for the fact that the SACP, a former Stalinist party, does seem to now mean them. The SACP does get more specific elsewhere, and when it does, it is clear that the liberal faction within it has now triumphed (at least for the time being). The party started out conventionally enough, but quickly moved to moderate positions on almost all issues[22]:

> We seek to abolish the huge differences in income, wealth, power and opportunity ... in espousing egalitarianism we are not arguing for a mechanical, and

enforced "gray" uniformity between all individuals.... We do not ignore that under socialism there will be a division of labour ... nor do we ignore the relative uniqueness of all individuals.... We do not seek to abolish these differences.... egalitarianism is about increasing, not decreasing, the individual [*9th Congress Draft Strategy* 15].

The party then moved on to the more economic aspects of its program:

For the SACP, socialism is about the socialisation of the predominant part of the economy. This is an essential condition ... this conviction, and its centrality in our strategic outlook, distinguishes us from most contemporary social democratic parties, whose horizons have become increasingly limited to social reform within the bounds of capitalism [*9th Congress Draft Strategy* 16].

So far this was just conventional Marxism-Leninism, but there was more:

In the past, we tended to see socialism as nationalisation plus state planning. Socialisation of the economy is a much broader and qualitatively richer concept. It shifts the emphasis away from a simplistic concentration of the legal forms of ownership, toward emphasizing the real empowerment of the working people.... A predominant and varied public sector [is key].... [P]ublic sector enterprises should enjoy a degree of autonomy ... [though] democratically elected government would have ultimate powers.... [E]ach public sector enterprise should also be subject to competition from alternative sources.... [There will be] a significant and growing co-operative sector. There would also be a private sector under socialism, mainly made up of small and medium firms, with an important role to play, notably, in the provision of goods and services [*9th Congress Draft Strategy* 15–16].

Such admissions should not be surprising, considering the changes the SACP had already made. Still, for one of the most orthodox Marxist-Leninist parties left in the world, such ideological modifications were significant. The SACP, though, could not seem to condemn its Stalinist past without qualification:

In the early phases of infrastructural development, central planning achieved some remarkable success in the Soviet Union. But the administrative command style of planning proved to be brutally undemocratic, inefficient, wasteful and hopelessly inadequate to the demands of an increasingly modern economy.... On the other hand, even modern capitalist economies cannot function without significant levels of government planning and co-orientation, despite rhetoric to the contrary [*9th Congress Draft Strategy* 16].

The party then went into some detail on how this socialist economy would actually operate:

Planning will be subject to a variety of democratic processes, including negotiation. It will also be subject to regular assessment and adjustments. The government will ensure implementation through inducements, pressures and instruction....

[But] markets will continue to have an important regulating and distributive function in a socialised economy, but they will not have the ultimate say. Significant areas of society will need to be wholly or substantially de-commodified.... Price and distribution will not be determined by sheer market forces [*9th Congress Draft Strategy* 16].

This is not all that new. The reforms in Czechoslovakia in the 1960s (under the guise of "Socialism with a Human Face") and later different ones in Yugoslavia in the 1980s utilized such democratic, market-hybrid socialist solutions, and with some success, at least when compared to the rest of the East Bloc (Dyer 1).[23]

The SACP had little else to say about its economic plans for the far future. It did state what its current economic plans called for: better internal redistribution, major economic restructuring, better "coordination," and a generally more "people centered" public policy. It added that "health-care, education, housing, the environment, culture and information should not primarily be commodities" (*9th Congress Draft Strategy* 17). Few specific details were given, but the few that were listed include: catering to social needs, the democratization of management, a bottom-up approach to economic reform, an increase in labor-intensive industries, increased productivity via training, better redistribution, a breaking-up of the monopolies, and more programs for women workers (*9th Congress Draft Strategy* 17).

The SACP was being much more specific about what economic reforms, in both the short and long term, it wished to initiate. Details, though, were still lacking. The SACP intended to seriously modify a highly complex market economy; this was a risky endeavor that needed to be planned carefully. It is true that much of what they wished to build was new and cannot be readily tested. Still, some of the plans made at the 9th Congress were fundamentally experimental.

The 9th Congress

The 9th Congress proceeded with few hitches or surprises. The author was able to attend and record the entire congress, the first historic congress since apartheid fell.[24] It took place during April 1995 over a period of four days, starting early and going relatively late into the night each day. It consisted of four main events: keynote speeches, the election of the Central Committee and officers of the party, policy meetings, and various social and cultural events. Though it could be argued that this congress was merely a public exercise to affirm what had already been decided much earlier in private, this would be an overstatement and unfair to the huge strides this formerly Stalinist party has made in making itself accessible to the public. Some things were indeed decided beforehand, but what well-run political party anywhere does not pre-arrange some topics for public consumption? As we shall see below, the SACP was surprisingly open and proficient at exercising party democracy.

The speeches presented at the Congress were similar to speeches given at communist congresses for decades with a few notable exceptions. The more mundane speeches were given by domestic communists, domestic allies, and foreign allies. The domestic communists were basically regional notables reporting on progress and problems in their respective regions while getting the spotlight for a few moments. The importance of this spotlight, though, should not be underestimated. Such exposure can be and was used by these people back home to show they were "connected" with the central command.[25] Still, for the purpose of this study, these speeches had little value. The one thing they did indicate is the extent to which the SACP had in fact become a "normal party" with mundane problems: everything from constituent worries to local political bickering was brought out during this phase (9th Congress AT). This was a far cry from the hard days of the underground, when open and public debate was neither possible nor desired.[26]

The domestic allies that spoke at the congress consisted mostly of ANC, COSATU, and various civics leaders. The ANC notables were led by President Mandela, whose speech will be examined more thoroughly below. Other ANC leaders (often communist party members themselves) reported on various aspects of the new administration, mostly in a positive tone. The reports ranged from economic to social to political issues. Since the ANC/SACP alliance had few outstanding or controversial issues at that point, these speeches were not all that important. Mostly they discussed local successes, occasionally warned of "counterrevolutionary" forces, and reported on various wildcat strikes that the unions had launched. As a matter of fact, the party's union allies did have some important issues to bring up. The alliance with COSATU was still solid, but there were issues that COSATU notables cited, and not always in a delicate and diplomatic way. They argued, for example, that now that the alliance had finally taken power, it was time for a more massive redistributive project to be started. They also hinted that the RDP was not being implemented thoroughly ("Reconstruction and Development Programme" 1; 9th Congress AT).[27] Finally and most controversially, they cited the need for more strike action, formal if possible, but wildcat if needed (9th Congress AT).

Though the both the ANC and SACP supported strikes in theory and often in practice, the many wildcat strikes that had been initiated by local unions, both in and outside of COSATU, had been criticized by the ANC for their destabilizing effect on the fragile economy. The unions naturally saw all of this as, at best, restricting their options and, at worst, a betrayal. In an earlier forum, the mine workers' union even suggested that a "workers' party" might be necessary. Though this was highly unlikely, it was a setback for both the ANC and SACP (and especially for the latter, which sees itself as just that), which had incorrectly assumed full union support. In any case, the speeches made by union officials hinted that the rank and file needed to be heard on this and many other economic issues (9th Congress AT). In general, the unions were making the same point they had been hinting at for some time: the alliance needed to address workers' problems more seriously (Masondo).

The civic organizations that had closely aligned with ANC in the United Democratic Front of the 1980s also had a small role at this communist congress. These grassroots organizations were often based in the black townships and had fought bravely against apartheid. They had longstanding ties to both the ANC and the SACP. Various leaders, officials, and others who had worked in the civic organizations made relatively perfunctory speeches. The only issue these speakers brought up again concerned the plight of the poor, nonwhite masses of South Africa. Many of the civic groups of the 1980s had begun to fade by the time of this congress in 1995. Still, the ANC had not been able to meet the expectations of the civic groups or the people they represent. Much later, the civic groups formed an umbrella organization to address these concerns, the South African National Civics Organisation (SANCO) (Schrire 139).

Before moving on to the speeches that related directly to SACP policy, the long-standing communist tradition of having "international comrades" sing each other's praises at their congresses needs to be noted. This remains fascinating simply because the SACP continued this tradition, but also because of who did (and did not) show up. In the heyday of international communism, scores of other communist parties would show up at one another's congresses year in and year out. With the fall of international communism and the collapse and/or conversion of many local communist parties, this practice is no longer the same. Only a few foreign dignitaries showed up at this congress (and later ones). An informal measure of the popularity of these dignitaries was the amount of applause they received as they took the podium. Using this admittedly crude system, one would have to conclude that the

Cuban regime was still quite popular amongst the SACP in 1995 (9th Congress AT).

Cuba's popularity is not surprising if one considers Southern African history. Members of MK actually served with Cuban troops in Angola against Angolan and South African troops. Not only were the Cubans reliable allies in this fight, but they also earned the respect of the MK guerrillas with their military exploits in Angola (Ellis and Sechaba 183). The SACP was also close to the Cuban regime because it has long been a bastion of Soviet "Third World communism," unlike other surviving communist regimes such as North Korea, which had a more isolationist orientation and at times a Maoist slant. In addition, as noted above, the 7th Congress of the SACP was held in Cuba.

The Cuban ambassador, Angel Dalmav, with whom I spoke before his speech, made it clear that Cuba was still concerned about the "unjust embargo" against its regime that America had maintained for more than thirty years.[28] In his speech, he pointed out that the Cuban regime saw the new South Africa as a potential ally against "First World domination" (9th Congress AT). This was overly optimistic, considering the relatively conservative economic policies the ANC had so far proposed,[29] but it was ironic to note that South Africa was now the nexus of a left-of-center geopolitics after decades of right-wing, racist rule. The next most popular speaker, not surprisingly, was from another surviving communist regime, Vietnam.

The Vietnamese dignitary, Le Huy Hoang, was also well received by the SACP delegates. His message was basically the same as the Cuban one: the need for the underdeveloped world to unite against "big capital" and "Western domination."[30] As they did for the Cubans, the delegates cheered after every denunciation of European and American "imperialism" (9th Congress AT). There is some irony here as well since one of the ANC's first major foreign policy acts was to rejoin the English Commonwealth, albeit for economic, if not political, reasons ("Ready to Govern" 1). Other communists also got some attention.

The SACP and the Communist Party of the Soviet Union (CPSU) had been close allies for decades and therefore it is not surprising that the SACP cheered the remnants of this once supreme communist organization. The dignitaries from what was once the center of "world revolution" were treated with respect and even excitement, but not as much as the Cubans or the Vietnamese (9th Congress AT). This may be due to the fact that these two regimes are part of the last communist holdouts against capitalism, but it is also because the CPSU discredited itself in the eyes of some parties during the collapse of communism. As noted earlier, the twists and turns of Soviet policy in the early 1990s went too far for even the SACP. By 1991 and as noted before, the SACP even *denounced* the mother party of communism, the CPSU ("The Class Struggle Is Alive and Kicking" 16). Thus, even though these neo-Soviets were still viewed as allies by the SACP, they were seen as tainted ones. The Russian communists at the Congress said little of importance, leaving untouched the SACP's seemingly low opinion of them. The Russians discussed the poor situation in former Soviet Union, how working class people had been betrayed by the "Yeltsin Clique," and how proud they were that they were allies of the SACP (9th Congress AT).

Finally, the absence of the largest and most powerful communist regime must be noted. The Chinese Communist Party (CCP) did not attend the Congress and this was no surprise, at least at that point. Ever since the Sino-Soviet split in the late 1950s, the SACP took an unwavering pro–USSR line against the Chinese (as it did the CCP's sometimes allies the Yugoslavians, Cambodians, and Albanians). Though such decades-old battles have become moot with the disintegration of the USSR and the easing of such obscure ideological debates, the SACP had little to no contact with the CCP (and vice versa) by 1995. There had been hints since the 1980s that the ANC has had feelers out to the Chinese (Carter and O'Meara 17). Still, the other more pro–Soviet delegates (such as the Vietnamese) would have been uncomfortable with Chinese communists there.[31] Regardless, with the massive capitalist penetration of the rest of Africa by Chinese corporations, the Chinese have become closer to the ANC and SACP since 1995; as will be detailed below, they are now welcome at SACP congresses.

Other than these domestic and foreign speeches, there was also the keynote speech by President Mandela and a few notable ones by various SACP officials. The very fact that the president of South Africa was even at the congress is significant.[32] As a matter of fact, the congress was covered on television by the South African Broadcasting Company (SABC), which also highlighted Mandela's speech. Basically, Mandela made it clear that (a) the alliance was indeed alive and strong but (b) that there were real differences between the ANC and SACP. Mandela started with praise:

> It is not given to a leader of one political organisation in a country to sing praises to the virtues of another. But that is what I intend to do today. If anything, this signifies the unique relationship between the African National Congress and the South African Communist Party. It is a relationship that has detractors in abundance; a relationship that has its prolific obituary scribes. But it is a relationship that always disappoints these experts. Because it was tempered in struggle. It is written in the blood of many martyrs. And, today, it is reinforced by hard-won victory [Mandela 1995, 1].

He then went on to talk of the alliance itself:

> More often than not, the ANC's defense of its alliance with the South African
> Communist Party is interpreted as sympathy with the Party's long-term goals
> and an attachment to a so-called "failed ideology and system." Individuals and
> groups who profess to be democrats lose all rationality when gripped by the
> venom of anti-communism. We in the ANC are driven by a different logic. Our
> commitment to democracy means, first and foremost, recognising the right of
> parties across the political spectrum to operate freely and canvass their views
> without hindrance. And we do not apologise for the fact that our alliance with
> the Party is also based on the warm sentiment of experience in struggle against
> Apartheid [Mandela 1995, 1].

But it was not just sentiment that kept these two very different parties
together:

> Whatever seemingly powerful friends we might have today, the ANC cannot
> abandon those who shared the trials and tribulations of struggle with us. Yet our
> relationship derives from much more than historical sentiment and commitment
> to multi-party democracy. The African National Congress seeks to build a better
> life for all South Africans, especially the poor. In this endeavor, we can only ben-
> efit from alliance and critical engagement with organisations which have put this
> objective high on their agenda. The SACP is the foremost champion of the inter-
> ests of the working class and the poor [Mandela 1995, 1].

As stated in previous chapters, the SACP had become almost a leftist think-
tank for the ANC policy-makers:

> In this era of nation-building and reconstruction, the ANC and the country as a
> whole need creative ideas about how we achieve goals that have become a com-
> mon national value. And we know that the SACP has been, and will continue to
> be, one of the nation's important repositories of creative thinking about things
> that really matter [Mandela 1995, 1].

Then Mandela moved on to how the two organizations, though aligned, were
indeed different:

> Our alliance is therefore not a marriage of convenience. Neither is it a commun-
> ion of similar organisations, which differ only in name. We talk of an alliance
> precisely because we are two independent organisations with political platforms
> and long-term goals that do not necessarily converge. But there in the theatre of
> practical work, we continue to learn that there is more that unites us than
> divides us: in brief, a people-centred and people-driven programme of demo-
> cratic transformation. To realise this requires unity in action [Mandela 1995, 1].

Finally, Mandela again praised the SACP for its role in the transition:

> At the last Congress of the South African Communist Party, we were all still
> faced with the question of how to speed up negotiations and ensure an outcome
> that would be in the interest of the people. We can today with pride acknowledge

the role that the SACP played in the events that unfolded thereafter. Not least among them was the mass action campaign of 1992 as well as the negotiations that followed. In this regard, we would like to single out both Comrades Chris Hani and Joe Slovo, who, also as leaders of the ANC in their own right, played a central role in these efforts.... Over the past months, we have been grappling with the strengthening of the alliance in the new circumstances. We cannot claim to have succeeded in finding all the answers.... I am confident that this Congress will reinforce not only the Party; but also the ANC, COSATU and the rest of the democratic movement [Mandela 1995, 1].

So what did this all mean? Mandela said nothing all that new, but that itself was important. He affirmed the alliance but admitted that there were differences. He praised the SACP for its role in the armed struggle, the transition, and even in government, but did not even hint at a broader or more powerful role for the future. If anything, he did imply that in the far future the goals of the ANC and the SACP would diverge to such a degree that the alliance could end. These hints, though, were subtle and mostly ignored by the delegates. As a matter of fact, many of the delegates were impressed by the president; applause for him continued for a few minutes. I was able to meet Mandela after his speech for a few minutes, asking him about the alliance (strong), the future of South Africa (good), and his thoughts on the need for deeper social changes (necessary); he was impressive, polite, helpful. Other speakers were less well received.

Both SACP general secretary Charles Nqakula and chairman Dan Tloone were applauded and listened to, but neither stirred the crowd like these other speakers (or even the Cuban delegates). They went on to speak of the historic role of the party, how they were the voice of the proletariat, and so on. The delegates were so excited that they were in Johannesburg at the meeting of their party that any speech seemed special, but from my perspective there was little of substance from these two speakers (9th Congress AT). Before we go on to some of the other aspects of the Congress, one interesting incident does need to be related.

One of the more charismatic communist speakers was Comrade Blade Nzimande. A longtime Stalinist (who has since become much more moderate and leader of the party), Comrade Blade did wake up the crowd. He, too, spoke of the historic meeting of the party, but instead of delivering a relatively boring presentation, Comrade Blade galvanized the delegates. He made it clear that being a communist was a privilege that needed to be earned. He also held little back when denouncing the "class enemy"—the capitalists. He was one of the few speakers who did speak of a domestic class enemy (though many had mentioned "imperialism" and "international capital"). As a matter of fact, he literally stated at one point that though the current regime needed to work with the capitalists, the "class enemy would be liquidated if necessary" (9th Congress AT).

Not only was this a refreshingly frank (though more extreme) statement, but it also was not universally well received by the officers of the party sitting with Comrade Blade on the podium. As a matter of fact, the Deputy General Secretary and liberal Cronin looked down and shook his head as this was said.[33] As made clear earlier, the liberals of the party, led by Slovo and Cronin, had been battling with the Stalinists for almost a decade. Though the Stalinists had a few victories at the last congress (such as retaining the term "communist"), overall the liberals had won on most policy fronts. This was just one more example of the Stalinists speaking tough but ultimately having less and less say to a party helping to run a capitalist regime. And as noted, Nzimande has stayed the leader of the party since then, though only by moderating his views due to pressure from both the SACP liberals but also the ANC, and ultimately the reality of the South African situation.

The congress was not just speeches, though it could seem that way to anyone who attended the daily sessions. Every day there would also be much socializing at lunch. In the evenings there were various cultural events that not only celebrated the diversity of the new South Africa, but which were also quite rowdy at times (though never out of control). Finally, a large amount of souvenirs were sold, ranging from T-shirts to video collections.[34] There were also policy sessions and an election.

The policy sessions consisted of a number of meetings during one evening where delegates met with officers and "discussed policy." This part of the congress was one of the more interesting: this is where the delegates got to say what was on their minds with little or no self-censorship (9th Congress AT). The people debated everything from health policy to the fate of would-be "war criminals" from the old nationalist regime. What was mostly brought up, though, was the dismal economic progress since taking power with the ANC. It was true that very little had "trickled down" to the nonwhite, poor masses that the SACP represented ("Commentary on the 1996/97 Budget" 1). The delegates complained about the policies against wildcat strikes, economic austerity programs, and even the crime crackdown which affected their constituents (9th Congress AT).[35]

Though this was billed as "participatory democracy," there was more participation than democracy. The leaders of the party did get to hear what was honestly on the minds of the delegates. What did not happen was a real chance to modify any significant policies within the party; I did not hear of one major policy change coming from these meetings (9th Congress AT); though it should be noted that some of the suggestions were adopted years later by the party. Still, there was more genuine policy discussion than at most American political conventions (which I have also attended). Finally, considering that this was a party once ruled by Leninist "democratic-centralism," what did occur was still real and deep progress. The same can be said for the election of the new officers.

The election was controlled from the start to finish and the results surprised no one. As a matter of fact, the election was probably the most "Stalinist" element of the whole congress. The candidate nominations were seemingly quietly arranged before the congress, and though there was some overlap in who ran for what, after some insider horse-trading sessions, everything was settled.[36] Right before the elections took place, all the nominees ran *unopposed*. Thus, the actual voting was a mere formality and affirmation of the would-be new officers (9th Congress AT).[37]

Did this all make the congress in general a farce? The answer would have to be no. It is true that such elections certainly take away from the claims that the SACP was fully democratic in 1995, at least by any Western standard. Still, it is also true that nothing "sleazy" occurred, as it often does in more open party conventions in the West. In other words, there was no sign of money being passed around (though political favors were surely exchanged). What occurred here may not have been highly democratic or confrontational, but it was actually relatively open and did seemingly affirm the delegate choices. And again, Western party conventions are also often not the ideal of democracy, transparency, or morality ("Corrupt GOP Establishment" 1)

What did this Congress say about the role of the SACP in the future? If nothing else, this meeting showed that the ANC/SACP alliance was strong and that the SACP would have a role in the regime for an indefinite amount of time. It also demonstrated that a once staunch Stalinist-elite-driven party had become an open, mass party with a number of democratic procedures. Such a transformation was not only doubtful as late as 1994, but was seen by most rightists both domestically and internationally as literally impossible.[38] They were wrong on this; the SACP has indeed transformed itself into a rather conventional political party with a rather unconventional platform.

The 10th–13th Congresses (1998–2012)

Just as the 7th and 8th congresses built up to the crucial and historic 9th Congress in 1995, the 10th–13th Congresses (in 1998, 2002, 2007, and 2012 respectively) were all less historic due to the very fact the SACP had to just consolidate its positions, both ideologically and politically, but not actually create new policy. It still faced a rocky political road as the ANC changed leadership a few times. It also continued its pressure on the ANC to maintain a more leftist public policy, instead of the more centrist one the ANC has leaned towards since the late 1990s. But the 10th and later congresses all made statements reaffirming the SACP's commitment to the ANC (and COSATU) but also a rejection of capitalist imperialism. It also stated a path towards eventual socialism in South Africa, mostly by pursuing various leftist programs in the current capitalist phase but also becoming more independent from the ANC.

The 10th Congress in 1998 covered the standard bases for a communist party after the collapse of communism (the will to fight on, push back against neoliberalism, anti-imperialism, etc.), but as mentioned already, the SACP was one of the few communist parties in power at the time (admittedly as a coalition ally). Thus it had a few unique and more pragmatic things to present. Regardless, Mandela was still in office (and would be until 1999), the alliance was still consolidating power and taking over the post–Apartheid state, and thus this was still early days. For this section, I will summarize and then analyze the key documents and speeches that were put out by this and later congresses.

The 10th Congress opened with this summary, an analysis of the situation a few years after apartheid ended:

> This 10th Congress of the South African Communist Party has taken place at a critical and complex moment in the ongoing South African national demo-cratic revolution. This Congress has met after four years of ANC-led gover-nance, and it has provided us with an opportunity to take stock of the major achievements, on the real objective constraints and of the subjective shortcom-ings of the past four years....
>
> On the one hand, powerful forces in our country, the beneficiaries of apartheid wealth and privilege, allied with powerful external forces, are bent on blocking and subverting the ongoing radical transformation of our society. On the other hand, there is the real possibility and necessity of pressing fearlessly ahead with national democratic transformation....
>
> [T]he precondition for ongoing national democratic transformation is a pow-erful, robust Tripartite Alliance, based on a common strategic programme, and rooted in a common working class constituency—the overwhelming majority of our people who continue to be the victims of the apartheid legacy [*10th Congress Declaration* 1].

It then argued for a strong alliance *and* independence:

> This 10th Congress reaffirms its deep commitment to the ANC/SACP/ COSATU tripartite alliance. This commitment, rooted in seven decades of

alliance experience, is not simply a matter of history. It is, above all, a strategic imperative.

The SACP's commitment to the alliance is, in no way, a renunciation of our own autonomous, communist organisation, policies and programmes. On the contrary, a strong communist SACP is a precondition for a strong ANC and COSATU, and vice versa [*10th Congress Declaration* 2].

It then stuck to its symbiotic role of backing the ANC in the crucial 1999 elections (and not running itself):

This 10th Congress re-affirms the SACP position that we shall work tirelessly as Communists to ensure an overwhelming ANC electoral victory. This resolve is based on many strategic considerations. It is also based on our conviction that, in the first four years of governance, the ANC-led government has spearheaded major socio-economic transformation [*10th Congress Declaration* 2].

It went on to carefully reject the centrist Growth, Employment, Redistribution (GEAR) plan, which had by then mostly replaced the more leftist Reconstruction and Development Programme (RDP):

Reaffirms its belief that the overall thrust of GEAR is not the appropriate macroeconomic framework for our society, and this overall thrust must be rejected. We have resolved, in the light of this, to engage with our alliance partners, other components of the MDM, and government, to ensure that we develop an appropriate macro-economic framework [*10th Congress Declaration* 2].

The Declaration then wrapped up with its somewhat optimistic slogan, "This 10th Congress emerges unified behind our Congress slogan—Build Peoples Power, Build Socialism Now!" (*10th Congress Declaration* 3).

The 10th Congress Resolutions opened with a stand against imperialism, which it saw as a fundamental global issue, since the Soviet bloc had been gone for half a decade:

The SACP at all organisational levels must foster a consistent anti-imperialist outlook, within our branches, within our Party, within the working class and broader movement, and amongst the South African public in general. Practically this means, amongst other things, that in our political education work and Party media work consistent attention must be given to this. This is a task that all Party members must take up, where they live and where they work or study. Wherever possible we must seek to connect current international events to a broader understanding of global realities, and we must constantly counter the ideological impact of imperialist dominated media [*10th Congress Resolutions* 1].

It went on to call for solidarity with Palestinians, oppressed peoples in Africa, and as always with Cuba's resistance to U.S. imperialism. More interesting was its attack on a new threat in the developing world:

The struggle against backward, xenophobic and fundamentalist ideologies:
In conditions of imperialist global cultural hegemony, in many Third World
countries, there is the danger of populist appropriations of backward, xenophobic and fundamentalist ideologies by elites. Preying on the genuine distress and
alienation felt by popular forces, certain elites demagogically mobilise around
ideologies that present themselves as "anti-imperialist." In fact, these ideologies
are used to brutally repress progressive, left and working-class forces in these
societies. Cases in point are Iran and Sudan. The SACP expresses its full support
for the persecuted Tudeh Party in Iran, and for the Sudanese Communist Party
in Sudan. We call for an end to anti-communist persecution in these countries,
and for the emergence of a democratic, secular and genuinely anti-imperialist
politics to be nurtured in these societies. We commit ourselves to deepening
understanding within our own country of the dangers of backward fundamentalist ideologies [*10th Congress Resolutions* 1–2].

This hinted at the rise of Islamic fundamentalism in the 1990s and its reactionary nature, which ironically both the capitalist West and communists
opposed then and now (though with the advent of the U.S. "War on Terror,"
the SACP also opposes such "imperialist actions"). This of course does make
sense, since Marx himself was for progress, modernity, industrialization, and
so forth (*Political Report* 32). He saw capitalism as a useful tool in bringing
progress to the world, though he would of course argue it would become the
problem itself as time passed, necessitating the need for socialism. Still, both
Marxism and liberal capitalism oppose the fundamentalists in various regions
(Islam, Judaism, Hinduism, etc.) as reactionaries.

The SACP went on and called for a new "front" against all conservative
and/or reactionary forces in the world. It stated:

In the context of our Party's commitment to renew the socialist and communist
project world-wide, to develop and deepen solidarity between all forces struggling against neoliberalism, race and gender oppression, the SACP will maintain
and advance connections with our historical allies, other left, worker, and democratic parties and social movements, and solidarity movements. The SACP will
seek out all means to carry out this work, including the new possibilities offered
by communications technology. In the face of the depredations of neo-liberal
globalisation, the SAC commits itself to the struggle for the globalisation of solidarity [*10th Congress Resolutions* 2].

The 1990s was seen somewhat like the 1930s, where a front of leftist organizations had to unite against the rise of fascism, but here it would be an alliance
against "neoliberalism" (aka the "Washington Consensus," "Western imperialism," etc.). The SACP also hinted at the use of new technologies such as the
Web and its email and social media (which the SACP has indeed now successfully started to use).

The SACP moved onto GEAR, and though the party admitted it was rooted in the leftist RDP, GEAR did not go far enough, had not succeeded, and had trusted global markets too much. It stated, "The overall thrust of GEAR is not the appropriate macro-economic framework for our society, and this overall thrust must be rejected" (*10th Congress Resolutions* 3). It concluded that it needed to continue to work within the alliance to bring a more leftist economic paradigm to fruition. As one can see, the SACP already had real issues with ANC economic policy by 1998, but still had no intention of bolting from its partnership with the ANC. These tensions would come to a head within a few years under the centrist ANC leader Thabo Mbeki, but then recede under the current ANC leader, ex-communist, and still leftist Jacob Zuma.

The SACP then discussed its approach to theory and practice. It admitted that though it supported the nationalist phase of the revolution at that point, it had to always be within a "socialist framework." Thus, not only should socialism be aimed for, but even current decisions also need to be grounded in a socialist perspective. It stated these trickier issues needed attention: "the dialectic between reform and revolution; gender exploitation and reproductive labour relationship between state and capital in the present post-apartheid context; how to appropriately engage with globalisation; working class approach to the environment and sustainable development" (*10th Congress Resolutions* 4). Though this is somewhat theoretical for even its own membership, let alone the masses of South Africa, it gets at a real and practical issue: how to back a capitalist system with all of its issues and problems while fighting for socialism in the future. Why do this balancing act? The document stated it clearly: "The centrality of the ANC-led Alliance in bringing about peace and democracy in our country [is clear]" (*10th Congress Resolutions* 4). As noted in earlier chapters, the SACP decided a long time ago that it would work with the ANC before *and* after the democratic revolution and thus it needed to carefully work for both tactical (a leftist but liberal democratic system) and strategic (building towards true socialism) goals at the same time. The next congress would build on these themes.

The 11th Congress in 2002 was not crucial, though it affirmed the SACP's themes and goals. General Secretary Blade Nzimande made an opening political report summarizing much of the congress. He began:

> We are gathered for the 11th Congress of the South African Communist Party under the banner "With and For … the Workers and the Poor." This 11th Congress, the largest ever of our great and glorious Party, is a fitting tribute to the great and dedicated communist revolutionaries who built and shaped our Party over the last 80 years [*SACP 11th Congress Political Report* 1].

The two points here, fighting for the poor and lasting eight decades, should not be dismissed as mere rhetoric. As noted before, it is amazing that the SACP had survived and even thrived after so many domestic and international challenges. The issue of the poor is also noteworthy since by 2002, more and more South Africans were feeling the ANC had become too distant from the masses. The SACP here and elsewhere would make it clear that it would constantly fight for the poor people of South Africa.

Nzimande then made a clear declaration of the SACP's deep leftist beliefs, which had not reduced a decade after the collapse of communism (though it had shed almost all of its Stalinist vestiges):

> Let's remind ourselves of four very basic things:
>
> **One:** Ours is a struggle for socialism—a society in which political power and the predominant means of production are in the hands of the workers and the poor.
>
> **Two:** The struggle for this objective is, fundamentally, a CLASS struggle. In the words of the Communist Manifesto (words which we have not forgotten), "the history of all hitherto existing society is the history of class struggles."
>
> **Three:** These struggles are, fundamentally, struggles over the control and ownership of PROPERTY. "...Communists everywhere support every revolutionary movement against the existing social and political order of things. In all these movements they bring to the front, as the leading question in each, the property question, no matter what its degree of development at the time" (*The Communist Manifesto*).
>
> **Four:** But we are also South African communists, active here on our continent, Africa. In our theory, our strategy and our practice we continue to be fundamentally guided by the famous Cradock Letter written in February 1934 to the Central Committee by our former General Secretary, that great communist hero, Moses Kotane. "The Party," he wrote, "must become more Africanised, pay special attention to South Africa, study the conditions in this country and concretise the demands of the toiling masses from first hand experience. We must speak the language of the masses and must know their demands. Thus while it must not lose its international allegiance, the Party must be "Bolshevised"—become South African not only theoretically but in reality." Over the past 81 years, we have built such a Party. We have confounded our enemies, our critics, even some of our friends and former members. Today, the SACP, with its socialist objectives, its Marxist analysis, its activism and, above all, its rootedness in South Africa, exerts more influence than at any other time in its history [*SACP 11th Congress Political Report* 1–2].

The first three points are standard socialist/communist beliefs, though it is interesting that he cites Marx and not Lenin. The last point, though, is more interesting.

Here Nzimande made it clear that the SACP had to be rooted deeply within the South African context, that is, a developing country with a complex colonial history. This is *less* Marxist and *more* Leninist (*Political Report* 1). As pointed out in detail in earlier chapters, Marxism and Leninism have real differences and even contradictions. One of the largest is the ability (or not) to build genuine and sustainable socialism in developing nations. Marx was clear that socialism, the historic stage after fully developed capitalism, must start in the West, where capitalism had evolved the most. Lenin, though, argued that since capitalism was international, one could start socialism in the developing world (in his case, Imperial Russia) and then have the revolution spread to the West (back then, mostly Western Europe). Lenin tried to argue he was not contradicting Marx, but expanding upon him. Still, orthodox Marxists reject this line of thought (Montague 1).

But that second step, where socialist revolution spread from the developing world to the West, just never happened with Lenin's Soviet Union or its satellites (the military conquest of East Germany does not really fit here and the rest of eastern Europe was not developed). According to even leftist critics, this was partially due to not having the material basis to have "true socialism" in the first place in Russia. Thus, some form of developmental state capitalism with an authoritarian political system was created in the Soviet bloc, dominated first by the party then by dictators (and never by "workers' democracy," as Marx called for). Again, as pointed out earlier, the SACP has never fully jettisoned this Leninist stand, even though the party cites Marx more often nowadays (though obviously not his admittedly limited work on the developing world). The SACP even hints at a Stalinist notion of "Socialism in One Country," since though it desires world revolution, it admits to the resilience of tertiary global capitalism. Therefore, for South Africa to move towards socialism, it will do so partially alone (though a loose alliance of partially socialist states still exists and would presumably support this). This is still all very problematic for orthodox Marxists (Montague 1).

Next Nzimande argued that technology has indeed advanced, which was for the best. (Unlike some leftists who are anti-progress/modernity and verging on Luddite ideas, Leninists have always called for development, like Marx.) But he noted that current capitalist progress was not for the benefit of the many but for the few:

> Over the past 30 years, we have experienced unprecedented levels of technological transformation that have impacted the entire globe. Much of this change is (potentially at least) an advance for human civilisation. Satellite communications, e-mail and the Internet have established an infrastructure that creates the basis for instantaneous global information and communication for a new global

solidarity. But it has been driven by a particularly virulent and crisis-ridden strain of capitalist barbarism [*SACP 11th Congress Political Report* 2].

Most leftists would agree with this, though the term "barbarism" is stronger than many would use. Still, more fairly spreading the benefits of modern technology is not an alien concept beyond the SACP, or even South Africa.

He then attacked the world system of both capitalism and the geopolitics of the West, especially the U.S.:

> But now, as we meet in 2002, the truth is less easily evaded. Crony capitalism turns out to be international "standard practice"—Enron and their crony accountants, Anderson, Tyco, Global Crossing, Qwest Communications, World-Com, Merck, Bristol-Myers Squibb, Xerox, the list goes on and on. What we see is the emergence of new, modern global robber barons of neo-liberal capitalism!
>
> As in the past, one menacing response to these crises, has been increased military expenditure in the U.S., and a growing and dangerous propensity towards aggressive unilateralism. The U.S. has increased its military budget during this year to $396 billion, a whopping expenditure of more than $1 billion a day. War, especially a high-tech war, is a destructive means of propping up declining profits. The demonisation of foreign countries, leaders, cultures, and religions is a demagogic attempt to unify and distract disgruntled domestic electorates. The fundamentalism of neoliberalism, of U.S. domination is counter-posed to other fundamentalisms. Deplorable acts of terrorism are used to justify counter-terrorism acts like the bombing of civilians in Afghanistan. The so-called "war on terrorism" becomes state sponsored, hi-tech, terrorism in Colombia, in Palestine. In the South we get lectures on "good governance" and "democracy," while the U.S. conspires to overthrow popularly elected Venezuelan president, Hugo Chavez, and while the U.S. and its allies plan externally imposed "regime changes" in Iraq, in Zimbabwe. In the Palestine Authority, the Palestinian people are instructed to go to the polls and vote for a candidate of President George Bush's choice [*SACP 11th Congress Political Report* 3].

Though one does not need to agree with his clear leftist bias on these issues, he was correct that the "crony capitalism" would only increase until hitting a high point with the global "Great Recession" starting in 2008. And he was also correct that the U.S. "War on Terror" would only increase (in both Afghanistan from 2001 and Iraq from 2003, let alone on a smaller scale in many other countries), especially in regards to the U.S. military budget (from the $396 billion cited then in 2002 to almost $750 billion by the late 2000s).

Nzimande then argued that a new, loose "front" needs to be created, with communists of the world uniting with, learning from, and ultimately harnessing the late 1990s and early 2000s protests against globalization:

> Since our last Congress we have seen significant mass challenges to the current imperialist globalisation. Some of these challenges have been expressed in the

Seattle mass demonstrations, in Prague and Genoa and in the convening of the alternative World Social Forum. The participants in these and many other initiatives around the world are drawn from a diversity of backgrounds and ideological traditions. The strength (and potential weakness) of these mass anti-globalisation movements is precisely their pluralism and diversity.

We must certainly not under-rate the importance of these and other phenomena. These mass struggles mark an end to the so-called "end of history"! The challenge for communist forces globally today is to interact with this diverse but popularly rooted anti-capitalist sentiment. We need to learn and listen; we need to appreciate the creativity with which a wide range of forces, sometimes single-issue campaigns, has mobilised. But we need also to engage with these diverse forces with our own analyses of the crisis, and our own strategic vision of a struggle for socialism as the only sustainable direction to take humanity out of the current tragic impasse [*SACP 11th Congress Political Report* 3].

Again, this has been a communist, and SACP, strategy for decades: to aid (and/or use) other leftist groups and social movements for communist ends. The SACP is quite open about all this, so there is nothing insidious about it (contrary to their right-wing critics' comments). Plus, parties and groups of similar stripes have aligned in modern political systems for centuries.

Nzimande then argued that African development is for the best, but not under Western values and/or pressure:

One of the big challenges for our party is that of linking up with other progressive forces on the African continent, to engage the realities on the continent and the challenge of development. The SACP supports the concept of NEPAD [New Partnership for Africa's Development] as an important initiative to reverse underdevelopment and poverty. But we reject the notion that the development of the African continent should be traded off for notions of good governance that are premised on imperialist, neo-liberal conceptions and conditionalities similar to those of the failed and disastrous structural adjustment programmes [SAPs] forced on our continent [*SACP 11th Congress Political Report* 4].

This was a classic leftist argument against SAPs imposed by the International Monetary Fund (IMF) since the 1990s on various developing countries so as to get aid and advisement. This is not the place to fully address the complex issue of SAPs and their effectiveness and/or fairness, but the left has mostly condemned them as unfair and harsh; the SACP fits this global mold. The World Health Organization (WHO), hardly an "extremist group," mostly agreed:

SAPs policies reflect the neo-liberal ideology that drives globalization. They aim to achieve long-term or accelerated economic growth in poorer countries by restructuring the economy and reducing government intervention. SAPs policies include currency devaluation, managed balance of payments, reduction of government services through public spending cuts/budget deficit cuts, reducing tax on high earners, reducing inflation, wage suppression, privatization, lower tariffs on imports and tighter monetary policy, increased free trade, cuts in social spending, and business deregulation. Governments are also encouraged or forced to reduce their role in the economy by privatizing state-owned industries, including the health sector, and opening up their economies to foreign competition.

One important criticism of SAPs, which emerged shortly after they were first adopted and has continued since, concerns their impact on the social sector. In health, SAPs affect both the supply of health services (by insisting on cuts in health spending) and the demand for health services (by reducing household income, thus leaving people with less money for health). Studies have shown that SAPs policies have slowed down improvements in, or worsened, the health status of people in countries implementing them. The results reported include worse nutritional status of children, increased incidence of infectious diseases, and higher infant and maternal mortality rates [*Structural Adjustment Programs* 2013, 1].

Obviously other groups farther on the right would disagree with this overall negative assessment of SAPs. It is still telling that the SACP was in agreement with a legitimate and internationally recognized organization such as the WHO. The days where the SACP was just an outlying radical organization were fading quickly.

Nzimande then spoke of the 1990s as a time of struggle, success, but also solidification of gains. He argued that though bans on the ANC and SACP had been lifted and the groups did win the crucial 1994 All Race Election, it was only due to constant pushback against both domestic and global forces:

> The legalisation of our organisations also coincided with the extension of counter-revolutionary warfare by the apartheid regime against our organisations and our people. One important lesson from the period 1990 to 1994 was the manner in which the movement managed to effectively combine *three* key elements of struggle in the new situation. The first element is extensive internal and public debate about our transition; our Party was indeed at the cutting edge of these debates. The second key element was that all these debates and engagement during this period were underpinned by sustained mass mobilisation and struggles. Thirdly, all these struggles and debates cohered around the development of the RDP [Reconstruction and Development Programme]—one of the most extensive policy discussions within the ranks of our movement.
>
> Perhaps most importantly during this period, we defeated a particular type of transition that some global and domestic forces wanted to impose on South Africa—a combination of a centrist, low intensity democracy marginalising both the right and the left. This was defeated principally because the ANC and its left allies managed to mobilise as a single force, won the election and marginalised both the right and the ultra-right, whilst keeping the left-bloc of forces intact to drive the transformation process in the post–1994 period [*SACP 11th Congress Political Report* 4].

This was mostly correct, though somewhat overstated. It was true that the whole idea of the early Government of National Unity (GNU) right after the 1994 election was to "contain" the more radical elements coming to power, like the SACP and COSATU (and even leftist elements within the ANC). It was also true that a centrist public policy was pushed upon the new ANC administration from day one, for good and bad reasons. Finally, though the alliance did resist the most right-wing suggestions, it was also true that the leftist RDP would soon be marginalized and replaced with the Growth, Employment, and Redistribution Plan (GEAR) and later by the National Development Plan (NDP), neither of which the SACP fully approved.

He went on to talk of the huge electoral victory of 1999, which did solidify gains from the 1994 election. He argued:

> Since our last Congress [the 10th in 1998], there have been further major developments on the broader political front in favour of the NDR-bloc of forces. In 1999, the ANC increased its electoral majority from 62,5 percent to just under two thirds. In the 2000 local government elections—the first truly nonracial and democratic local elections—the ANC won 5 of the 6 metropolitan councils, and controls more than 80 percent of the municipalities in the country. These elections were won on progressive manifestos, including a commitment to provision of free basic services for the poor, an indigent policy, and an assertion that the state should be the preferred provider of social services [*SACP 11th Congress Political Report* 4].

This was mostly true: real gains were made, some of it due to the promise of more social programs, but also due to the fact the ANC now controlled the state, which can and did lend itself to campaigning. The opposition of that period, from the weak but liberal Democratic Party to the dwindling New National Party (NNP) to their weak alliance with other groups under the Democratic Alliance (DA) banner, all aided the ANC-led victory in 1999 ("Mandela Hails..." 1999).

But Nzimande then argued that with the 1999 electoral victory under their belts, the alliance needed to effect more radical economic and social changes (though as we shall see, this would not be the case). He stated:

> The key strategic objective of the SACP over the next five to ten years is to build a mass-based momentum for socioeconomic transformation that overcomes poverty, deep-seated inequality and systemic underdevelopment, launching our society onto a new path of growth and development. This mass-based momentum must be ANC-led, and working class-driven. To this end, we need to mobilise the active participation of the overwhelming majority of our people, working together with our allies, with government at all levels, and the mass movement. As an active formation in this struggle, the SACP will seek to advance, deepen and defend the NDR [National Democratic Revolution] and,

at the same time, build momentum towards, capacity for, and elements of social-ism [*SACP 11th Congress Political Report* 4].

This indeed had been the desire of the SACP since 1994, let alone 2002 when this was stated, but even today, this is still not the case. Not only is socialism not being built in any real way (though the SACP does indeed push for it), but also the current NDP plan is too centrist for the SACP and its leftist allies. This is partially due to the fact that the alliance is indeed "ANC led" and thus will not, and possibly cannot be, much more radical in its in approach to solving South Africa's serious social, economic, and even political problems. The SACP surely recognized that by 2002, and certainly does today (as we saw earlier, it said so subtly in its more current critical comments about the centrist NDP). But the SACP was and is limited in how much it can say, let alone do, on this issue since it is the minority partner in the alliance.

Nzimande then went to argue for more work against the HIV/AIDS epi-demic in South Africa, more power to the working class, the empowerment of women, and the integration of the rural poor into society (*SACP 11th Congress Political Report* 9–11). These are admirable goals, but they were almost truisms for the party and South Africa at that point. He then addressed a much more salient issue. Nzimande turned to the serious tensions within the alliance:

> We held our 10th Congress in the wake of heightened differences within the alliance over government's macro-economic policy framework, GEAR. These tensions were played out at that very Congress, as illustrated by one of the harsh-est criticisms ever directed at our Party by the ANC leadership. Tempting as it was to engage in an ongoing polemic against GEAR, as the SACP, we deliberately chose to focus our attention and role in the alliance on providing a way out of this stalemate, without at the same abandoning our critique of GEAR...
>
> During all our engagements within the alliance we patiently argued and pro-posed a need for the alliance to shift its focus towards the microeconomy (including investment in infrastructure) through the mobilisation of domestic resources based on an integrated, coherent and state-driven industrial strategy...
>
> During the latter half of 2001, the alliance experienced what was perhaps its most strenuous and conflictual period over the last few decades. This tension was brought to a head by the COSATU and SACP-supported, anti-privatisation strike of August 2001. As the SACP we had consistently warned for a few years before that the accumulation regime was based on turning around our economy on the altar of sacrifices made by the working class. We are pleased to report now that the series of bilaterals and alliance meetings, including the all-important Ekurhuleni declaration of April 2002, have taken us out of the dip, and set us on a positive path of finding a common approach...
>
> We believe that the manner in which we handled the differences by focusing on areas around which we can agree was the correct approach [*SACP 11th Con-gress Political Report* 12–14].

This was all related to the many and serious frictions between the ANC and SACP detailed in other chapters. But as he argued, the SACP (and COSATU) stepped away from the brink of dissolving the alliance by pushing a consensus agenda, stressing issues all three partners could readily agree on. This did work, but at the cost of never settling the deeper issue of where South Africa should go on privatization or when some form of socialism should be attempted (Mfuku 2006).

Elements within the ANC still agreed with many international economic actors that more privatization was needed, while the SACP and COSATU opposed it then and now. If anything, the SACP (and often COSATU) argued that more nationalization was the logical first step towards socialism (probably true, but highly unlikely in the near future due to the domestic and intentional factors). It should be noted that after 1999, the South African privatization program was given to a SACP member, Jeff Radebe, who continued to pursue it but more carefully and emphasized the need for it to serve "public needs"; this was surely due to some sort of quid pro quo between the ANC and SACP ("The Painful Privatization..." 1).

Nzimande then concluded with the issue of how a communist should see him/herself in the new South Africa. He stated pragmatically:

> In the midst of a persisting old legacy and sometimes confusing new realities, it is easy to lose your bearings. For instance, we need, as a country and economy, to attract foreign investment, and so it is perfectly natural that we should sometimes look at our society through the imaginary eyes of potential investors. "The fundamentals are in place," we might say. We need, as a country and economy, to attract tourists, and so it is natural that we should look at our society through the eyes of tourists. "Things are not as bad as they say"; we might want to assert. It is inevitable, and perhaps even necessary, that these things should sometimes happen.
>
> But we should never, never, never allow these perspectives to dominate our understanding, analysis or sensitivity. We must, above all, occupy the trench, not of tourists (as welcome as they are), not of investors—but of workers and the poor. This standpoint must inform our understanding, our analysis, and our morality. As communists, let us be very clear: WE are deployed, first and foremost, to the ANTI-capitalist sector. WE are deployed to the ANTI-private accumulation struggle. That is our profession. The class struggle is our primary listing. The workers and the poor are our core business [*SACP 11th Congress Political Report* 21–22].

This approach, stressing the realities of running a still capitalist South Africa while being communists, is something the SACP has struggled with since 1994. It argued that this is a "stage" towards socialism, which may indeed be the case. But this is still hard to understand for the party itself, let alone the people of South Africa, who then receive a somewhat complex and even garbled class message. Indeed, South Africa does need at this stage foreign (capitalist) investment to readily develop (and the SACP admits this also), but how can one readily attract that with communist rhetoric, let alone a communist agenda?

The SACP has argued that the capitalists are so needy of investment returns that they will take the risk with a leftist South Africa. And South Africa is so needy of said investment that it will risk working with such investment partners. This is a fair evaluation, but as one can see, hardly a trusting or stable long-term situation (though it is not rare; much of the developing world has a similar situation, with various leftist regimes balancing priorities, not unlike the ANC). Much of the ANC would like to stabilize this rocky environment with a more centrist public policy. The SACP, if anything, would like to push towards the left, even at the risk of the relationship with foreign investors. As mentioned elsewhere, this will come to a head eventually for the ANC and SACP.

The SACP also passed a few resolutions at this congress that need to be addressed before moving on. It started with this statement:

> 1. The SACP's strategic commitment to advancing, deepening and defending the National Democratic Revolution (NDR) as a crucial strategic objective in its own right, and as the most direct path to socialism in South Africa; and
>
> 2. The SACP's longstanding strategic commitment to the alliance, and to actively building a broad, mass-based ANC committed to the leading role of the working class within the NDR [*SACP 11th Congress Political Report* 1].

This was the SACP just again arguing that the current phase, led by the ANC, is the best way to eventual socialism. Those farther on the left (anarchists, Trotskyites, etc.) obviously deny this, but they have no real or practical method themselves to obtaining a "Socialist South Africa." Still, the SACP admitted that there is real friction within the alliance on how to develop the nation:

> 1. Notwithstanding our democratic political advances we have not been able to break out of an accumulation path that is, in many respects, unfavourable to working people and the poor; and
>
> 2. Our current situation has introduced new possibilities but also new challenges, including the emergence of new class strata within our movement.
>
> 3. Some of the recent difficulties within the alliance arise out of problems with policy, particularly economic policy, as well as a lack of a shared understanding on the relationship between the alliance and governance processes.
>
> 4. There is a need to create space for increased engagement within the alliance, including for self-criticism and constructive criticism [*SACP 11th Congress Political Report* 1].

This was a complex way of saying that the ANC-led alliance and its stress on the controversial centrist GEAR policies (especially privatization) had been resisted by the SACP and COSATU and that more debates were needed. It is unlikely the ANC agreed that GEAR was wrong-headed or that more debate was needed, but regardless, this whole set of tensions would drag into the NDP debate years later.

Finally, what the SACP resolved to do is interesting, since, as argued elsewhere in this volume, it showed the SACP was and is aiming for more independence from the ANC:

1. To take active steps to engage in a struggle to promote a working class hegemony within the NDR;
2. To expand the capacity of the SACP to make its own specific policy proposals on key national issues;
3. To establish mechanisms to more effectively utilise the large number of SACP members, who are public representatives, to promote SACP policy;
4. To work with alliance partners to ensure that the agreements reached at the Ekurhuleni Alliance Summit are implemented;
5. To advance campaigns that give socialist content to the NDR, including the eradication of poverty, dealing with unemployment and job losses, defending and extending the public sector, free basic services, support for the principle of the Basic Income Grant, land and agrarian reform, recognising unpaid reproductive labour and informal work, building a socialist co-operative movement [*SACP 11th Congress Political Report* 1].

This pushed the SACP agenda on a number of levels, many of them against ANC wishes. By saying the working class should be predominant, the SACP was arguing that other classes would not be, including the middle class, which the ANC has pandered to since being in power (which is not rare; catering to the middle class is almost universal in the West). Saying the SACP should have its own policies was self-evidently saying the SACP should not just help to develop ANC ones. Saying the SACP should use its members in the ANC and government is leveraging its "mole-like" situation (much to the chagrin of the ANC).

Finally, it argued that the SACP should push leftist public policies to help end social problems, all at the cost of more centrist policies for economic growth per se, which the ANC had stressed since the late 1990s. The 2002 Ekurhuleni Declaration was an agreement between the alliance members that though economic growth needed to be stressed for development (the ANC pushed for this), the gross social issues of South Africa had to still be addressed (the SACP and COSATU pushed for this) ("The Ekurhuleni Declaration..." 2002, 1). This would be reaffirmed again by the alliance in 2005 ("The

Declaration..." 2005, 1). These agreements helped end many of the damaging strikes and much of the heated public rhetoric between the alliance members, but it did not end the underlying tensions, which are based on real ideological differences. In any case, these were not radical statements, but they showed a real distance between the ANC and SACP, the most since the 1994 election.

The SACP then stated something that most Western economists would argue is economically contradictory. It said, "The state must intervene on behalf of the poor and stimulate socio-economic development by: Providing basic services, amongst others; regulate the private sector..." (*SACP IIth Congress Political Report* 2). All three of these actions would be seen as *hurting* economic growth by most Western, conventional economists (though they might admit it might still possibly help the poor in the short run). One does not need to be a libertarian to see the growth of the state, especially in these ways, as often detrimental to economic growth, for good or bad. The SACP has argued that it supports some form of "state capitalist approach," such as in Asia. This guided capitalist method has indeed worked well at times in Asia (China, Singapore, South Korea, even Japan to an extent), but few other places (Schuman 1).

This whole debate about how much a developing state should provide in social and welfare services versus how much it should invest in economic growth is not a settled one, though since the 1990s most Western economists argue for more investment for growth than welfare programs (though the more sophisticated ones do admit that an investment in "human capital" is also needed) (Ogunade). The SACP of course disagreed with a neo-liberal approach, and if there was any doubt, the SACP then called for:

1. The restructuring of the state that results in the privatisation of basic services and shedding of jobs be halted;
2. The state provide basic services such as health, housing, education etc. to the working class and the poor;
3. The state ensures that all state owned enterprises have and obligation to deliver of basic services to the working class and the poor;
4. The state ensures that all state owned enterprises have and obligation to deliver of basic services to the working class and the poor;
5. The state expands its programme of ensuring that civil servants put people first;
6. The delivery of services must focus on women and children, in particular [*SACP IIth Congress Political Report* 2].

Again, these may be desirable and possibly even somewhat obtainable goals for South Africa, but it is unlikely any of them could help with much needed economic growth. The ANC knew this and opposed most of them.

The SACP went on again to call for more public and private action against HIV/AIDS. This was a veiled attack against President Mbeki's highly controversial "revisionist" theories about HIV. The SACP then called for more agrarian reform, admitting that the party itself had not studied this issue enough (the SACP, like most Marxist-Leninist parties, emphasized the urban issues of developing nations much more than rural ones; this is in contrast to most Maoist parties). It also called for the reform and cleanup of various public bureaucracies that had not delivered needed services well enough a decade after the 1994 election; this too was a veiled attack against the ANC since they ran said bureaucracy. Finally, it said that South Africa should engage the New Partnership for Africa's Development (NEPAD) process more to ensure African development (*SACP 11th Congress Political Report* 3–5). The 12th SACP Congress would continue these themes.

The SACP's 12th Congress (2007) started with a major document aptly named *The South African Road to Socialism*. It began by stating:

> As we convene at this 12th National Congress of the SACP, we are all well aware that the first decade of freedom is now well behind us. It is a decade of important victories—the achievement of democratic rights, the consolidation of a non-racial, democratic state and constitutional dispensation, the redistribution of considerable resources by way of low cost housing, water and electricity connections and some 12 million social grants.
>
> But it is also a decade in which the stabilization and return to growth of the capitalist economy has strengthened established big capital—the very forces who shaped a century of colonial and apartheid oppression and minority accumulation. Despite legislative gains, the working class has suffered from one million job losses in the formal sector, and from wide-scale casualisation. A million farm-workers and their families have been evicted from commercial farms in the past decade. Some 37 percent of the work force is unemployed and social (mainly racialised) inequality has deepened. Rural women and women living in peri-urban settlements continue to bear the brunt of poverty and the crises of underdevelopment. Conditions in our often under-resourced and overcrowded public schools and public hospitals are dire.
>
> Things are certainly better than they were before 1994. We must celebrate what we have achieved. We must build upon it. But we cannot simply continue to march to the hymn of "the revolution I on track," or "today is better than yesterday," and therefore supposedly "tomorrow will be better than today." There is nothing pre-ordained, or guaranteed about progress. The future of our country is deeply contested. And that contest is, fundamentally, a CLASS contest.
>
> Will our 1994 democratic breakthrough promise only to deceive? Will our democratic gains become stunted and undermined by a neo-colonial (of a special type) stagnation in which a new elite is simply absorbed by an old elite?
>
> Will earnest social delivery, without systemic transformation of the economy, be overwhelmed and undermined by that untransformed economy?

These are not idle questions. There are countless examples of promising post-colonial societies losing their way a decade or so into their independence [*The South African Road to Socialism* 1].

In other words, South Africa had made real progress since 1994, but by 2007, not only did so much more need be done but that right-wing elements, upper-class actors, and structural issues could and have reversed some achievements for the poor of South Africa. It was a subtle attack against some within the ANC who had indeed stressed past achievements more than current issues, and who had argued that a more radical approach, which the SACP wanted, was not the best route.

Interestingly, the document then explained how the SACP, since 1928, has needed to be a close but independent partner with the ANC. It stated:

> Almost 79 years ago, meeting in Moscow between August and September 1928, the Sixth Congress of what was then the Communist International, resolved that the Communist Party in South Africa should (and we quote): *"pay particular attention to the embryonic national organizations among the [African majority], such as the African National Congress. The Party, while retaining its full independence* [we repeat: **"while retaining its full independence"**], *should participate in these organizations, should seek to broaden and extend their activity. Our aim should be to transform the African National Congress into a fighting nationalist revolutionary organization against the white bourgeoisie and the British imperialists, based upon the trade unions, peasant organizations, etc., developing systematically the leadership of the workers and the Communist Party in this organization* [we repeat: **"developing systematically the leadership of the workers and the Communist Party in this organization"** ... *The development of a national-revolutionary movement of the toilers of South Africa ... constitutes one of the major tasks of the Communist Party of South Africa."* [*The South African Road to Socialism* 2].

This book has talked a great deal about the symbiotic nature of the ANC/SACP relationship, but this document, quoting a decades-old statement, sums it up brilliantly. But the document then went farther, pointing out the relatively large schism that had grown between the ANC and SACP a few years before, in the mid–2000s:

> Two weeks ago, cde [comrade] Thabo Mbeki [president of South Africa] opened the ANC's National Policy Conference. Speaking in his capacity as ANC president, cde Mbeki said that the ANC/SACP/COSATU alliance was a strategic and necessarily enduring alliance. He said:
> *"The objective reality in our country is that the NDR cannot succeed if it does not contain among its motive forces our country's socialist, trade union and civic movements."*
> We welcome this clear strategic statement which was warmly endorsed by the nearly two thousand ANC delegates. We also note that this statement marks an

important shift from formal ANC positions of just four-and-a-half [*sic*] years ago. At the ANC's 51st National Conference in Stellenbosch in 2002, a new Preface was added to the 1997 ANC Strategy and Tactics document. This Preface characterized ANC policy as in opposition to two ideological currents— "neoliberalism" and what it called "modern ultra-leftism." Both were identified as essentially "counterrevolutionary."

The attack on what was loosely labeled "modern ultra-leftism" was, in fact, a thinly disguised attack on the SACP and the policy positions emerging from our own 2002 SACP Congress. All loose references of this kind to "modern ultra-leftism" have no disappeared from the ANC's current draft Strategy and Tactics document. That is good. The ANC's hundreds of thousands of members know very well that the threat to the NDR and to the ANC itself does not come from the SACP and its policies. It comes from the powerful private conglomerates whose wealth and power were accumulated under white minority rule. It is the same wealth and power that is now used to menace, cajole and bribe our new democracy [*The South African Road to Socialism* 2].

This was probably one of the most honest admissions by the SACP that there had been real and serious tensions between it and the ANC since 1994. Though officially reversed since then, the ANC position that the SACP is "too leftist" will not go away. The SACP was right that various capitalist actors (domestic and international) will continuously pressure the ANC on the SACP, as long as the ANC is in power and South Africa remains fundamentally a capitalist nation. Obviously, the SACP would like to change that last factor, creating some type of socialism within South Africa, but it admits that cannot come about for some time. The SACP may, one day, have to become independent and challenge the ANC at the polls to resolve this issue, but that too is seemingly far off.

The SACP then argued in this important document how for the past decade, since GEAR started in the late 1990s, the ANC had ignored the SACP on some key issues, at least at first. It stated:

So (for the record) let us state quite clearly that, as in the past, so in the present the SACP has certainly not sought to "impose" anything undemocratically upon the ANC, nor "delegate" socialist tasks to it. But of course we are seeking to influence the ANC and its mass membership in a constructive, open and non-factionalist manner. We are seeking, without apology, to underline the imperative of many socialist-oriented policies and programmes in order to advance, deepen and defend the very NDR itself in the present phase of struggle.

And, judging from the recommendations emerging from the ANC's national policy conference two weekends ago, the SACP has had considerable, if sometimes belated, success in this regard.

When, in 1996 government introduced its GEAR macro-economic policy and told us it was "written in stone," the SACP raised serious concerns. We didn't (as is often falsely claimed in the media) dismiss the need for the careful management of our foreign currency reserves, our inflation rate, or our budget deficit. But we did strongly criticise the notion that macro-economic management was virtually all that government could do while leaving the rest to the market. We called (and we were the first in SA to call) for an **industrial policy** that addressed the skewed character of our economy. We said that macroeconomic policy should be aligned to industrial policy. Our views were dismissed at the time.

When government's GEAR macro management policies failed to produce a major flow of productive investment into our country, there was a move to a massive privatisation drive. Once more, the SACP opposed this move, and we called instead for the forging of a **democratic developmental state** capable of driving socio-economic transformation. Again we were among the first in South Africa to elaborate this perspective. Again our views were dismissed, or rather given passing lip-service at the time.

We are pleased to say that our government now treats both industrial policy and the developmental state as cornerstone strategic objectives. The ANC delegates to the ANC policy conference strongly confirmed and elaborated on these broad strategic objectives [*The South African Road to Socialism* 3].

This was again an important set of statements: the SACP was making it clear that for almost a decade, it had been ignored on crucial issues and now the ANC had reversed its position. This is not the place to argue whether GEAR or other programs had objectively failed economically (it is a mixed bag), but it is telling that the SACP in 2007 felt it necessary to state publicly how it had been disregarded far too many times by the ANC.

The document then went on to argue that the congress needed to define what the SACP, and SACP alone, needed to do first, then broaden the goals to the alliance. It was also clear that at least aspects of socialism needed to start sooner rather than later: "Firstly, it is important for us as communists, in the midst of the struggles to deepen, consolidate and advance the national democratic revolution [NDR], that we never for once lose sight of our goal to achieve a socialist South Africa. In fact, as we say in our draft programme, the very consolidation of the NDR [National Democratic Revolution] requires some socialist measures in the here and now" (*The South African Road to Socialism* 4).

It then stated a subtle formula to show it does support aspects of the NDR but wanted far more:

The SACP is of course not part of the national democratic revolution merely as a stepping stone to socialism. The attainment of the objectives of the NDR is something that is of fundamental importance and in the deepest interests of the working class. The total liberation of the African people in particular, and blacks in general is an important objective in itself, that ensures that the working class itself is completely freed from the burdens of colonialism of a special type. However, at the same time, as the SACP we know that we can never attain the total liberation of Africans and black people under capitalism. This is simply because capitalism continues to reproduce some of the key features of colonialism of a special type...

It is on the terrain of the national democratic revolution that we are struggling for a socialist South Africa; hence the continued relevance and importance of our programmatic slogan "Socialism is the Future, Build it Now" [*The South African Road to Socialism* 4].

This is a common far left argument that one should fight specific injustices now (racism, sexism, etc.), but also fight for socialism in the long term, since capitalism is the root of many of those injustices and thus needs to be overthrown eventually (though the timetable is often as ambiguous as it sounds).

It then stated, "In pursuing a working class led NDR, we are guided by our Medium Term Vision (MTV). Our MTV enjoins us to lead a process of building working class hegemony in key sites of power" (*The South African Road to Socialism* 4). Which seems to mean that as time passed, the NDR would become more worker-led and thus more socialist (but even today, this has not become a reality). The SACP then stated that the working class needed to be empowered enough, through its unions (thus COSATU), to push back against the upper class and certain elements within ANC; this process has been done (*The South African Road to Socialism* 4–5).

The document then went on to show how globally the U.S. had become more imperialistic by 2007 (due to the "War on Terror") which was a loss for the world socialist movement. However, domestically the alliance had won more local and national elections, which was a win for socialist and working-class forces at least within South Africa. It also argued that women, rural workers, and other marginalized groups have been aided by these domestic victories in South Africa. But it did worry about the South African "middle strata" (middle class), which was still mostly white (with the few middle-class blacks being squeezed in harder economic times). Finally, the SACP argued that the South African "bourgeoisie" (upper class) was almost entirely still white, except for some co-opted black elements, and was still a clear class enemy of the working class. The party of course concluded that what was needed was not more "black bourgeoisie" but less bourgeoisie in general (*The South African Road to Socialism* 6–8, 9).

The document then discussed politics and the alliance. It admitted that the SACP had not run in any elections and had always backed the ANC at the polls since 1994, though it also stressed how it helped pick ANC candidates that did run for the alliance. Also, it argued that some of those ANC candidates were also SACP members, and thus the SACP has helped run the country. But then the document argued this:

> The modalities of the SACP's participation in elections are not a matter of timeless principle. As an independent political party, the SACP has every right to contest elections in its own right—should it so choose.
>
> The 2005 SACP Special National Congress established a Central Committee Commission to research this whole area and to make recommendations to this Congress. The CC Commission tabled its report to the CC earlier this year. Amongst other things it noted that, internationally, capitalist dominated societies are an extremely unfavourable electoral terrain for Communist Parties. There is not a single example of a Communist Party, on its own, winning national elections within a capitalist society—let alone using such a breakthrough as the platform to advance a socialist transformation [*The South African Road to Socialism* 12].

This was the first time the SACP admitted publicly that it was not viable to run separately in the elections. This was an accurate and surprisingly honest statement. This has been argued by this author elsewhere, and the alliance itself knew it, but the SACP usually did not admit this openly.

The SACP then stated that the legislative branch was too weak, the executive had too much power, and that capitalist special interests have captured too much of the power in South Africa. Plus, the SACP saw elections as a "bourgeoisie formation" and should not be the only place power is taken by a communist actor (which hinted at social movements and/or other more ominous developments). Finally, the SACP wanted party members, sitting as ANC members in various state positions, acting more like *communists* (*The South African Road to Socialism*, 21). This last statement was telling also, since it might mean the SACP was forming an informal caucus within the ANC (something it had yet to do). Still, a half-decade after this document was released, such changes do not seem to have occurred between the ANC and SACP, for good or bad.

The SACP began to wrap up this historic document by discussing ideology. The party admitted that though ideology is ultimately formed by the material conditions around someone, as any Marxist would argue, it went on to say that "false ideologies" have been created by the capitalist media for its own ends. The SACP felt this process needed to be fought at all levels for the class consciousness of the working class to improve (*The South African Road to Socialism*, 14). This was and is probably true, but as many postmodernist authors argue, these so-called false ideologies are quite resilient and might indeed shape reality for the masses.

The SACP then moved on to international linkages, saying that it had many ties in Africa and throughout the developing world, but it stressed Cuba and, surprisingly, China too. As noted before, the SACP and China have had cool to cold relations since the early 1960s due to the Sino-Soviet split of that period, with the SACP clearly siding with the Soviets. Still, since the collapse of communism, China is not only the most powerful "communist" state left, it is also a model of "state capitalism," which the SACP would like to emulate in South Africa (*The South African Road to Socialism*, 14–16). It stated a general goal:

> Our main strategic objective in our international relations should be to contribute towards building a left, socialist movement and solidarity networks in Southern Africa, Africa and the developing world, in that order of priority. The aim of such a movement should immediately be to fight neoliberalism, U.S. unilateralism, promote world peace and advance the struggle for building developmental states with and for workers and the poor as a platform to build a momentum towards and capacity for socialism [*The South African Road to Socialism* 17].

This 2007 message of building an intentional leftist front has been stressed elsewhere by the SACP, and though such fronts do exist, communists per se have little say in them. Some right-wing American commentators would argue the opposite—that communists secretly control such fronts—though with little or no hard evidence (Ungar 2009).

The document ended on party needs and structures. The SACP made clear that when a party member acts as an ANC member, they no longer have leeway to oppose official SACP policy. This was important, since it was implied for many decades that the SACP members within the ANC should obey ANC orders. It admitted that this could be complicated to implement but was needed (and another sign of pulling away from the ANC). It also called for more resources for the party and no more "freelancing" of members in the capitalist economy. It then moved on to "party democracy," which had changed little since key reforms in the early 1990s:

> [O]ur Party does indeed believe and practice inner party democracy. There is no party cadre who is prevented from making her/his point of view in our structures. This is a practice we must foster in order to strengthen inner party democracy. BUT, views and opinions must be made in a constructive manner, respecting the principle of democratic centralism, with the aim preserving the unity of the Party and in a disciplined and loyal manner. Inner party democracy does not mean ill-discipline, undermining the collective decisions of our structures, and recklessly acting in a manner that divides and embarrasses the SACP.
> But the converse is also true, loyalty to the Party, democratic centralism and the imperative of maintaining Party unity must not be used to suppress legitimate expression of different views within the Party or to sideline comrades. This

Congress must however reaffirm the primary principles of democratic central-ism. This means that there must be free debate and flow of ideas inside the Party, but once decisions have been taken all members are bound to implement those decisions. This includes loyal implementation of these decisions by all, including those who might have argued against such decisions before they were taken.

No-one should use the excuse of inner party democracy to deliberately go against and undermine decisions that have been collectively taken by our struc-tures. Such actions are not a reflection of inner party democracy, but acts of ill-discipline. Democratic centralism also means that decisions of higher structures take precedence over, and are binding to, lower structures. But this is not an imposition, and that is why senior representatives from lower structures are always represented "ex-officio" in higher structures, as part of ensuring inner party democracy as well as ensuring lower structures do have input into higher structures [*The South African Road to Socialism* 17]!

This was the same formula used for decades by the SACP, basically saying that there would be more debate and voting within the party, but that once a deci-sion was made, almost absolute obedience to it was needed, especially from lower organs within the party. This was still basically Leninist "democratic centralism." Not sharing these internal debates was also emphasized, especially with the "bourgeois media," which the party argued cannot be trusted (which may indeed be true in the case of the SACP). This is all indeed a form of democracy (which is a broad concept), but a tad remote from the types prac-ticed by most Western parties elsewhere (or even within South Africa, like the Democratic Alliance). Still, it is not the secretive Stalinist patterns that did exist within the SACP before the early 1990s. Finally the document con-cluded that its alliance with the COSATU was closer than ever (partially due to tensions with the ANC) and that the relaunched Communist Youth League (CYL) was thriving but had some tensions with both the ANC and SACP (*The South African Road to Socialism*, 19–20).

The historic document concluded on the alliance and the ANC:

> Throughout this political report, and to a certain extent in our Draft Political Programme, we have raised the question of the centrality of our alliance in the current phase of the national democratic revolution. But at the same time we have warned that we should avoid the dangers of either mythologizing the alliance or turning it into a museum, both incapable of confronting the chal-lenges facing our NDR in the current period.
>
> Our alliance has been incredibly weakened since the adoption of GEAR in 1996, as most of our energies have been spent on disagreements rather than on a common programme. Our alliance has tended to function better during elec-tions as proven by the two election campaigns we have been involved in since our 11th Congress in 2002 [*The South African Road to Socialism* 20].

This was again surprisingly honest, showing that the SACP recognized that at least factions with the ANC have real and possibly fundamental disagreements with the SACP. And though those issues of the early 2000s were officially over by 2007, the deep-rooted factors behind them still existed. It went to the very controversial issue of Vice President Jacob Zuma, who had numerous scandals and who fought with other factions within the ANC. The SACP mostly backed Zuma (possibly due to his former communist career and/or realizing he could be the next president) and though costly at the time (since Zuma was accused of rape and corruption), it paid off as Zuma eventually became leader of the ANC and president of South Africa.

The 12th Congress also passed resolutions. Many of the points were covered by the above document, so there is no need to go into detail again. Still, some of these resolutions reflected the serious tensions between the ANC and SACP as noted above:

> 3. That the strategic Medium Term Vision (MTV) of the South African Communist Party is to secure working class hegemony in the State in its diversity and in all other sites of power.
> 4. That electoral politics are an important but not an exclusive terrain for the contesting of state power.
> 5. Working class power in the state is related to working class power in all other sites, including the imperative of developing organs of popular power, active forms of participatory democracy and social mobilisation.
> 6. That the structures of the SACP and our cadres have confronted many problems with the way in which the alliance has often functioned, particularly with regard to policy making, the lack of joint programmes on the ground, deployments and electoral list processes [*SACP 12th Congress Resolutions* 1].

The language here was a tad stronger than in some of the SACP's past pronouncements, possibly reflecting the frictions with the ANC and/or frustration with the slow pace of real social and economic changes in South Africa. It stated that there should be a "working class hegemony" and that there are other options than elections for taking power. As already noted, these can be read as using social movements to pressure the system (which is probably what was meant), or more provocatively, that the working class could seize power or create a "dual power" system like the Russian Bolsheviks did with the early soviets (workers' councils) in 1917. It is hard to know what was meant, but it is it still telling it was said publicly. Finally, the party again stated the difficulties in working with the ANC and the state organs it controlled.

The SACP went on to say how the public sector needed to be rebuilt, more investment in education and health care was needed, and finally that the SACP needed to be more independent from the ANC and the state. It declared:

that SACP cadres who are deployed as ANC elected representatives, or as public
servants must continue to owe allegiance to the Party and cannot conduct themselves in ways that are contrary to the fundamental policies, principles and values of the SACP. The same principle applies to SACP cadres in other
deployments, including within the trade union movement, community organisations, etc. [*SACP 12th Congress Resolutions* 1].

This was important: once again the SACP was making it clear that as an organization it intended to be much more autonomous from the ANC and it
expected its members to be so also. This was mostly directed at the ANC, but
it also mentions unions and civic organizations, so COSATU and others were
being warned (which was rarely done, since the SACP has had much less issues
with either of these groups than with the ANC).

The SACP then went on to make clear that though it had no intention
yet of running separately in the next set of elections, it wanted much more
say in how the campaigns would be run. It declared "that the SACP contests
state power in elections in the context of a reconfigured alliance" and proposed
"an electoral pact with our alliance partners, which could include agreement
on deployments, possible quotas, the accountability of elected representatives
including accountability of SACP cadres to the Party, the election manifesto,
and the importance of an independent face and role for the SACP and its
cadres within legislatures" (*SACP 12th Congress Resolutions* 2). These were
important steps to gain more say in campaigning, but they also could have
been the first warning signs of running separately sometime in the future.

The SACP went on to state that though South Africa had made some
progress in transforming the economy, overall fundamental change had yet
to occur. It said, "The South African economy, notwithstanding important
changes, preserves the systemic features of its formation and consolidation
within a colonial and special colonial framework" (*SACP 12th Congress Resolutions* 2). And by definition, the ANC had allowed this to happen and thus
the SACP felt a need to act more on this crucial issue. The SACP did make it
clear it knew the ANC inherited a system built on racism and inequality, but
there was still the need to make many more changes, such as an emphasis on
more manufacturing, more infrastructure spending, extensive land reform,
improved banking regulations, and more investment in educational and job
training (*SACP 12th Congress Resolutions* 3–6). It added, "In order to advance
the agenda of building working class power we need an active democratic
developmental state, buttressed by a mobilised national democratic movement
in which the working class increasingly plays a leading role. A South African
developmental state should seek to roll back the domination of the mineral

energy-finance monopoly capitalist complex" (*SACP 12th Congress Resolutions* 7).

Continuing, the SACP stressed the need for even greater strides against the entrenched patriarchy and the resulting sexism throughout South Africa. It also emphasized the role of the civic organizations here and how the SACP needed to work with them more. It noted how race, class, and gender were all intertwined throughout South African culture (*SACP 12th Congress Resolutions* 8–9). But it also talked about the SACP's role in international affairs, and how it needed to align with other progressive, socialist, and leftist actors, parties, and states to fight neoliberalism, imperialism, and antigreen forces (*SACP 12th Congress Resolutions* 10–11). Interestingly, on the environment, the SACP was against "biofuel" (due to rising food costs), for "clean coal" if done right (due to South African coal reserves), and for safe alternatives such as hydropower (as most green groups are) (*SACP 12th Congress Resolutions* 12). The positions the SACP took at this meeting would be repeated at their last one, the 13th Congress.

The SACP's last congress since the writing of this book was in 2012. This was its 13th Congress and again it made no historic changes, but continued some of the more salient trends from the last decade or so. I will review the Political Report and Declaration given (no resolutions document was issued for this congress). Again, I will offer only brief summaries since many of the issues and themes are now clear to the reader and are little different since the 10th Congress. The *Political Report* started out with the standard (though genuine) militant rhetoric and broad overview we are now familiar with:

> Indeed as we open this Congress we need to say for all to hear that we are gathered here as South African Communist Party delegates—we are alive, we are well, we are militant! Everywhere across our country, in our region and in international forums our Party's influence is to be felt. Since our 12th Congress we have more than tripled the membership of our Party and it now stands at its highest ever—at over 160 000, from 51 000 in 2007! Not only have we grown the membership of our Party but also we have grown its stature and influence, and it commands the respect of millions of the workers and poor of our country. Indeed we have to focus our discussions at this Congress on enhancing the quality of our membership...
>
> [F]ive years ago, we set ourselves very clear tasks—that of building working class hegemony and influence in all key sites of power, with the priorities being in the economy, the workplace, our communities, in the state, on the terrain of the battle of ideas and in the international sphere [*Political Report* 1].

One of the most striking things here is the large increase in membership. The SACP has indeed thrived: from having a few thousand members in 1990, to around 75,000 in the mid- to late 1990s, to an interesting decrease for awhile to 50,000 or so, and finally to the new high of 160,000. As the document itself stated, the quality of the some of the new members may be in question, but the higher quantity does show how the SACP was meeting its goal of being a mass party.

The document went on: "The key task for this Congress is to discuss how to improve the quality of our presence in all key terrains and fronts of struggle. This we call taking responsibility for the national democratic revolution—we are not a left-wing, oppositionist clique observing the unfolding struggle from the outside. We will criticize where criticism is required, but always as active revolutionary participants in the trenches of struggle" (*Political Report* 2). The party planned to attack three main issues: "In consolidating and deepening of the national democratic revolution it is absolutely essential that we anchor our struggle around tackling the triple challenge of unemployment, together with racialised and gendered poverty and inequality in our country" (*Political Report* 2). The SACP saw the ANC as in agreement: "Delegates [at the last ANC conference] agreed that what is now required is a radical shift, a second phase in the ongoing transition from Colonialism of a Special Type towards a truly united, non-racial, non-sexist, democratic South Africa. Many SACP cadres contributed actively to shaping this characterization" (*Political Report* 2). There is little doubt on the last statement that the SACP members within the ANC had been pressuring the ANC to be more radical and leftist.

How was this to be done? The SACP stated, "For the SACP building working class hegemony in all key sites of power and influence must remain the key strategic objective in the current period" and "another key feature of the second phase of the transition must be a more enhanced role of the state in economic development, incorporating strengthening the economic role of the state, not only through state owned entities, but through interventions by the state in directing the private sector towards developmental outcomes and objectives" (*Political Report* 3). This was a large pushback against the more neo-liberal privatization plans of GEAR and later the NDP.

The SACP went on to argue against half-measures, corruption within both the state and the alliance, and the threat of global capitalism and its current and deep crisis (*Political Report* 4–6). The SACP then denounced foreign influences (special interest politics, longer campaigns, etc.) on the politics of South Africa. "Our revolution is also faced with the threat of what we can call the creeping 'Americanisation' of our politics, coming from a variety of sources" (*Political Report* 6). The SACP also made clear that American notions of "the state" as "being the problem and not the solution" must be resisted. It naturally saw the growth of the state as crucial for building socialism (*Political Report* 6).

The SACP then started to restate some of its fundamental ideological positions, since it felt that others either misstated or misunderstood them:

> It is therefore important that we start reminding ourselves about who we are as the SACP. We are the political party of South Africa's working class, seeking to represent the most advanced elements from within its ranks. We are a Marxist-Leninist Party, but an African Marxist-Leninist Party. More particularly, a South African Marxist-Leninist Party, rooted in the realities and trenches of the South African revolution. We are not a Marxist-Leninist non-government organization or some sectoral workers' organization. We are a party that is deeply interested in political power, we seek to be the political organizational form of the most advanced elements of the working class [*Political Report* 8].

This was nothing new per se, as we have seen in earlier chapters, but it just showed that though the party had jettisoned its Stalinist elements more than two decades ago, it still saw itself as a Leninist party, and not some sort of social democratic one or a leftist think tank. It quoted Slovo himself on how the party should lead the working class and the working class should lead the National Democratic Revolution (NDR). Thus, the party needed to recruit more from the union movement, and not just sit within the ANC (*Political Report* 10, 11). Obviously some within the ANC saw these statements as being destabilizing and/or threatening.

But that would have been the least of the ANC's worries. The SACP then stated:

> Our 12th Congress adopted the "South African Road to Socialism" as the programme of the SACP for the next five years. At the core of SARS has been our medium term vision—building working class hegemony in all key sites of power and influence—with priority being given to building working class hegemony and influence in the state, the economy, the workplace, the community, ideologically and in the international sphere [*Political Report* 12].

Again, this statement could be seen as relatively innocent, as building up workers' influence within the alliance, or it could hint much more ominously that the SACP wants to dominate key sectors of South Africa. The ANC surely wondered about this through back channels but this would obviously not be reported. More reassuringly, the SACP then stated that regardless of some details, overall the ANC had put the state in the center of the NDR again:

> The identification of five priorities for our movement and government, the adoption of an industrial policy action plan, the New Growth Path, the NDP, notwithstanding some inadequacies—all represent important advances at a

policy level for our overall strategic tasks of transformation. Of late, the massive infrastructure plans announced by government have, at least in conceptual and policy terms, redefined the role of the state in the current phase of the national democratic revolution. underpinning these policy breakthroughs has been an assertion of the role of the state and the need to build its capacity to drive development—which is a far cry from the conceptions and practices of a minimalist state of the 1996 class project [*Political Report* 14].

This was mostly correct: the more right-wing elements of the ANC under Mbeki in the late 1990s had been replaced by more left-wing ones of Zuma, which the SACP approved.

The SACP saw the alliance as deeply rooted in communities, unions, and civics, which helped prevent it from going too astray (*Political Report* 16). Though the party showed some optimism about less privatization, less emphasis on Black Economic Empowerment (BEE) programs, more land reform, and the like, it still saw the possibility of the ANC backsliding again, as it had in the late 1990s and early 2000s (*Political Report* 18–19). It argued that the party's Red October Campaigns were effective tools against such backsliding (*Political Report* 21). With that, the SACP also stated, "It is the duty of the SACP, as custodians of progressive media to continue the critique of mainstream bourgeois media, which has now increasingly positioned itself as part of the opposition forces to our movement and government" (*Political Report* 23).

It went on to discuss its deepening ties to other leftist and/or socialist actors, parties, and states throughout the world. It again stressed Cuba and China as key international players (somewhat overstating Cuba's role). The praise towards China showed again that the last vestiges of the Sino-Soviet Split were over for the SACP (*Political Report* 23). But it also critiqued the direction of the so-called Arab Spring: it moved from being mostly a semi-progressive mass movement for democracy to often being a manipulated one, by various Western imperialist or local fundamentalist reactionary forces, depending on the country. It cited the current Syrian Civil War as an example of imperialist powers using local proxies for their own goals (*Political Report* 24). With President Obama officially backing factions within the war in the summer of 2014, this is certainly true to an extent.

The SACP went on to call for a pushback against worse work conditions, the privatization of education, and in general a rationalization of South African society for the sake of profit. It saw the need to mobilize the youth for these causes, since they have more at stake than most. It also addressed the need for much improved state health care for the people of South Africa

(*Political Report* 26–30). To do this, a systematic fight against corruption was called for. It argued that overall the capitalist system itself was corrupt and was the root of the problem. Thus, the party called for an immediate battle against conventional corruption but also renewed its call for socialism, which would fight its root causes (*Political Report* 31). Finally, the SACP went into detail on how South African land reform was needed for centuries, that apartheid only made it worse, but that not nearly enough had been done since 1994 to rectify it (*Political Report* 32–33).

The SACP then went over again its complicated relationship with its partner the ANC. Though that relationship hit a low in the early 2000s, and was seemingly on the mend since the last congress in 2007 and Zuma becoming president in 2009, there were still tensions in 2012. It stated:

> Indeed the functioning of the alliance continues to be highly uneven at subnational levels. In a number of cases it is because of tensions between the ANC and SACP structures, arising out of fights for positions and power...
>
> Although most of the problems at these levels emanate from the ANC side, some of our own SACP structures are not entirely innocent themselves. This has been the case for a very long period and this is a matter that needs to be given added priority. The key task in front of the alliance is that of ongoing mass work on the ground...
>
> The SACP is indeed satisfied with the current leadership of the ANC and the manner in which it has sought to foster and deepen the unity of the alliance. So do we also note with satisfaction some important progress made by government under the leadership of President Zuma. We can only wish that this relationship and commitment to the alliance and its improved working relationship continues and is further deepened [*Political Report* 34].

As one can see, the ANC and SACP still have some friction (especially at the local level), but one could argue that things have not been this good for more than a decade. Still, as the SACP made clear earlier in the document, it needs to be more independent and leftist as it works within the ANC.

The SACP also discussed its normally good relations with COSATU, which if anything, have gotten closer over the past decade as both fought with the ANC (though sometimes for different reasons). It stated:

> Our relationship with COSATU, overall has continued to be good, and has taken place at a number of levels. We continued to have very good relations with a number of COSATU affiliates, especially around joint cadre development initiatives as well as support for each other's campaigns. A number of COSATU affiliates have also contributed in many ways materially to the campaigns and activities of the SACP [*Political Report* 35].

But it continued:

The only issue that created serious tensions between COSATU and the SACP was that relating to the manner in which the deployment of SACP cadres was raised in the public domain without raising this matter with the SACP first. Nevertheless after bilateral discussions we managed to resolve this matter in a manner that has contributed to the further strengthening of our relations. Unfortunately the NUMSA [National Union of Metal Workers of South Africa] leadership seems to have continued to raise this matter in a manner that seems to be directed at discrediting the SACP, its leadership and its decisions, and seems to be aimed at negatively harming the image and integrity of the SACP rather than improving relations amongst ourselves. We have told NUMSA in a very forthright manner that it is not the custodian of the decisions of the SACP, nor should it seek to act as such in future. As the SACP however, and as the vanguard Party of the working class, we must not allow ourselves to be irritated and diverted by some of this behaviour, but instead we need to be focused on strengthening relations with COSATU and all its affiliates. We all know that enemies of the working class will always attempt to drive a wedge between communists and the labour movement. We must protect this relationship with all we have [*Political Report* 35].

This referred to NUMSA more than COSATU per se, though the former is part of the latter. NUMSA was known for being more radical and promoting wildcat strikes, which the alliance usually did not approve of (especially the ANC but also the SACP). As the SACP stated, one of the bigger issues here was not the specifics of this situation (which involved strikes and the ANC), but how NUMSA attacked the SACP publicly. Also, the SACP argued that *it* led the working class, not any one union or even COSATU; obviously COSATU and its unions might disagree on this point. As noted before, this issue got so serious that NUMSA suggested forming a "working class party" at one point. The SACP obviously saw no need for another party of the proletariat, and more politically, perceived such talk as a threat (though not yet a serious one) (Masondo 1). Still, the SACP and NUMSA did agree on some issues, such as the NDP being centrist and harmful for the country.

The SACP went on to discuss whether the South African National Civics Organisation (SANCO) should be formally brought into the alliance [*Political Report* 36]. Though the alliance has always backed the work of the civics (various civil society organizations that fought apartheid), SANCO itself was not part of the alliance. The alliance of the ANC, SACP, and COSATU had a decades-long history, and bringing in any new partner would be complicated and politically problematic. This SANCO issue would not be resolved at this congress.

The SACP turned to the issue of its increased size and influence, and how this was mostly for the best but how it attracted the attention of its enemies. It stated:

Since 2007 our membership has grown and the stature and influence of the SACP over this period has also increased. Whilst our class enemies and detractors have continued to belittle us, they know that the reasons for attempting to do as such is because they are deeply worried about the continuing growth and influence of the SACP. Precisely as an attempt to try and isolate and therefore weaken us, they continually goad us to stand on our own, to move out of the alliance and go our own way. It is as if being part of the alliance is not going our own way. They goad us in this direction precisely because they are scared of our influence and as one of those few parties that have continued to grow despite the collapse of the Soviet Union [*Political Report* 37].

As this whole book has argued, the SACP is unique amongst surviving communist parties after the collapse of communism. Some adapted and become social democratic parties, others disbanded, and most just faded from influence. The SACP has indeed been special in how it has stayed both communist but also politically influential. The SACP went on to explain how it was a political school for the alliance, how it helped build up the unions, and how it has always presented a leftist perspective for new public policy. But it also made clear that those things are not as important as being the leader of the working class and building socialism. It then argued, "Party building must also be informed by the absolute necessity to build independent Party presence and influence in the various fronts of struggle and society as a whole" (*Political Report* 37). Since the early 2000s, the SACP started pushing over and over the issue of independence from the alliance and especially the ANC. This, at the least, shows a widening between the SACP and its partners. At the most, it could be preparation for full independence and even running separately in the elections, though again, this seems far off.

The 13th Congress wrapped up with a declaration:

We, 2000 Communist militants, have met over the past four days as delegates to the SACP's 13th National Congress in Ongoye, KwaZulu-Natal. We are drawn from 3,298 SACP branches across the length and breadth of our country and from the ranks of the Young Communist League of South Africa. As delegates, we represent more than 150,000 SACP members—marking an unprecedented three-fold increase in the Party's membership since our 12th Congress just five years ago [*Declaration of the 13th Congress* 1].

The party was obviously proud of its growth in the 2000s, and as pointed out before, having 160,000 members in 2012 was impressive. The SACP went on from there to decry the global "Great Recession" that had started in 2008 and how it had added misery to South Africa, which was already struggling with it legacy of Colonialism of a Special Type. It declared that these values helped it fight for South Africa in such hard times:

Our disciplined unity in the midst of an alliance facing many challenges; our Marxism-Leninism; our principled commitment to Communist values of solidarity and to fighting all negative tendencies—including individualism, self-enrichment, and corruption—all these attributes of the SACP and its cadres place an enormous vanguard responsibility upon us, now more than ever [*Declaration of the 13th Congress* 1].

Much of that is common leftist rhetoric, but it is refreshing to read how the party was still openly Marxist-Leninist and even anti-individualism, something few leftist parties would even hint at in the West. It then stated in conclusion:

As we rise, today, at the conclusion of the largest ever, and one of the most united congresses of the Communist Party in South Africa, we declare once more that
SOCIALISM IS THE FUTURE!
WE ARE NOT WAITING FOR THAT FUTURE—WE ARE ACTIVELY BUILDING THAT FUTURE, HERE AND NOW!! [*Declaration of the 13th Congress* 2].

This was an appropriate way to wrap up a communist congress, dedicated to changing South Africa at its very core. Though the SACP has fought consistently for some sort of socialist future since 1994, we have seen how it has had serious setbacks with its own partner, the ANC. From the late 1990s to the early 2000s, especially under President Mbeki, the alliance was definitely strained. But after two key conferences with the ANC, and, more to the point, the election of the ex–SACP member Zuma to the South African presidency, such issues mostly ended. The SACP still did not fully get its way with the development of the NDP, but it certainly influenced the debate.

Conclusion

What does the future hold for the SACP? The SACP has adapted to a severely changing (and occasionally hostile) environment. First and foremost, it had to adapt to the fact that it was no longer an illegal, underground party. Then it had to take on the (ironic) role of often being the "moderate" in the negotiations between the nationalists and the ANC. This has included navigating the changes in the ANC leadership and their public policy (RDP to GEAR to NDP). Finally, while it performed those transformations, it also recreated itself, moving from a Stalinist, underground party to a democratic, mass-based communist party.

The lifting of the ban on the party was of course to the SACP's advantage, but it presented numerous problems. It forced the left and right wings of the party to settle some long-running debates once and for all. For decades, the party had been guided by Joe Slovo and his clique. As outlined here and in other chapters, his then moderate faction pushed for a negotiated settlement with the nationalist regime. This was unpopular with the far leftists (Stalinists), such as Harry Gwala and Blade Nzimande, who argued that such a settlement would leave the vast majority of South Africa's population under capitalist rule (which was accurate but seemingly inevitable). Until the ban was lifted, such debates became academic since the SACP could do little one way or another. Once the negotiations with the NP started, this debate became very real.

The moderate Slovo did win and personally help create both the Sunset Clauses that gave much to the nationalists even if the NP lost the would-be All Race Elections (which, of course, it did) (van Heerden 5). These clauses, though, allowed such elections in the first place and defused any chance of a civil war. The structures and policies of the SACP were also shaped by the moderates within the party. Though they tarnished some of the SACP's hard-earned reputation of being a "hardcore communist organization," that was the point. Slovo knew that if the party was to survive, it would have to become a mass-based, democratic leftist party.

This transformation is still incomplete, but significant progress has been made. There are still elements within the party that are not devoted to a fully Western democratic South Africa, even as a stepping-stone to socialism. It is also true that the party itself still retains fragments of its Leninist democratic-centralist past. Overall, though, the SACP has transformed itself. It has also become much more democratic and open to public scrutiny. Finally, the public has started to accept this "new" SACP for what it is: a legitimate player within the pluralist system of the new South Africa.

Conclusion

This book set out to show how a communist party could not only survive the collapse of communism, but also even thrive. The SACP used both domestic and international events to increase both its political base and its power in the ANC-led regime. The SACP's huge increase in membership and its all-important alliance with the ANC are the two most salient aspects of the SACP's successful strategy to remain relevant. How did the SACP accomplish this?

To a certain extent, the fact that historic domestic affairs overshadowed other significant international events allowed the SACP to be "reborn" during a period of extraordinary change during the late 1980s and early 1990s. If in 1989 the rightwing and hardcore nationalist president P.W. Botha had held on for at least another decade, the new South Africa would have been put off for at least that long, if not longer. This would have meant that what was then the underground SACP would have had to face the collapse of communism in a totally different, and more difficult, context. Instead of having numerous new domestic bases of support to call upon, the SACP would have been small, isolated, and still hunted as "International Communism," its sole supporter, disappeared. The SACP might have survived such a transition, but it would have had a much harder time doing so. Without global support, the SACP would have faced the darkest time in its long, hard history. If the inverse had happened, the SACP would have also faced a very different future.

If the ban on the SACP had been lifted in 1990, but International Communism had not collapsed, the new South Africa might have been reshaped very differently. Instead of the reforming *and* reformist SACP aiding its centrist ally the ANC in the early 1990s, the still relatively Stalinist SACP would probably have been a negative influence on the ANC and the all-important negotiations with the nationalists. Thus a historic moment might have been missed by everyone in South Africa. Even to consider briefly these two alternative scenarios makes it clear how both the international and domestic changes positively affected the fate of the SACP.

In the final analysis, it seems that domestic events were the greater of the two key sets of factors affecting the SACP in the last decade. On the one hand, though the collapse of communism did push the SACP towards even greater reforms, the SACP had already shown signs of change in the mid-to-late 1980s, before anyone suspected that International Communism would soon cease to exist. Also, even without any internal reforms, the SACP would have played at least a similar role in the events that led up to the 1994 All Race Elections in South Africa. In other words, even a "Stalinist" SACP would have aided the ANC in its talks with the National Party in the early 1990s, though it would not have been as flexible or helpful.

On the other hand, regardless of the fate of International Communism, if the ban on the SACP and ANC had not been lifted in 1990, the history of the SACP and all of South Africa would have been much different. Being forced to stay an underground party would not only have slowed any reforms within the SACP, but may have even hardened it. The ANC would of course not be ruling South Africa and thus everything would be different for the SACP. Naturally, all of this is speculative, but it seems that domestic changes were the more significant of the two.

Still, external factors, whether domestic or international, were only one aspect in the transformation of the SACP from a small, cadre-based revolutionary organization into a modern, mass-based democratic party. These external shocks did shape the reforms that the SACP self-initiated, but in the end it was the SACP that reformed itself and without direct prompting from any other actors. On the international front, the Communist Party of the Soviet Union (CPSU) under Gorbachev may have served as some sort of role model for a while, but relations had become so strained by 1991 that the CPSU played no direct role in the transformation of the SACP (and by then, the CPSU was hardly a role model for any other party as it imploded). On the domestic front, the ANC did play a role in the SACP's changes, but also only indirectly. Though it seems that some of the more moderate SACP leaders also had strong ANC ties, overall this connection did not play a major role. Slovo, Hani, Cronin, and their ilk were the major "liberal" reformers of the SACP, and there is no evidence that any of them were pressured by ANC leaders to remake the SACP. Naturally, their exposure to the more moderate and centrist ANC was important, but that exposure was seemingly no more than an influence, not a catalyst or guiding hand.

With this in mind, one must conclude that international, domestic, and internecine factors all played a role in the SACP's survival and transformation. The internal factors should not be underestimated. Though the external shocks certainly mattered, if the SACP had not been ready for change, events would surely have turned out differently. The SACP could have been marginalized by state repression, or it might have converted itself into a social-democratic party (which almost happened), or it could have just slowly faded away as a weak parasite, living off its host the ANC. What did happen was that several key decisions were taken by a more liberal faction within the party, decisions which allowed the party to grow in a challenging environment.

When International Communism started to break up in the late 1980s, the SACP almost immediately distanced itself from the CPSU. At first, this actually may have been more of a knee-jerk Stalinist reaction to Gorbachev's "liberal" reforms than some far-sighted and informed move. But this critical stance quickly became a more analytical attack on poorly thought-out CPSU reforms that the SACP accurately predicted would fail. The SACP especially condemned the "regional settlements" initiatives that the Foreign Department of the CPSU was pushing throughout the world, including southern Africa. The SACP correctly concluded that these settlements helped the USSR far more than its former local allies, such as the ANC-SACP alliance. The SACP did not end there in its criticism of its former patron, but became distracted when its ban was lifted after forty long years.

President De Klerk's sudden (and cunning) political move to legitimize all the formerly illegal and underground parties changed everything for the SACP within South Africa. As International Communism collapsed, the SACP suddenly found itself legalized and faced with unprecedented challenges and opportunities. Though being legal and "above ground" had self-evident advantages, it also meant that the small, secretive cadre-based party would have to adapt. Communist parties that had been persecuted in the past had transformed themselves (i.e., Eurocommunism), but the SACP faced some unique hurdles. It was smaller than many other communist parties, even other underground ones. It was also far more Stalinist than most other communist parties of the 1980s and 1990s. Thus, between its structural and ideological disadvantages, the SACP had much to transform to stay relevant.

As it turned out, the SACP was up to the task. As it began to condemn first Gorbachev and then Yeltsin (for different reasons), the SACP also started to plan and then quickly implement internal reforms. At the 7th Congress in the late 1980s it hinted at such changes, but at the 8th and especially 9th congresses, the SACP completed its own metamorphosis, and later congresses would solidify these improvements. It moved away from the conspiratorial, cell-based model on which it had relied for forty years to become a more mass-based, semi-open party. Notwithstanding these changes, the SACP is still not quite a "normal Western party"; it still has secretive elements and it still relies heavily on its symbiotic relationship with the ANC. It also seriously calls for a socialist future for South Africa, which should never be forgotten. Still, the party did effect real and significant structural changes and purged its Stalinist roots.

The SACP, once one of the most Stalinist and pro–Soviet communist parties in the "Third World," denounced Stalinism, the CPSU, and its own mistakes at its 9th Congress in 1995. It admitted that it had been too dogmatic, too blindly loyal to the CPSU, and finally, out of touch with local factors. However, when the dust settled after a short power struggle between "Stalinists" (Gwala, Blade) and "Liberals" (Slovo, Hani, Cronin), the party decided to abandon Stalinism but also reject "reformist" social-democracy to adopt a middle position which I call neo–Leninism. It reached back to its earliest roots, before Stalinism corrupted International Communism and the SACP. It recast itself as a traditional Marxist-Leninist party, but one that voluntarily accepted the new parliamentary system that was being created around it (something more orthodox Marxists could even accept).

Though the SACP, even the liberal faction, still reserves the right to use violence to overthrow capitalism in South Africa, at this stage it has committed itself to a nonviolent, democratic route to power. Just as International Communism was disappearing, the first All Race Elections were being planned for South Africa. As the SACP escaped the collapse of communism, it prepared for a brave new future within a nonracial, democratic South Africa.

These extraordinary events occurred in less than a decade. The SACP dodged an international disaster and took advantage of a historic domestic event, all without losing much of its own unique character. Still, the SACP faces significant hurdles in both the near and far future. The ANC-SACP alliance has held state power since 1994, and though there is still no fundamental weakening of this alliance, the SACP must decide what it is to do in this next phase in South Africa's transformation. Since 1994, it has played the role of the loyal (if not sometimes critical) leftist ally of the ruling party; this arrangement has worked surprisingly well for both parties (though it did hit a low point in the early 2000s). The SACP will continue to play this role indefinitely, but in both the short and long term it faces major decisions regarding its alliance with the ever more centrist ANC.

The SACP still sees the National Democratic Revolution (NDR) happening in two stages. The first is the current one, where the local, progressive bourgeois nationalist party (ANC) takes control from the colonial power (in this case, the domestic Afrikaners) and starts to correct the more egregious wrongs that exist (such as apartheid). On this level, the ANC has done an outstanding job by dismantling the decades-long system of racism with relatively little violence or upset. Still, the larger issues of economic disparity between white and black and rich and poor remain; plus, the ANC seems to have few permanent answers for these problems. The SACP, though, believes it does.

During this first stage, the SACP will continue to aid the ANC in transforming the country as much a possible within a democratic-capitalist context. Sooner or later, though, the SACP will need to start to significantly distance itself from the admittedly multiclass ANC and its centrist public policies. From strikes to education to privatization schemes, the SACP already disagrees with the ANC. These differences will only grow unless the ANC and/or the SACP change their fundamental positions, and neither shows signs of doing that.

With the second stage, when socialism is actually started, the SACP sees itself forced to distance itself from the ANC (again, unless the ANC changes radically, which is unlikely). What this means exactly is unclear, but it is self-evident that during this latter stage the Marxist-Leninist SACP will have to break with its more moderate partner. How and when this will happen is not even hinted at by the SACP, but in its literature and in candid interviews with the author, the SACP is clear that it wishes to build true socialism in South Africa, which no multiclass alliance will ever do. Only a revolutionary workers' party, which the SACP sees itself to be, can accomplish this historic and daunting task. Thus, it is obvious that the ANC-SACP alliance is inevitably doomed, at least if it stays on its current course.

Such a fate, though, is far off, even according to the SACP. In the meantime the first stage, which stresses cooperation and compromise, will continue. During this lengthy period (possibly decades more), the alliance will probably continue with few major disagreements. There have been hints by the SACP that it may even run *separately* in elections from the ANC in the future. If this happens, it indeed could be the beginning of the end of the alliance. Still, even such a step remains largely speculative. With the nation and the ANC led by someone other than the almost universally respected Mandela (neither Mbeki nor Zuma were of equal stature), the SACP now faces hard choices. In the past the party proved to be able to deal with such turning points, and judging from all the available evidence, it seems to be preparing to confront such choices once again.

Chapter Notes

Introduction

1. The SACP was historically referred to as the Communist Party of South Africa (CPSA). The name change occurred after its banning and major reorganization in the 1950s. I use SACP throughout the book unless context dictates that the name CPSA should be noted.

2. This issue is not to deny that communism still exists throughout Asia (China, Vietnam, North Korea, and so forth). Not only are these states not aligned with one another, but for many historical reasons they have often been considered separate from the communist world of the East Bloc—except in the 1950s, when they were artificially and incorrectly linked together in a monolithic bloc of communist nations.

3. The *Broederbond*, formed in the early 20th century, was a semisecret society of Afrikaner Boer leaders dedicated to advancing the interests of the country's Afrikaner population. Many top cultural, economic, social and political Afrikaners were members. This society helped engineer the National Party's electoral victory in 1948 and remained a secretive "advisory council" to the regime for the next forty years. It was weakened by the NP's reforms during the 1980s and officially dissolved by the time of 1994 All Race Elections.

4. The SACP even shares COSATU's large and fortress-like headquarters in Johannesburg, which I was able to visit in 1995 to do research.

5. Though there is a now a Russian Communist Party, and various other communist parties and organizations throughout the Russian Federation, the historic CPSU was dissolved by Yeltsin and Gorbachev soon after the 1991 coup.

Chapter 1

1. This mostly refers to the Marxism of the western European intellectuals who opposed the "revisionism" of both Eduard Bernstein, who stood for a more reformist Marxism, and Lenin, who called for more radical and conspiratorial Marxism (McLellan, Chapter 1; Gwala 1991, 7).

2. One example of this that comes to mind is the Shining Path guerrilla group in Peru, which claims to be Marxist though it recruits peasants in a developing nation and funds its revolution with drug deals; Maoist would be a better description (Strong 1992). This is hardly the workers' revolution that Marx envisioned. As Laqueur stated, "At first sight, Marxism-Leninism is an unlikely doctrine for providing spiritual guidance to the Third World" (Laqueur 18).

3. Though, of course, there have been and are many leftists, parties, and organizations that denounce Leninism while still being Marxist, such as Rosa Luxembourg's revolutionary organization of 1920s and the Socialist Labor Party of America today.

4. It is a well-known fact that even the term "Leninism" was created by Stalin after Lenin's death (though Lenin himself had distorted orthodox Marxism for years before his passing). Stalin would go on to create a cult of personality around the founder of the Soviet system for his own political needs (Ulam, Chapter 7). Though by the end of Stalin's reign these phenomena would be known collectively as Marxism-Leninism-Stalinism, the latter name would drop away almost immediately after Stalin's death, the term once again becoming Marxism-Leninism (Medvedev 66). Still, the unique and unorthodox contributions of Stalin

to "Leninism," such as "Socialism in One Country" (which Lenin would never have espoused, being a dedicated internationalist) remained part of the Soviet definition of Marxism-Leninism.

5. Leon Trotsky, Bolshevik latecomer and archnemesis of Stalin, wrote far more on this subject. He referred to the effects of "combined and uneven development" as allowing a relatively backward nation such as Russia to have a socialist revolution. He discussed how Russia, though mostly a peasant nation, had huge concentrations of proletariat in relatively modern plants due to foreign capital investment, and how this created an explosive class situation which would allow Russia to leapfrog over western Europe in a revolutionary sense.

6. As noted above, the party was also called the Communist Party of South Africa (CPSA) before 1950. I use SACP in most cases, regardless of the time period, since the name change involved no splintering of the party or other effects and therefore has no political significance.

7. The SACP origins were in geographically spread out socialist and leftist discussion groups, socialist and communist parties, and other organizations (Johns 1994, 13–15).

8. Ironically, the SACP was hardly acknowledged by the Comintern until 1928. It was oddly grouped under the same branch of the Comintern that handled the "African American Problem," apparently because both dealt with "Africans" (Johns 1975, 212–213). The fact that the U.S. and South Africa had little to do with each other meant little to an already parochial and Soviet-dominated Comintern. Such ignorance of local conditions only grew worse as years passed and the Comintern became a sad extension of Soviet foreign policy, instead of the instrument of world revolution that it was created to be.

9. The SACP was mainly a workers' party at first, which meant that it recruited mostly whites, who made up the majority of the industrial proletariat at the time. As a former chair of the SACP stated, "Under the circumstances prevailing in South Africa at the time, it was inevitable that it was whites who would take the lead in the formation of a Communist Party" (Dadoo 32). This resulted in a seemingly racist move when it backed the 1922 Rand mine strike, for one of the demands of the white mine workers was not to allow blacks into the mines (which would supposedly lower wages and displace white jobs). The SACP

later admitted that such a position was improper, regardless of the fact that the (white) working class demanded it (Ellis and Sechaba 22).

10. Though, as we shall see in detail in later chapters, it has *never* been made clear if the SACP is to peacefully co-opt the ANC or forcibly overthrow it, when the "objective conditions" call for a "move to socialism." Naturally, the SACP was unclear on this subject when asked about it by the author (Cronin AT interview, 1995).

11. As we shall explore at length in Chapter 4, the SACP did not fully condemn Stalinism until 1991.

12. This process lasted for years as Wolton and his clique purged the SACP. These purges, though, ended at the 7th World Congress of the Comintern, "which marked a crushing defeat for dogmatic, ultraleft tendencies in the communist movement" (Lerumo 71–75).

13. Though what is now called South Africa has had some form of racist regime since the Dutch landed in 1652, the coming to power of the National Party in 1948 crystalized Afrikaner political power and allowed for the formal creation of Grand Apartheid ("separate development"). Under earlier Dutch or English rule, the racism had been mostly informal, local, and/or ad hoc in its administration.

14. This is not to say that the SACP controlled the ANC at this point, or at any point. As Chapter 3 will detail, the SACP *never* controlled the ANC; at most it influenced the ANC's highest circles, and even this was not the case most of the time.

15. It should be pointed out that the "Unlawful Organizations Bill" or "Suppression of Communism Act" literally stated that all parties and organizations that agitated for any form of "social change" could be defined as "communist" (Lerumo 89). Not only was this obviously an incorrect definition of communism, but it meant that even liberal opposition to the regime, in the form of the Progressive Federal Party (PFP) and its successor the Democratic Party (DP), would be at times branded "communist," though they espoused a more free-market-oriented form of capitalism than even the nationalists ("FW, There's One Thing..." 1992b, 3).

16. At first, the MK prided itself in not attacking any "soft targets," concentrating on economic ones such as power plants. In 1995, I even visited one of the plants that had been attacked and was then fortified. But as the ini-

tial successes of the early 1960s wore off, the MK more and more turned to the use of violence against soft targets, such as soldiers with civilian casualties sometimes (Lodge 1983, 284). This was used effectively by the nationalist regime to turn many white liberals against the ANC and SACP.

17. For years, the chief of staff of MK was none other than Joe Slovo, probably the most famous communist in South Africa by the 1990s (Lodge 1983, 239). As Daniels added, "[Slovo] is still generally regarded as the *éminence grise* and master tactician behind the ANC's drive for complete ascendancy.... [But he] was polite, mild-mannered and affable, even avuncular" (Daniels 20). Even some in the black population, much of whom admired MK for its resistance against the racist nationalists, were shocked to learn in 1990 that Slovo was *white*, since MK was known to be a "black organization." Of course, there have been rumors for decades that Slovo was an officer in the Soviet KGB and though this has been denied, Laqueur was right when he said, "The KGB is an important tool in the penetration and consolidation of Soviet influence" (Laqueur 1983, 37).

18. Not unlike the legendary Bolsheviks, the SACP was also penetrated by police spies regardless of all the security precautions it took. Starting with the huge setback of the Rivonia Trial in 1960, the nationalist security forces would constantly harass the SACP (Vermaak 115–116). Even the leaders of the SACP admitted that they greatly underestimated the effectiveness and ruthlessness of the nationalist secret police (Lerumo 108). Still, the SACP did have extensive security, especially compared to the ANC. As Weyl claimed, "By the early 1960s, the South African Communist Party was efficiently organized on an illegal basis" (Weyl 117).

19. Leninism is not simply another name for Stalinism (although some authors feel it is), but Leninism can create ideological and structural foundations for a totalitarian regime such as Stalin built (Frost 2).

20. Leon Trotsky, exiled CPSU leader, makes one of the best critiques of the concept of "Socialism in One Country" in his attack of the whole Stalinist Soviet system, *Revolution Betrayed*. He argued convincingly, and almost with prescience, that if the Russian socialist revolution did not spread to western Europe, it would not be able to sustain itself except through crude, dictatorial methods that would

eventually fail. Trotsky only underestimated the timing in his calculations (and the ruthlessness that Stalin would use to hunt him down and brutally murder him through a secret agent).

21. Though the SACP has never bought into personality cults per se and even officially denounced them at times, they have treated their martyred leaders in a more than just respectful manner (though western parties at times do this also; see U.S. Republicans and their treatment of Ronald Reagan). I saw evidence of this at the 9th Party Congress, where numerous posters bore the portraits of both Joe Slovo and Chris Hani, the party's two greatest leaders. Still, when I asked for a photo of Deputy General Secretary Jeremy Cronin after an interview, he stated that they disapproved of such things because of the "cult issue" (Cronin AT interview, 1995).

22. Ironically, the Chinese Communist Party condemned this "de–Stalinization" campaign of Khrushchev's, calling the Soviets "revisionists" and reserving the right to see Stalin as a "great man of history." This was, of course, due to the fact that Chairman Mao himself had taken on much of Stalin's cult of personality and did not want to delegitimize his own rule by condemning Stalin's (Kautsky 1968, 97–98).

23. The lifting of the ban was a shock to the SACP and the general public (Cronin 1992, 41). Though there had been secret talks between the ANC and the regime since the mid–1980s, lifting the ban on the SACP was another thing entirely. Communism was often portrayed as "the root of all evil" in South Africa, with everything being blamed on it (or on communism's "fellow travelers"). But the regime had no choice, for as shown in Chapter 3, the ANC and SACP are intimately intertwined and lifting the ban on one and not the other would have been nearly impossible.

24. The former Italian Communist Party (PCI) is a perfect example of this issue. Since it already was a long-standing member of the moderate Eurocommunist tradition, it was relatively easy for it to rename itself and move to its current left-of-center position after the collapse of communism.

25. The openness may have been unprecedented for the SACP, but there was still a staged atmosphere to some elements of that Congress. I must admit, though, that the work sessions that took place at the 9th Congress were not only open to debate, but I was allowed full access to many heated discussions (9th

Congress AT, 1995). Still, Mokonyane, a vocal leftist critic of the alliance, added, "The ANC has never operated democratically, and the Stalinists in SACP have never even aspired to" (Mokonyane 78). But no one can deny there is *more* democracy within the SACP since its reforms began, and few political parties have full democracy, even in the West. This can be seen in the U.S. by Tea Party critiques of the Republican Party and its lack of real internal democracy in recent years.

26. Some leftist critics would deny this point, seeing the party as just plain selling out to the capitalists: "The SACP, particularly, is neither nationalist nor socialist nor communist—neither revolutionary nor reformist (in the radical sense). It is dead wood with a lot of creatures imbedded" (Mokonyane 125).

27. Some critics do not believe that this socialist stage will ever come, at least with the ANC/SACP in power: "The SACP ... is pretending that the sell-out this time is alright [*sic*] because it is the first stage of the insanity called 'a two stage theory' ... after this, the big one, socialism, it is alleged, will be reached. The idiocy is to jettison the real one in order to clasp at a sick man's dream"; and "even the never-learning SACP will soon realise that their Two Stage Theory is fallacious and unscientific" (Mokonyane 85, 98).

28. It should be noted that before its banning in 1950, the SACP was indeed an open and mass party, in name if nothing else, and won a few seats in the Cape Province Assembly (Ellis and Sechaba 21).

29. For months in 1995, I was gently rebuffed by the SACP's Head Office secretary when requesting lists of SACP officeholders during the 1980s, seemingly for security reasons since other, admittedly less sensitive information had readily been provided by the party whenever requested. Since then, the SACP has been more open on such issues.

30. Slovo, speaking for the party, reserved the right to reject democracy: "There may be moments in the life of a revolution which justify a postponement of full democratic processes" (Slovo 1990, 39).

31. Yet, as late as 1992, Slovo stated, "The ANC remains a mass nationalist movement ... the ANC does and should not demand a commitment to a Socialist South Africa as a precondition to membership. [The SACP, on the other hand,] is not a mass movement; it represents the aspirations of a single class—the proletariat" (Bundy 54). While a mass party (like

the new SACP) is not a mass movement (like the UDF of the 1980s), Slovo's comments do show that backing a multiclass party like the ANC can create fundamental conflicts for the SACP.

32. The SACP reaffirmed its belief in this mode of analysis as late as the 1989 "Path to Power" program (Lodge 1983, 173).

33. The argument was made not through high-level theory but mostly though empirical evidence, showing that one of the core axioms of this Leninist theory, that the industrialized nations extract raw goods and sell processed ones to the developing world at a high profit margin, is simply not the case. Numerous works have also shown that this rather simplistic assumption that imperialism causes war is also incomplete, if not just plain incorrect at times (Smith 25–66). This is not to say that there is no exploitation between the West and other nations, or that wars are never fought over resources, just that it can be much more complex than this earlier conception of it argued.

34. The Eurocommunist parties, ever since their inception in the 1970s, have steadily moved away from all aspects of Leninism, including its theories on imperialism. They still often take an anti–American stance due to vestiges of this theory, but they do not speak of the ills of imperialism as they used to.

35. Some Black nationalists in South Africa overtly ignore the fact that liberal Western whites (especially in Northern Europe) led the boycotts and embargoes against the nationalist regime in the 1980s. Still, after decades of ignoring apartheid and even having strategic trade agreements, Western liberals must have been seen as a little late to the party on opposing racism in South Africa to such Black nationalists.

36. The once powerful Afrikaner *Broederbond* was formed to fight British economic power. Its members saw such entities as the Masons and "International Jewry" as a threat (Goodwin and Schiff 175, 209).

37. Stalin dissolved the Comintern during World War II to prove to his capitalist allies that he did not really want their countries overthrown in communist revolutions (at least for the duration of the war). This passage, from the decree dissolving it, is telling: "Any sort of international centre was bound to encounter insuperable obstacles in a working class movement ... [the Comintern] has even become a hindrance to the further strengthening of the

national working class parties" (*South African Communists Speak* 179–180). It was a hindrance to Soviet foreign policy during the war. Needless to say, soon after this declaration, the SACP agreed with this decision.

38. These ties started in the early 1920s, as this passage from an early SACP manifesto shows: "The party will derive great strength and inspiration from its connection with the world communist international, as presented by the Russian Communist Party" (Lerumo 120).

39. All Comintern parties had to adhere to the twenty-one points of the Comintern declaration, of which one included opposing capitalist imperialism. And as Johns added, "The CPSA never questioned the ultimate authority of the Comintern" (Johns 1975, 207).

40. The survivors include China, North Korea, Vietnam, and Cuba (dismissing "socialist" and/or "far left" nations such as Venezuela). Vietnam and Cuba, longtime allies of the Soviet Union, still have close ties to the SACP (9th Congress AT, 1995). Still, the West has always seemed to ignore these communist nations as evidence that communism did not completely collapse in the 1990s.

41. Many of which attended their 9th Congress in Johannesburg in 1995. Most spoke of a need to maintain ties during this "hard time" for leftism throughout the world (9th Congress AT, 1995).

42. The nationalist regime made the assumption with some justification that the SACP was part of some huge international communist network, especially since during the 1930s Comintern agents literally controlled aspects of SACP policy (Lerumo 71–75). By the time the Nationalist Party came to power in the late 1940s, though, this would no longer be the case, let alone decades later.

43. Hani went so far as so say in 1991, "We see ourselves as a democratic-socialist party" (Goodman 13). Such sentiments were rejected by a surprising but short resurgence of the more Stalinist elements in the party. The seemingly powerful duet of both Slovo and Hani were outvoted at the 8th Congress when they pushed for a formal declaration of "social democracy" ("Eighth Party Congress..." 1). Of course, as Laqueur stated, "According to official Soviet sources communist parties are working class (in theory, if not always in practice), Marxist-Leninist, and democratic-centralist ... lower on the scale are the revolutionary-democratic parties" (Laqueur 1983, 6). The

more Stalinist elements in the SACP clearly agreed with this assessment.

44. The early SACP even became entrapped in the racial politics of South African capitalism. As mentioned, it supported a "white strike" in the 1920s, where one of the demands of the white mine strikers was *not* to allow lower-paid blacks into the mines, which the bosses wanted to lower production costs (Ellis and Sechaba 14). Since that strike, and the fateful Comintern 1928 decision, the SACP has avoided such unsightly racial entanglements, arguing that capitalism is to blame for most of South Africa's race problems. Thus, it argues, eliminate capitalism and the race problem will solve itself eventually.

45. Thanks to the over-enthusiastic purges by Comintern agents of all "rightist" elements within the SACP, such acts crippled the SACP for a decade and aided it in becoming a classical Stalinist party, which it mostly stayed until the mid–1980s (Lerumo 72).

46. The SACP lent fighters via MK to help leftist forces in Angola and Namibia during the 1970s and 1980s (Ellis and Sechaba 89).

47. Besides its long affiliation with the ANC, the SACP also joined the Congress of the Democrats in the 1950s and the United Democratic Front (UDF) of the 1980s (Lerumo 196; Molapo 20).

48. The ANC/SACP alliance will be further examined in the next chapter, but the more leftist factions within the SACP did object to the ANC suspending guerrilla activities but maintained party discipline when the SACP decided to back this ANC decision. But as a more Stalinist member of the party asks, "What happened to armed struggle?" (Moloba 16). It should be noted that the radical Pan Africanist Congress (PAC) remained an advocate of violent revolution, condemning the ANC's position as a "sell-out" even after the All Race Election of 1994.

49. Ironically, MK Chief of Staff Chris Hani was probably the greatest asset that MK ever "gave" the SACP. After rising in MK and the SACP simultaneously but gaining fame in the former, he became the most popular leader of the SACP in the late 1980s and early 1990s until his assassination by a Polish right-wing zealot in 1993 (Taylor).

50. It is unclear what conditions would force the SACP to take up violence again, especially now that their ally the ANC exclusively runs the government since the ending of the Government of National Unity (GNU) in

May 1996. Obviously, they could be referring to the overthrow of the ANC regime itself, but the SACP would have no reason to admit that at this point.

51. The SACP Central Committee itself admitted in 1992 that such terms have historical "symbolic meaning" and therefore need to be kept for that reason alone ("Eighth Party Congress..." 1). Of course, no one disagreed that such terms are symbolic, but that is the point, for they have both positive *and* negative connotations, to say the least.

52. Some within the SACP disagreed with this commitment: "Given the nature of the ANC now, it will never support the insurrectionary approach ... but the SACP should support it because it is the path to power" (Molaba 20). Obviously, the writer also had doubts that the SACP would rebel against its seemingly more conservative ally, the ANC.

53. This commitment to democracy was seriously questioned by the Nationalists, most whites, and even many blacks due to the very undemocratic behavior and human rights abuses the ANC demonstrated in its military camps in Angola and elsewhere (Ellis and Sechaba 28). The ANC still defends most of its behavior in these camps as necessary discipline within a military context. This issue has yet to be fully settled, though after decades it is no longer brought up on a regular basis and the SACP was not seriously touched by it.

54. Such support for apparent class enemies was not even disapproved of by the Soviets; as a matter of fact, they ordered it. "The SACP's theory of a two-phase struggle corresponds with Moscow's [plans]" (Legum 112).

55. This party power was given to it in both the so-called Stalin Constitution of 1936 and the revised Constitution of 1977. This guarantee was reversed voluntarily by the Gorbachev regime and practically erased from history after the 1991 coup that allowed Boris Yeltsin to actually *ban* the CPSU from politics (Lebedev 2–3).

56. Mervyne Frost agreed, "There are embedded in Lenin's theory of state and society understandings that if acted upon would tend to erode democratic practices and favour the emergence of one party rule" (Frost 2).

57. This view is opposed by such former Stalinists as Blade Nzimande, who argue that civil society and its organizations are only part of the capitalist stage of history, and therefore simply cannot be the perfect tool for bringing about socialism (though he does not deny their

importance in other ways, such as reaching out to the masses) (Nzimande 65–71).

58. This issue was, of course, totally denied by the National Party for decades, since it has always seen the ANC, unions, and civics as mere instruments for a communist takeover, even though there has been little direct evidence of such massive influence by the SACP.

59. These Soviet invasions, especially the latter, so shocked some of the European communist parties that they contributed to the creation of Eurocommunism (Franqui 14).

60. Slovo did claim that years ago the SACP had criticized, in a qualified and quiet way, some Soviet policies (Slovo 1990, 45).

61. One of the last of the "Baltic Marxists" within the party, Slovo served the SACP, the MK, and the ANC for decades. Though he supported the Stalinism of the Soviet Union for years, and some claim that he was even a former KGB officer, he would become a crucial "liberal" by the mid–1980s for bringing democratic reforms to this once authoritarian party (Francis 57; Lodge 1983, 177).

62. Adam felt, "The paper amounts to a distancing of the SACP chairman from an embarrassing past without addressing the causes of the crime" (Adam 30). This seems a little harsh to me. Still, Slovo did dodge some issues. Overall the work is quite honest, especially considering the sensitivity of the subject for the South African communists.

63. Such liberals as Cronin and Hani did note that South Africa can still learn things from socialist countries such as Cuba, which is not known for its democratic traditions (Lodge 1983, 176). Hani stated, "Well, I think we have to look at the socialist countries, at Cuba, and see how they handled some of their problems ... these countries went a long way towards addressing the problems of social injustice" (Goodman 15).

64. To give the Stalinist Gwala his due, he did further argue in the article that it was the backward conditions of Russia and not the tenets of Leninism that created the admittedly repressive Soviet system (Gwala, 1990). This, though, ignores the Orthodox Marxist position that the two factors of Leninism and backwardness are intimately tied and not in contradiction.

65. Such radical contemporaries of Lenin as Rosa Luxembourg resented and rejected this elitism (Luxembourg 276).

66. I might add that the SACP gave this Stalinist a relatively positive obituary: "Harry

Gwala, SACP and ANC stalwart, died after a long illness on 20th June 1995" (Nqakula, 1).

Chapter 2

1. As former SACP Chair Yusef Dadoo stated in 1979, "[The SACP] has no interests separate from any contingent of that alliance [between the ANC and SACP] ... this approach does not stand in conflict with our belief that our party has an independent role to play" (Dadoo xvii).

2. Even the long-time president of the ANC, Oliver Tambo, admitted as much: "It is true that the ANC has members of the Communist Party. There has been an overlapping of membership all along the way" (Bardis 104).

3. This, of course, was not what the right-wing in South Africa believed. At the very least they saw the ANC as heavily influenced by the SACP; at the most, these rightists saw the ANC as a mere front for a communist takeover (Vermaak 1966). Though overstated, this latter view would fit standard Soviet policy for its "daughter" parties: "Front organizations ... manipulated by the communists, have been a crucial part of Soviet strategy" (Laqueur 1983, 8).

4. As Tom Lodge, a leading expert on the SACP, pointed out, "In exile ... the party regularly received financial help from the Soviet government" (Lodge 1983, 174).

5. Of course, such high-placed defections, especially from an organization like the SACP, are not likely, considering the extremely harsh discipline of that organization (Ellis and Sechaba 202). Since the 1960s Rivonia Trial, the few members that have left the party have been at most mid-level operatives who knew little of the organization. Still, nowadays, it is more likely to happen.

6. Even with them, the overall military effectiveness of MK was often questioned, especially by South African Defense Force (SADF) officials, but also even by some alliance leaders. As Bardis commented, "Given the amount of money, the training facilities, weapons, etc., invested by the USSR and its allies in the ANC, the ANC's [MK] performance has been poor" (Bardis 111). Vanneman agreed: "Moscow has a well-known disdain for African insurgents [MK].... This disdain emanates from the ANC's poor security and its inability so far to carry out sabotage on a very large scale" (Vanneman 21).

7. As noted above, the rather extensive and well-stocked SACP headquarters is located in COSATU House, owned and controlled by COSATU.

8. "Today this succor has disappeared, as have in-kind contributions from Eastern European administrations" (Lodge 1983, 174).

9. It is ironic that these East Bloc regimes' control of their own people was lost so quickly and thoroughly, thus showing that some totalitarian states may after all be surprisingly "weak" states.

10. The SACP was even forced to move its printing presses from communist East Germany to London and then to South Africa ("We Have to Move House" 1990, 15). The GDR had been a longtime supporter of the SACP, as Albright explained: "The GDR has become a major supplier of arms and training to those engaged in active guerrilla conflict" (Albright 11).

11. This issue was demonstrated at the São Paulo Conference ("Our Eighth Congress" 42; Cronin AT interview, 1995).

12. It is no longer called the South African Defense Force (SADF) but the South African National Defense Force (SANDF). This is more than a semantic change, since the once-hated MK has been integrated, roughly, into the old SADF, changing its composition and, in some experts' opinion, lowering the military's effectiveness.

13. From whom South Africa will buy weapons in the future is unclear. The nationalist regime prided itself on arming itself to a great extent, but with ever-greater budget problems the new regime will need to find cheap, if not effective, weapons (Stedman 128). The Chinese would be a natural fit both financially and politically.

14. It might be added that Deputy President Mbeki's famous revolutionary father, Govan Mbeki, is a longtime Communist Party member and attended the 9th Congress as an honored guest (9th Congress AT, 1995). But Govan Mbeki has also been called an apologist for Stalinism in the Soviet Union (Lodge 1983,175). Also, and much more suspect, is the fact that Weyl has stated that Nelson Mandela was "one of the two most able Bantu Communists in South Africa" (Weyl 118). It must be added that the idea that Mandela was "communist" per se has almost universally rejected by all sources the author has seen.

15. Even though Slovo claimed in 1991 that, "if and when elections come, we as a party will certainly participate" (Slovo 1991, 5).

16. Hani noted in 1992, "Our party is grow-

ing rapidly in the rural areas," which indeed has been a weak spot for the party (Hani 15).

17. The ANC has about 640,000 members and many auxiliary organizations, such as its Women's and Youth leagues (Lodge 1983,174).

18. The regime emphasized the SACP's atheism, its "terrorist" activities, and even its "foreign connections." Communism was often depicted as a "foreign ideology" that would corrupt both white and black society (Vermaak 129).

19. One older black man, with whom I talked soon after I arrived in South Africa in 1995, was very uncomfortable even discussing the SACP. This was probably due to the fact that though the ANC had been in power for almost a year, for decades a white person asking about "communism" was a suspicious character at the least and possibly some sort of undercover agent who posed a real danger.

20. Another older black man whom I talked to stated that the SACP was not only "dangerous" but "corrupt." I thought he may have been confusing the ANC, known for its graft, with the SACP, which normally has a reputation for honesty and discipline. But he was sure the SACP was indeed "the problem." This position was the exception, though, not the rule, since the SACP had a rather clean image in this regard.

21. Many Marxist-Leninists have been seen as "atheists," though in 1989 the SACP did announce, "We recognize the right of all people to adopt and practice religious beliefs of their choice" ("Path to Power" 114).

22. Still, a "dangerous" reputation can be an asset for the SACP. "Large numbers of people admire its leaders and sympathize with [the SACP's radical] goals" (Lodge 1983, 174).

23. As Nel recalled, "In spite of the patently racist nature of the strike, the CPSA supported the action" (Nel 66).

24. Even the most famous South African communist of recent times, Joe Slovo, was born a Lithuanian, which is obviously not Russian, but for the regime's propagandists, it was close enough (Adam).

25. All of this is interesting since in general the Nationalist Party had always been very careful *not* to be anti–Semitic. This was partially strategic, for South Africa had close (if not secretive) ties to Israel for decades (United Nations Centre against Apartheid). It goes deeper than that, however, with some authors speculating that the very devout Afrikaners see themselves not unlike the ancient Jews of the Old Testament, that is, a persecuted, devout, and a chosen people (Thompson 82). Still, when it came to fighting communism, the nationalist regime held little back and sometimes used anti–Semitism.

26. The SACP has made it clear in various declarations that though elections have a role in their grand strategy of bringing socialism to South Africa, it is only one of many tools. These "tools" also include supporting the ANC, pushing leftist public policies, building up the unions, and other such projects (Cronin AT interview, 1995).

27. Obviously everyone does not agree with this conclusion, as this excerpt from a resignation from the SACP makes clear: "The party is simply tailing the ANC. The party is a subcommittee of the ANC" (Molaba 1993, 16)

28. Though the SACP practices only one type of communism, most South Africans do not differentiate between the schools of thought, rivalries, and sectarianism rife within the left. Vermaak continued the practice of seeing the SACP as the local "branch" of "international communism" (Vermaak).

29. Henze stated in 1988 that "A largely white- and Jewish-dominated South African Communist Party (SACP) serves as an instrument for exacerbating tensions and encouraging polarization that aims to exclude all but extreme solutions—or any solutions at all" (Henze 50). This statement is incorrect. It is now known Slovo was crucial in the secret talks with the nationalists of the late 1980s and encouraged compromises like the Sunset Clauses of the 1990s. And the accusation that the party was "white" (let alone "Jewish") has been always been false. By the 1940s, the mass of the SACP was certainly black, but it is true that some of their most outstanding leaders such Abram Fischer and the then young Joe Slovo were white (though other famous leaders were and are black). This gave the regime ammunition, allowing it to claim that the communists were a "white, foreign influence" on "innocent bantus" (read: blacks) in South Africa (Vermaak 11).

30. The British Empire's domination of South Africa in the early 19th century and the bloody Boer War at the end of that century (in which close to 30,000 Afrikaner civilians were allowed to die by the British in the world's first concentration camps) embittered the Afrikaners against all things English (Mallaby 24).

31. Interestingly, like many communist parties, the SACP has not only deemphasized atheism but has also often stated to one degree

or another that it is not an enemy of religion and often promised freedom of religion (Slovo 1994). Given the East Bloc example of in theory guaranteeing "religious freedoms" but in practice ruthlessly persecuting religions and their members, it remains to be seen whether the SACP is serious about its promises of religious freedom. Still, most communist parties have moved away from atheism as a fundamental tenet and the SACP has never persecuted anyone for religious reasons.

32. Even the British were considered "foreigners" by the sometimes xenophobic Afrikaners (Goodwin 302–303). However, this makes the definition of "foreigner" almost meaningless, since most of the British had been there for over a century when the nationalists took power in 1948.

33. This would mostly apply to the early 1930s when Comintern agents such as Wolton dominated and purged the SACP at the orders of the Soviet Comintern (Lerumo 71–75).

34. Especially since the SACP prided itself on not being a mere elitist revolutionary party but a truly mass-supported one, which was unlike other leftist revolutionary organizations in South Africa.

35. The SACP, for obvious reasons, does not use the term "infiltrate" when it refers to the ANC. But the "dual membership" issue has never been a secret.

36. It should be added that the nationalists had long been under extreme domestic and international pressure, both political and economic, to lift the bans on the ANC, SACP, and other parties and "allow" an election in 1994.

37. This passage from the charter (1955) does appear socialistic, but the ANC has not mentioned it in years: "THE PEOPLE SHALL SHARE IN THE COUNTRY'S WEALTH! The national wealth of our country, the heritage of South Africans, shall be restored to the people; The mineral wealth beneath the soil, the Banks and monopoly industry shall be transferred to the ownership of the people as a whole; All other industry and trade shall be controlled to assist the well-being of the people" (ANC website, 1995).

38. It might be added that at least one commentator, Michael Radu, thinks Slovo wrote this document and Panos Bardis believed that the ANC wanted to create a "Marxist state" (Bardis 98; Radu 63). There is no proof that Slovo wrote the charter, and the ANC has obviously not even created a social democratic state, let alone a socialist one.

39. The SACP agreed with this, stating the need to control "mining, heavy industry, banks and other monopoly industries ... [and the] state ownership of large-scale farms" ("For a Democratic Victory..." 103–104).

40. The SACP has been cautiously critical of this ANC policy for obvious reasons: "The SACP views with suspicion and concern most of the mindless advocacy of wholesale privatisation that is being articulated in SA" ("No to Mindless Privatisation" 1). It is unclear if the SACP would support any form of privatization, even in a limited way.

41. As noted, Slovo and Chris Hani are the most obvious examples, but Jay Naidoo and Govan Mbeki are also striking examples of this dual membership phenomenon.

42. The ANC's centrist economic policies during the mid- to late 1990s were almost universally hailed by the relatively conservative South African and global business press as moderate, proper, and austere.

43. But this Second Stage was openly mocked by some: "Even the never learning SACP will soon realise that their Two Stage Theory is incorrect and unscientific" (Mokonyane 98). But beyond this simple attack, Mokonyane said little more about the Two Stage Theory.

44. As a matter of fact, in the early 1990s, "The SACP's immediate demands [were] for an interim government of national unity," which is exactly what was created after the 1994 elections ("The Way Forward" 44). For a communist party to call for a government that included the elements of the old regime shows real political flexibility.

45. However, I can attest that strikes were the major issue on the mind of many rank-and-file members to whom I spoke in 1995, especially those who attended the 9th Party Congress. Many of them, though not openly defiant, did wonder why the "fighting vanguard" of the working class was not supporting various wildcat strikes. The SACP, though sympathetic to the strikers and their demands, was backing its ally the ANC, which, as the new head of government, opposed the disruptive strikes and worried about the economy (9th Congress AT, 1995).

46. Undoubtedly this milder term was adopted because its current ally, the ANC, would be, by definition, the target of the inevitable transformation/revolution since the ANC does lead capitalist South Africa.

47. Or at the least, the current more liberal

ruling clique of the SACP is generally devoted to such democratic ideals.

48. In theory, some of the more extreme conspiracy theorists that see the SACP behind everything could argue that the divergence of ANC/SACP policy is merely a facade created by the "all-powerful" SACP to throw off observers. In should be noted, though, that there is literally no evidence to support this proposition.

49. Lodge suggested that SACP members have been criticized in the past for putting ANC work ahead of their SACP duties (Lodge 1992, 172). It is doubtful that this was a widespread problem, for there seems to be no evidence to indicate that it was. Still, the SACP recently made clear that SACP members had to act "more like communists" when serving within the ANC.

50. As a matter of fact, the right-wing critics of the SACP have said these numbers are understated. The right-wing newsletter *The Eye* claimed in the 1990s that the SACP had always held the majority of seats in the ANC's NEC. But the gross bias of such a source is clear and should be considered. And there is the fact that both Cronin and Lodge have stated that some communists in the ANC are "lapsed" and thus of little value (Cronin AT interview, 1995; Lodge 1983, 176). How many members have "lapsed" is important but there is no way to know at this point. In theory, the current president, Zuma, would even fit this category.

51. Though this statement could be easily denied, citing the "top-down mentality" in the ANC (especially within the African training camps), the organization still maintained some form of democracy (Francis 64).

52. Slovo said in 1991, "I for one am committed to the proposition that [after the first legal congress] there will be no secret party members" (Slovo 1991, 5). As far as I can tell, this pledge has been maintained by the party, though by its very nature, such a thing is hard to verify.

53. Until the 1960s, the regime had been able to penetrate the SACP almost as effectively, with the Rivonia Trial proving this (Kotze 135). After that disastrous event and its aftereffects and with the beginning of the guerrilla struggle, both the ANC and especially the SACP increased their security measures extensively. Still, the ANC was less successful in this endeavor than the SACP.

54. The causes which the SACP chose to champion are reflected by the type of leaders the SACP had at the time; Lodge estimated that 75 percent of them were intellectuals (Lodge 1983, 172).

55. As many critics of the Stalinist East Bloc have pointed out, the ruling communist parties of these states claimed to hold the same principles as the SACP, but in reality "political need" often meant that they sacrificed their principles on such issues as women's rights (there had never been a woman on the Soviet politburo), children's needs (the infamous Rumanian orphanages), and environmentalism (Chernobyl).

56. And as Francis added, "Nelson Mandela has never been a member of the Communist Party, although he has acknowledged the influence of Marxism on his thinking and political activities" (Francis 59). If he was or was not part of the SACP is a long historical debate; the nationalists claimed he was (though with obvious political motives). There is no hard evidence to believe he was ever a "communist," let alone a SACP member.

57. One of Mandela's first public speeches after his release had the SACP banner, with a bright red hammer and sickle, flying in the background. I personally remember seeing that image in 1990 and thinking it sent a powerful message.

58. There seems to have been a skirmish in the ANC in the late 1980s, as Mandela was about to be released and the SACP was beginning to moderate itself. Vanneman explained, "Whatever the outcome of this succession struggle between the ANC's militant and moderate wings, Moscow's chief instrument, the SACP, is getting stronger" (Vanneman 23). As it turned out, there was no clear-cut "win" for either the moderate or militant wings. Mandela was released and dominated the ANC as a centrist, but the SACP did hold onto its influence.

59. Still, the SACP had faith: "The main force of the progress of humanity remains the transition from capitalism to socialism... [But] capitalism in the advanced imperialist countries has proven to be more resilient, more capable of weathering the enormous structural crises into which it has periodically plunged in the twentieth century, than most Marxists originally imagined" ("The Way Forward" 41). Though if anything this was an understatement, this comment still shows that the SACP saw capitalism's eventual fall as inevitable, like any party that believes in the "scientific" nature of Marxism-Leninism.

60. Though COSATU does feel somewhat

betrayed now that the ANC no longer holds to its old semi-socialist positions. Goodwin reported that in an earlier alliance conference document, the state "would assume the leading role in the reconstruction of the economy" (Goodwin 12). This no longer is the case, much to the relief of the World Bank, the International Monetary Fund, and international capital.

61. This is unlike the National Mineworkers' Union (NUM), which had unsuccessfully called for a break from the alliance and the formation of a new "Workers' Party" to replace the SACP ("South Africa" 556–557). Others have more recently made this argument, though there has been little traction to it.

62. Unlike COSATU, most other South African unions fear such "communist penetration" and have bans on it (Lodge 1983, 175).

63. This is like the recent "state asset restructuring plan," also known as privatization, which was attacked by both the unions and the SACP, which usually avoids criticizing such high-level ANC policy ("Say No to Privatization" 1).

64. If anything, the SACP is gradually gaining strength among the unions as it slowly loses strength with the ANC (Lodge 1983, 173). This makes sense, as the SACP pushes for a base among workers and becomes more and more independent from the ANC.

65. For years pundits have predicted a split between the ANC and SACP. As early as 1990, some authors saw the split coming relatively soon, though many years later there is still no concrete sign of this supposed break (Ottaway 1990).

66. Take, for example, this comment on economic policy from the Nationalist Party: "Dynamic growth is required for sustained socio-economic development—the RDP and other plans cannot succeed without a vibrant economy. The free market and private enterprise is the only viable path to ongoing economic progress. Experiments with outdated socialism will only lead to disaster" ("National Party Manifesto," 1995). Ironically, the National Party seemed to have not realized that the ANC was closer to its economic program than the above statement would imply.

67. This is a South African term that refers to those of "mixed racial origins," which often include white, black, and even Malay roots. "Coloureds" received slightly better treatment in comparison to "pure" blacks under apartheid and therefore are resented by some seg-ments of the black population. It might be added that though the Coloureds themselves see their "racial group" as indeed distinct and unique, the ANC's official policy is that the entire "Coloured race" is merely a nationalist creation to divide the nonwhites of South Africa (Ozinsky 42). Though this may have been true decades ago, the Coloureds, who often speak Afrikaans and have little to do with other nonwhites, remain a separate group at this point.

68. Officially, this has been the case for the SACP since its inception in 1921 and practically since 1928. Slovo famously took a position on the ANC NEC ("Members of the Interim Leadership Group" 19). Others then sat on it, including Cronin until very recently. Regardless of all of this, as was shown above, the SACP has had tremendous influence over the ANC for decades.

69. It should be noted that the SACP made the argument that King Goodwill Zwelethini, the nephew of Buthelezi and "traditional" ruler of the Zulus, had no real desire for secession from South Africa, unlike his uncle. It was unclear exactly what the king wanted, since he had, at the very least, played the IFP and ANC against each other more than once to gain political advantage for himself (Neuhaus Chapter 10).

70. There has been a serious debate in South Africa about exactly how long the "Zulu Nation" has existed. The Zulu leaders themselves claim many hundreds of years, but an SACP author makes the counter-claim that only in modern times did a true, cohesive "nation" actually exist (Lubisi 1993). The SACP, though, has much to gain by arguing that the Zulu nation is a modern creation, for it weakens their claim for an independent country, which the both SACP and ANC reject.

71. It is interesting to recall that the when the National Party walked out of the GNU when the new and final constitution was ratified in May 1996, the IFP stayed in the government, even though it still boycotted meetings, commissions, and the like when it wanted to.

72. Though the IFP, NP, and FF made it sound as if the ANC favored some sort of centralized state, the ANC has actually made huge compromises on this issue. The ANC used to push for a "unitary" state, but agreed to a federal system in the last and current constitution. Still, there are different degrees of federalism, and obviously the IFP wanted more regional autonomy.

73. Such extremists currently have little to

no electoral clout and only the potential for political disruption. The PAC and other black nationalist organizations such as AZAPO are also very small with a poor national structure and few followers (PAC interview AT, 1995). And at a crucial time in 1996, the PAC chairperson stepped down for various political and organizational reasons (ANC Press Releases, May 1996).

74. Though the ANC claims to be "winning the war" against corruption, all indications show that it is still a serious and possibly a systematic problem (Baqwa 1995; "Political Report").

75. Though Bundy did state, "The SACP has linked itself so closely in alliance with the ANC that one prominent party official speaks of the party's 'dissolving' itself in the national liberation movement" (Bundy 52). It would be interesting to know who this party official was, because this is totally contrary to the direction the SACP is now taking; if anything, a slight separation is being hinted at. In any case, this "prominent party official" could have been one of the "hangers-on" to whom Cronin referred and who had quit the party soon after the ban was lifted in 1990 (Cronin interview AT, 1995).

76. Or, as a black nationalist critic of the new regime said, "South Africa [is now] ... a hand-maiden of capitalist/imperialist forces" and "The ANC/SACP are no longer debating issues as far as capitalism is concerned. They have accepted it *in toto*." But this author was wrong when he went on to predict, "It is more likely (and signs of this are abundant) that the ANC/SACP state would introduce a heinous Stalinist autocracy" (Mokonyane 28, 62, 65). Though there has been a lack of economic and social transformation, the move to democracy in South Africa has been a success, if not a flawed one.

77. With the unions still defusing strikes and the ANC getting 66.4 percent of the vote in the 1995 local elections, both events were improbable then, if not now (Masondo 29).

Chapter 3

1. It might be added that Slovo himself was "connected" to the CPSU, at least according to Peter Vanneman. Vanneman claimed, "Slovo is usually credited with a major role in military policy and is often characterized as a KGB agent.... A Secretary General of the SACP, he is close to the Soviets" (Vanneman

21). Much has been written on this matter, especially in questionable right-wing papers, as Ian Grieg made clear: "There is some indication that the KGB and its military equivalent have embarked upon a policy of infiltrating agents into various 'liberation movements'" (Grieg 170). On Slovo's supposed KGB status, we may never know the truth, but even Slovo admitted the he was close to his Soviet allies, though this hardly means he was a member of KGB or even the CPSU.

2. The term "orthodox" is somewhat misleading, since there has always been a relatively wide degree of ideological variance among communist parties (and Marxists in general). It is still useful to use the term to distinguish between fully Marxist-Leninist parties that have some form of connection to the Soviets as compared to various socialist, Marxist, Maoist, anarchist, and other parties of the left.

3. Bukharin, the famous Soviet theoretician, at the 1928 Comintern meeting even went so far as to hint the SACP leaders were "racist" (Johns 1975, 224). Later S.P. Bunting, Edward Roux, Bill Andrews, and Solly Sachs, all outstanding leaders of the SACP, were all purged by the leftist agents of the Comintern (Lerumo 72; Ludi 8).

4. Even the popular leader S.P. Bunting, who re-created the SACP in the late 1920s, was cited as having rightist tendencies for having "contacts" within the government; "Buntingism" was condemned (Lerumo 73; Roux 255). Most of the rank-and-file members saw this as ridiculous. "Bunting remained ... the great leader, the one [the rank and file] knew ... [Bunting] has a white skin but a black heart" (Roux 101). Ironically, Bunting had pushed for the admittance of blacks into the SACP when others had thought it a premature move (Ellis and Sechaba 13).

5. This ultraleft faction included Douglas Wolton, Molly Wolton, Lazar Sachs, and Louis Joffe (Roux 96).

6. S.P. Bunting was even "rehabilitated" in 1936, a surprisingly short period considering the severity of his purge (Roux 102).

7. It has been rumored that the democratic powers sent their delegation to the Soviet Union on a boat that was literally slow. Soviet leaders reportedly saw this as a snub by the Western leaders.

8. The fact that Stalin apparently wasted this time, at least militarily, is not the issue. The official, and seemingly true, reason for the treaty was to buy time to build up Soviet de-

fenses against an attack from any capitalist power, be it Nazi Germany or the other Western powers. In the industrial sector it did do just this. But for various other political reasons, Stalin killed 50,000 officers in the late 1930s and generally handicapped what little military leadership was left in the USSR.

9. It is true that some of the Afrikaner organizations and institutions were supportive of the German fascists during the war, though nothing much came of such backing.

10. According to Ludi, the SACP increased its power over the ANC under these adverse conditions: "Dominion of the African National Congress probably became an accomplished fact during the war years" (Ludi and Grobelaar 9).

11. The SACP did save some face among blacks by leading numerous campaigns for black rights and by constantly demanding that "natives" be armed and sent to fight the Axis forces. These demands, of course, were rejected by the regime, but once again the SACP was at the forefront of the battle against racism, and blacks did notice this (Lerumo 81–82).

12. England, which had been the primary "menace" to the Soviets for years, was now seen as a pawn for the new imperialist power of the world, the United States. This is a more negative take on the famous "special relationship" between the U.S. and UK.

13. One must not forget the Sino-Soviet conflict that arose in the 1950s and continued to one degree or another for thirty more years. This did affect the South African situation in one small way: "Red China" dallied with the PAC against the Soviet-aligned ANC during the 1970s and early 1980s. With the quick decline of the PAC in the 1980s, this whole issue soon became moot. Recently, the SACP and the Chinese Communist Party (CCP) have become closer.

14. It needs to be added that "African Marxism," which accurately claimed to be "unique," is more of a centralized developmental program than true Marxism or Leninism.

15. It should be pointed out that the Soviets had a somewhat low opinion of its African allies. Albright claimed, "Moscow rejects the claims of these parties to 'genuine' Marxism-Leninism, and regards them merely as 'revolutionary vanguard' parties" (Albright 7).

16. The Soviets did have a diplomatic presence in South Africa until the 1950s, when the then-new nationalist regime, vehemently anti-communist, finally expelled the Soviet diplo-mats. Interestingly, even though the nationalists charged these diplomats with spying and subversion, they stressed the "crimes" of having parties, inviting "bantus," and serving them alcohol (though the last-named was actually a crime under apartheid).

17. Still, as Laqueur himself admitted, Soviet influence was still extensive in Africa, including such nations as Congo/Zaire (1960), Ghana (1966), Mali (1968), Sudan (1971), Equatorial Guinea (1977), Somalia (1979), and Zimbabwe (1980) (Laqueur 1983, 189). Ultimately though, as Henze points out, all this Soviet advice and assistance to Africa produced some debacles: "In 1984–1985 Ethiopia produced the most dramatic example of the effects of Soviet-style Marxism in the great famine" (Henze 39, 47).

18. Though the negotiations were officially between the ANC and the Nationalist Party, in the later stages it become obvious that SACP members, including Joe Slovo, were some of the leading negotiators on the "ANC" team.

19. Ironically, some notables in the U.S. State Department thought that the Chinese, not the Russians, were the real threat in the long run for most of Africa (Henze 40). At the time, the Pan Africanist Congress (PAC) was the closest party to the Communist Chinese. But this is now a moot point, with the PAC quite insignificant and its ties to China almost nonexistent (PAC interview, AT 1995). Still, by the 2000s, it has turned out that once "revolutionary and radical" China was the actor to gain the most from all of this, as it has made massive investments, not provided revolutionary funding, throughout Africa. And as noted, the SACP and China do have ties now and the SACP sees China's current "state capitalism" as a model for South Africa.

20. Such Andropov reforms as a "crackdown" on alcoholism was not exactly what the Soviet Union needed in its last years of relative stability (though alcoholism was indeed a serious problem). It is ironic that this supposedly totalitarian state could not stop its own military personnel from drinking excessively, with rumors of them literally stealing alcohol from their own jets' brake tubing.

21. Vanneman, though, claimed that Slovo resisted glasnost and perestroika at first and then came around only later (Vanneman 23). I have found no other collaborating evidence for this, but it seems logical that a longtime Soviet supporter such as Slovo would be initially resistant to such liberalizing ideological changes.

22. Over the years and by the 1980s, communist parties that strictly adhered to the Soviet line became rarer and rarer, as various sectarian splits, domestic reforms, and political fatigue greatly reduced the ranks of Stalinist parties.

23. Though the communist "bloc" in the East (i.e., China, Cambodia, Laos, Vietnam, and the Democratic People's Republic of Korea) existed, it was fractured along ideological and geopolitical lines and was mostly ignored by the SACP. Though the SACP would occasionally mention the Chinese ties to the Pan African Congress, the Cambodian conflict, and the economic reforms of China, overall the entire Asian communist world was mostly ignored. As Albright noted, China had little interest in South Africa: "On Beijing's resulting ladder of geo-political priorities, southern Africa has occupied a low rung" (Albright 32).

24. The fact that the Soviet GDP growth went from a decades-long 5 percent to 0 by the early 1990s was a clear sign that the USSR was indeed in critical economic trouble (Nel 88).

25. Mokonyane, a longtime critic of the Soviets, the SACP and the ANC, agreed: "The USSR became the most decisive purveyor of an unscientific, un-dialectical and erroneous analysis of the capitalist system world-wide.... [The Russian] revolution was wrongly characterized as a socialist revolution by Stalin ... that Russia was ever anything approaching socialism can no longer be argued by anyone seriously" (Mokonyane 38).

26. It would appear that members of the former CPSU, the Soviet African Institute, and other former Soviet bodies still maintained ties with the SACP throughout the 1990s (9th Congress AT, 1995).

27. Though it seems common sense that one party should never just copy another party, especially from another country, it is remarkable for a formerly Stalinist party to admit it. It should be noted that even during the Comintern days there was some lip service given to the need for "accommodating the party to local needs," but this was in direct opposition to the forced Stalinization of all communist parties.

28. Though there was no Western conspiracy to "overthrow" the regimes of the East Bloc, it is also true that one would suspect there was such a scheme from the almost gleeful expressions of Western media pundits as events unfolded in the early 1990s.

29. Not only is it true that communist Ger-

mans lived relatively well, but it is also true that even Poland had a higher per capita standard of living than the Soviet Union ("The World Factbook..." 1). These facts were something the CPSU obviously kept from its own people over the many decades of its rule.

30. This "KGB" coup was handled surprisingly poorly. The fact that central communication points were not seized (Gorbachev even called Western leaders from his "house arrest") and lethal force was not used against Boris Yeltsin were just two of many mistakes made by these apparent amateurs (Oberdorfer 1991).

31. As a matter of fact, Gorbachev was apparently told what to say and do in the Supreme Soviet by Yeltsin at the close of the coup. This spectacle was broadcast worldwide for everyone to see. After more than seventy years, the CPSU had faced its final disgrace, as it soon disintegrated.

32. This is a classic excuse for every poor decision of dictators, and insightful of how even this "new" SACP held back, to a degree, when condemning Gorbachev.

33. This last point needs to be explained and qualified. First, the SACP dropped the insistence on a violent revolution due more to changed domestic factors than international or ideological issues. Second, it did not entirely drop the idea of revolution. The SACP made it clear many times during the lengthy negotiations in the late 1980s that it reserved the right to resort to violence if necessary. Deputy General Secretary Cronin also made this clear during his interview with me in 1995 (Cronin AT interview, 1995). Finally, at its last congress in 2012, the SACP argued that elections were not the only option open to the party (though this could have just meant social movements and other nonviolent methods).

34. Though Slovo did say in 1992, as he was condemning Gorbachev: "As an independent party of social democracy..." (Slovo 1992, 26).

35. The collapse of such a crude and bloody regime as Romania's was probably no shock to the relatively sophisticated SACP leadership, who had already adopted a number of "liberal" reforms and had condemned communist "political tyranny."

36. Simon Stevens of the SACP did try to weakly link class morality with human rights in 1992 (Stevens 124). The attempt was half-hearted and seemingly not convincing to anyone concerned, since it was never cited again.

37. The SACP summed up the new situation well: "The balance of world power has

changed very rapidly in the last three years....
[The] two-bloc world system has now more or
less collapsed. The imperialist world, led by the
United States, has emerged more powerful and
confident. Generally, these developments are
not favourable for progressive forces" ("The
Way Forward..." 41).

38. In late 1992 the SACP did approvingly
publish some material on the newly reformed
CPSU. It stated, "The CPSU of Gorbachev
and Yeltsin, Yakovlev and Shevardnadze no
longer exists. But the CPSU of millions of
communists dedicated to the ideals of social
justice is alive.... The draft [for the 29th CPSU
Congress] commits the party to struggling for
power along constitutional lines, in elections"
("Russia Moves to Relaunch CPSU" 56–57).
Though the CPSU would ultimately dissolve,
the Russian Communist Party has made a mar-
ginal political comeback.

Chapter 4

1. An article in the SACP's *African Communist* argued that though rare, a few industries can indeed be privatized without major
harm, but many still cannot be without betraying the interests of the working class ("No to
Mindless Privatization" 1).

2. One can see this issue even in America:
some local African American organizers have
decried busing because it disrupts the local
community too much.

3. There was an actual GDP decline during the last decade of nationalist rule ("State
of the Economy," 1994).

4. On many rural plantations during
apartheid, the white owner was held responsible for educating his or her workers. Not surprisingly, this often resulted in extremely low
to nonexistent educational standards for these
rural black children ("The Write Stuff" 1).

5. This was done when the South African
navy asked for new corvettes and was told that
there was not enough money for them. The
military claimed that South Africa's national
security was jeopardized by this decision, but
they still did not get the ships. Still, the navy
almost won on this issue, and other interests
have often defeated the more radical suggestions of the ANC.

6. As with other aspects of Grand Apartheid, when it was dismantled by de Klerk at
the national level, local city councils resisted
educational desegregation strongly (Ottaway
1992).

7. In the mid–1990s, an anarchist organization at the University of the Witswatersrand
called ARM fully admitted that all the anarchist organizations combined had little to no
influence on the ANC regime, though they
were of course hopeful about the future (ARM
AT, 1995). Since then, these groups have faded
from the political scene.

8. But educational fees have not been low-
ered enough, at least according to many of the
blacks at the University of the Witswatersrand
and other universities, who rioted in 1994 and
1995 over many issues, including financial aid
(Campus Obligations, 1998). In 1995, the author himself saw the results of the infamous
"Operation Litter," where students would literally "trash" the campus as a form of protest.
Though usually harmless, such protests did go
to extremes when expensive plumbing was destroyed and valuable computers were thrown
into pools.

9. Again, in the universities, nonwhite students now scramble to take engineering, economic, and business courses which they believe
will get them better jobs and ensure greater social mobility. The SACP can hardly deny this,
at least at the level of the individual, but the
party rightly points out that only a handful of
nonwhites get such educational opportunities.

10. Though they have a racist past, these
Model C Schools are what many nonwhites desire for their own children (Nzimande).

11. Though seemingly progressive, the
CPSU clearly had not adopted modern inclusive language. This, and many other policy issues, proved that the CPSU had hardly eradicated sexism amongst its own ranks, let alone
society.

12. Although no one would deny that before the collapse of communism the SACP
planned to emulate the Soviet model, regarding education and other policies, now it is not
always so clear since the SACP has abandoned
so much of its Stalinist and even Leninist past
(see Chapter 4). Though it has shown no sign
of discarding its common Leninist position
that people are highly malleable, it may be
forced to in the future for pragmatic reasons.

13. Many whites to whom I talked in 1995
said they had heard blacks talking about how
they soon would be living in the "master's
house" when the ANC took power. And
though this obviously did not take place, it is
likely many of the blacks who held this position
were disappointed that they still lived in the
back of their "master's" garage (which is very

common for urban, live-in servants) like they always have.

14. All of this chaos would surely promote such parties as the Zulu-dominated IFP (and maybe even the Coloured community) to take advantage of the situation and reject ANC authority.

15. Though this is in contrast to "ultraleft" organizations and parties (such as the Trotskyites, the Workers' Party, and Anarchists), which demanded that some form of socialism to be built as soon as possible (ARM AT, 1995). The SACP claimed then and now that such demands are not only dangerous in the delicately balanced political environment but are also disastrous in economic terms if attempted.

16. The SACP had been close to its Cuban allies since the outbreak of the civil war in Angola, and the SACP congress had to be held outside South Africa for obvious reasons. This, though, was seen as a rejection of moderation by some authors. "Despite its newly professed anti–Stalinism in 1989, the SACP held its 7th Congress in one of the last Stalinist redoubts, Havana" (Adams 33).

17. At this point, the SACP did not see the regime as willing to negotiate. The recently "retired" P.W. Botha was far too hard-line to ever negotiate directly with the ANC, let alone with the SACP. In might be added that P.W. Botha was put on trial for illegal activities against dissidents during his reign (*Daily News*, National Public Radio, January 22, 1998). And though the then newly elected National Party leader, de Klerk, had already hinted at some reforms, his hard-line tenure as education minister in the 1980s was hardly a good sign at the time.

18. The main slogan everywhere at this congress was "Socialism Is the Future! Build It Now!," which is not only catchy but also quite telling. How far into the future this socialism was, was only hinted at, but the need to "build it now" was certainly a common theme. This often meant working with the ANC's RDP (since faded away) and, in keeping with the new emphasis on bottom-up democracy, to aid the civics in their goals. These are admirable activities, but both are also surprisingly innocuous for a revolutionary communist party.

19. Though this sounds like a prudent position for any political party, it is a major concession for a faction of a communist party to disregard semantics to gain political ground.

20. Cronin himself told me during a lengthy interview in 1995 that though the term "social democracy" was not adopted, many social democratic ideals had indeed been incorporated into the SACP, which was quite correct (Cronin AT interview, 1995).

21. Cuba demonstrates this change well. Once it lost its million-dollar-a-day subsidy from the Soviet Union, it collapsed economically. If not for renewed support from "socialist" Venezuela, it might have collapsed fully by now (or, at the least, reformed itself more extensively).

22. Though such positions may not seem moderate to the reader, for a formally Stalinist party, they are indeed. And the aforementioned "far-left formations," such as Trotskyite and anarchist organizations, have indeed condemned the SACP for "selling out," as detailed in Chapter 2.

23. It might be added that the decentralization that was also allowed during this phase may have contributed to the bloody civil war that broke out in Yugoslavia in the 1990s.

24. Due to a number of limitations, I could make only an audio recording of this important event. Still, the material filled almost a score of ninety-minute cassette tapes and comprehensively covered all public meetings (and many private ones). This collection appears to be the only full record of the congress available to researchers.

25. It might be noted that parts of the congress were even televised throughout South Africa, though the coverage was understandably light when compared to the ANC National Congress that had been held a few months before in 1995.

26. The underground period, which lasted for almost forty years, included the very real danger of capture, long imprisonment, and too often torture and death ("Path to Power" 10). Deputy General Secretary Cronin told me in 1995 how he had been jailed for seven years, often in solitary confinement (Cronin AT interview, 1995).

27. Ironically, since this congress, the RDP was dismantled and replaced first by the new GEAR economic program (which has also ended) and then later by the new NDP. What little "socialism" existed within the RDP was then nonexistent. This has become even more pronounced in the past decade.

28. I was actually quite impressed by the personal and political demeanor of the Cuban ambassador. I could see clearly the genuine outrage that many developing-world dignitaries feel against the United States. Though, at

times, he spoke in communist jingoisms, he genuinely seemed to believe that America had some sort of irrational hatred toward his country (and compared to how America has treated China, Vietnam, and other communist nations, he may have been partially correct, though the Cuban lobby in Florida makes it less irrational and more about special interest politics in a key primary state).

29. The Cubans surely know that the new South Africa, even the SACP itself, asks for international capital, as even the Cubans have begun to do ("Reconstruction and Development Programme" 20). Both regimes are being forced to recognize the power of neoliberalism that has swept the globe since the mid–1990s.

30. A few years later, even communist Vietnam would be asking for international investment, even from its former archenemy the United States.

31. It might be noted that the popular Cuban and Vietnamese delegates would also have been displeased with a Chinese presence since both sided with the Russians during the Sino-Soviet Split. Vietnam even fought a short, though bloody, border war with China in 1979.

32. The fact that the young Mandela may have been anticommunist adds irony to this whole affair (though this has not been well established).

33. As with many communist parties and regimes, such subtle indications are the only signs of true public "debate" that an outside observer is allowed to see (and often even these are staged, though often without the other faction's knowledge).

34. The SACP videos were snatched up quickly and I had to take great pains to obtain the cash needed to purchase them for research

and educational purposes. This was harder than it sounds, since the congress was held in a distant suburb of Johannesburg that had no ATM machines or banks in 1995. The SACP, of course, did not take credit cards (at that point). It might be added that these videos were also problematic, for though they were of a surprisingly high quality, they were recorded in the obscure PAL-M video format (used only in Brazil, South Africa, and parts of the Middle East). I eventually obtained a multi-format VCR from a foreign friend back in St. Louis, Missouri, where I lived at the time.

35. Not unlike in America, a crackdown on crime is popular but still controversial, for it often has racial undertones. It is usually nonwhites that are rounded up, and even if they are guilty, the local community still sees an oppressive (often white) police force taking away nonwhites.

36. The author personally saw Cronin and others constantly moving to and fro, seemingly arranging everything at the congress before it happened.

37. This is not unlike at the 7th, 8th, and many other congresses of the SACP and other communist parties ("For a Democratic Victory" 14).

38. It might be added that most of these conservative organizations, such as the AWB, HNP, and even the NP/NNP, all claimed that the communists cannot be trusted within the government (AWB and HNP AT, 1995). Whether what is now left of these organizations will ever trust the SACP is academic; the party has proven itself as a reliable and invaluable component of the regime for the last few years.

Selected Bibliography

Books

Alba, Victor. *The Communist Party in Spain*. New Brunswick, NJ: Transaction Books, 1983.

Albright, David. "The Communist States and Southern Africa." In *International Politics in Southern Africa*. Edited by Gwendolen Carter and Patrick O'Meara. Bloomington: Indiana University Press, 1982.

Bardis, Panos. *South Africa and the Marxist Movement*. Lewiston, NY: E. Mellen Press, 1989.

Barrell, Howard. *MK: The ANC's Armed Struggle*. London: Penguin Forum Press, 1990.

Baskin, Jeremy. *Striking Back: A History of COSATU*. Johannesburg: Raven Press, 1991.

Bell, David Scott. *Eurocommunism and the Spanish Communist Party*. Brighton: Sussex European Research Centre, 1979.

Bundy, Colin. "Alliance, Exile and Armed Struggle: The SACP from 1961 to 1991." In *The History of the South African Communist Party*. Ed. Colin Bundy. Cape Town: University of Cape Town, Department of Adult Education and Extra-Mural Studies, 1991.

Buston, Thomas. *Gorbachev*. New York: Stein and Day, 1985.

Campbell, Kurt. *Soviet Policy Towards South Africa*. New York: St. Martin's Press, 1986.

Carter, Gwendolen, and Patrick O'Meara. *International Politics in Southern Africa*. Bloomington: Indiana University Press, 1982.

Checa, Genaro Carnero. *Korea Rice and Steel*. Pyongyang: Foreign Languages Publishing House, 1977.

Communism in Africa. Bloomington: Indiana University Press, 1980.

Contending Ideologies in South Africa. Grand Rapids: W.B. Eerdmans, 1986.

Dadoo, Yusuf. "Introduction." *South African Communists Speak 1915–1980*. London: Inkululeko Publications, 1981.

De Villiers, C.F. "Russia in Africa." In *The Communist Strategy*. Edited by C.F. De Villers, F.R. Metrowich, and J.A. Du Plessis. Johannesburg: Department of Information, 1975.

Doder, Dusko. *Shadow and Winter*. New York: Random House, 1986.

Ellis, Stephen, and Tsepo Sechaba. *Comrades against Apartheid*. Bloomington: Indiana University Press, 1992.

Fic, Victor. *Peaceful Transition to Communism*. Bombay: Nachiksta Publications, 1969.

Forman, Lionel. *A Trumpet from the Housetops*. London: Zed Books Ltd., 1992.

Franqui, Barbara. *Eurocommunism in Spain*. Long Beach: California State University, 1983.

Gann, L.H. *Hope for South Africa?*. Stanford, CA: Hoover Institution Press, 1991.

Gevisser, Mark. *Thabo Mbeki: The Dream Deferred*. New York: Jonathan Ball Publishers, 2007.

Goodwin, June, and Ben Schiff. *Heart of Whiteness*. New York: Scribner, 1995.

Gorbachev, Mikhail. *Gorbachev's Speeches and Writings I*. Oxford: Pergamon Press, 1987a.

_____. *Gorbachev's Speeches and Writings II*. Oxford: Pergamon Press, 1987b.

Greig, Ian. *The Communist Challenge to Africa*. Parow: SAFF, 1977.

Gumede, William Mervin. *Thabo Mbeki and the Battle for the Soul of the ANC*. Cape Town: Zebra Press, 2007.

Henze, Paul. "The Soviet Impact on African Political Dynamics." In *The Red Orchestra: The Case of Africa*. Edited by Denis Bark. Stanford, CA: Hoover Institution Press, 1988.

Johns, Sheridan. *Chasing Votes: The Communist Party and Elections, 1929–1950*. Cape Town: Centre for African Studies, University of Cape Town, 1994.

Jumba-Masagazi, A.H.K. *African Socialism*. Nairobi: East African Academy, 1970.

Kautsky, John. *Communism and the Politics of Development*. New York: John Wiley and Sons, 1968.

_____. *Moscow and the Communist Party of India*. Cambridge: Technology Press, 1956.

Keylor, William. *The Twentieth-Century World*. New York: Oxford University Press, 1996.

Kotze, D.J. *Communism and South Africa*. Cape Town: Tafelberg Publishers Ltd., 1979.

Kunert, Dirk. *Glasnost, New Thinking, and the ANC-SACP Alliance: A Parting of Ways*. Bryanston: International Freedom Press, 1991.

Laqueur, Walter. *The Pattern of Soviet Conduct in the Third World*. New York: Praeger, 1983.

Legum, Colin. "The USSR and South Africa." In *The Red Orchestra: The Case of Africa*. Edited by Denis Bark. Stanford, CA: Hoover Institution Press, 1988.

Lerumo, A. *Fifty Fighting Years*. London: Inkululeko Publications, 1971.

Lodge, Tom. *Black Politics in South Africa Since 1945*. London: Longman, 1983.

Ludi, Gerard, and Blaar Grobbelaar. *The Amazing Mr. Fischer*. Cape Town: Nasionale Boekhandel, 1966.

Malhotra, Avtar. *What Is the Communist Party?* New Delhi: Communist Party, 1970.

Mallaby, Sebastian. *After Apartheid: The Future of South Africa*. New York: Times Books, 1993.

Mandela, Nelson. *Long Walk to Freedom*. New York: Little, Brown and Company, 1994.

Masani, Minocheher. *The Communist Party of India*. New York: Macmillan, 1954.

McCauley, Martin. *The Soviet Union After Brezhnev*. New York: Holmes and Meier, 1983.

McLellan, David. *Marxism*. Oxford: Oxford University Press, 1989.

Medvedev, Roy A., and Zhores A. Medvedev. *Khrushchev: The Years in Power*. New York: W.W. Norton, 1978.

Meer, Fatima. *Higher Than Hope*. New York: Harper Perennial, 1988.

Meredith, Martin. *Mandela: A Biography*. New York: Public Affairs, 2010.

Metrowich, F.R. *Africa and Communism*. Johannesburg: Voortrekkerpers, 1967.

Mfuku, Nkosana. "Privatisation and Deregulation Policies in South Africa." Thesis, University of Western Cape, 2006.

Mokonyane, Dan. *The Big Sell Out*. London: Nakong Ya Rena, 1994.

Mujal-Leon, Eusebio. *Communism and Political Change in Spain*. Bloomington: Indiana University Press, 1983.

Muzaffar, Ahmad. *Myself and the Communist Party of India, 1920–1929*. Calcutta: National Book Agency, 1970.

National Development Plan 2030: Our Future—Make It Work. Johannesburg: Sherino Printers, 2013.

Nel, Philip. *A Soviet Embassy in Pretoria?* Cape Town: Tafelberg, 1990.

Neuhaus, Richard John. *Dispensations: The Future of South Africa as South Africans See It*. Grand Rapids, MI: William B. Eerdmans Publishing, 1986.

Ngubane, Jordan. *An African Explains Apartheid*. New York: Praeger, 1963.

Nizami, Taufiq. *The Communist Party and India's Foreign Policy*. New Delhi: Associated Publishers House, 1971.

Ogunade, Adeyemi O. *Human Capital Investmenting in the Developing World: An Analysis of Praxis*. Kingston: University of Rhode Island, 2011.

Ottaway, David. *Afrocommunism*. New York: Africana, 1986.

Overstreet, Gene. *Communism in India*. Berkeley: University of California Press, 1959.

Pierson, Christopher. *Marxist Theory and Democratic Politics*. Berkeley: University of California Press, 1986.

Pike, Henry. *A History of Communism in South Africa*. Germiston: Christian Mission International of South Africa, 1988.

Raditsa, Leo. *Prisoners of a Dream*. Annapolis: Prince George Street Press, 1989.

The Red Flag in South Africa. Johannesburg: Jet Printers, 1990.

Roux, Eddie. *Time Longer Than Rope*. Madison: University of Wisconsin Press, 1964.

Roux, Eddie, and Win Roux. *Rebel Pity and Life of Eddie Roux*. London: Rex Collins, 1970.

Rubinstein, Alvin. *Moscow Third World Strategy*. Princeton: Princeton University Press, 1990.

Russoc, James. *On the Threshold of Government*. New York: St. Martin's Press, 1982.

Saul, John. *Recolonization and Resistance in Southern Africa in the 1990s*. Trenton, NJ: African World Press, 1993.

_____. *Socialist Ideology and the Struggle for Southern Africa*. Trenton, NJ: African World Press, 1990.

Schrire, Robert. *Adapt or Die: The End of White Politics in South Africa*. New York: Ford Foundation, 1991.

Sena, Canakya. *Communism in Indian Politics*. New York: Columbia University Press, 1972.

Sinha, Viveka. *The Red Rebels in India*. New Delhi: Associated Publishers House, 1986.

Smith, Tony. "The Underdevelopment of Development Theory Literature." In *The State and Development in the Third World*. Edited by Atul Kohl. Princeton: Princeton University Press, 1986.

Sonnenfeldt, Helmut. *Soviet Politics in the 1980s*. Boulder, CO: Westview Press, 1985.

South African Communists Speak 1915–1980. London: Inkululeko Publications, 1980.

South African Communists Speak. London: Inkululeko Publications, 1981.

Spain Organizes for Victory. London: Communist Party of Great Britain, 1937.

Stedman, Stephen. *South Africa: The Political Economy of Transformation*. Boulder, CO: Lynne Reinner Publishers, 1994.

Strong, Simon. *Shining Path: Terror and Revolution in Peru*. New York: Times Books, 1992.

Thompson, Leonard. *The Political Mythology of Apartheid*. New Haven: Yale University Press, 1985.

Trotsky, Leon. *Revolution Betrayed*. London: New Park Publication Ltd., 1973.

Ulam, Adam B. *Stalin: The Man and His Era*. Boston: Beacon Press, 1973.

Urnov, Andrei. *South Africa against Africa*. Moscow: Progress Publishers, 1982.

Vanneman, Peter. *Soviet Strategy in Southern Africa*. Stanford: Hoover Institution Press, 1990.

Vermaak, Christopher. *The Red Trap*. Johannesburg: A.P.B. Publishers, 1966.

Wely, Nataniel. *Traitors' End*. Cape Town: Tafelberg-tigewers, 1970.

Periodicals

Adam, Heribert. "Eastern Europe and South African Socialism: Engaging Joe Slovo." *South African International* 21, no. 1 (July 1990).

Akhalwaya, Ameen. "The Communist Party Manifesto." *African Report* 35 (September/October 1990): 43–47.

"American Schools Still Heavily Segregated by Race, Income: Civil Rights Project Report." *Huffington Post*. September 20, 2012.

"Anglo-American: Our History." Angloamerican.co.za, 2012.

"BEE Legalises Theft (from Blacks)." *Mail & Guardian,* November 26, 2010.

Beilenson, John. "The Failing Strength of Western Europe's Communist Movement." *Scholastic Update* 199 (September 1986).

Beresford, David. "Zuma's Missing Years Come to Light." *The Times* (UK), February 22, 2009.

"Blade Nzimande, SACP Minister of Basic Education, Speaks About Intellectualism." *South Africa Today*, April 18, 2013.

Brigland, Fred. "New President Will Fight AIDS with Science." *The Scotsman* (Edinburgh), September 26, 2008.

Bushin, Vladimir. "Soviet Policy on South Africa." *African Communist* Second Quarter, no. 125 (1991).

"Campus Obligations." *The Star,* November 13, 1998, p. A12.

"Capitalism vs. Socialism." *African Communist* Fourth Quarter, no. 119 (1989).

Cargill, Jenny. "Naidoo Interview." ANC website, 1997.

"The Case of S.P. Bunting." *African Communist* Fourth Quarter, no. 119 (1989).

"The Class Struggle Is Alive and Kicking." *African Communist* First Quarter, no. 120 (1990).

"Collapse of Communism." *CQ Researcher* 3, no. 10 (March 12, 1993): 224.

"Confusion in Jay Naidoo's Offices After Cabinet Reshuffle." ANC website. March 1996.

Conquest, Robert. "The Moscow Coup." *National Review*, September 9, 1991.

"Consolidating Our Strategic Unity—The SACP's 9th Congress." *African Communist* Second Quarter, no. 141 (1995).

Contreras, Joseph. "Compromised by Comrades." *Newsweek*, August 12, 1991, p. 43.

_____. "Mandela Loses Control." *Newsweek*, April 26, 1993.

"Corrupt GOP Establishment." *Veil of Politics,* 2013.

Creamer, Martin. "National Development Plan Fatally Flawed, Cronin Tells Godsell." *Mining Weekly*, May 27, 2013.

"The Crisis in the Socialist World." *African Communist* Second Quarter, no. 121 (1990).

Cronin, Jeremy. "The Boat, the Tap and the Leipzig Way." *African Communist* Third Quarter, no. 130 (1992).

_____. "Bolshevism and Socialist Transition." *African Communist* First Quarter, no. 136 (1994).

_____. "Lenin Is Not a Statue." *African Communist* Fourth Quarter, no. 127 (1990).

Crowe, Sarah. "White South Africans Learn Zulu—and Much More." *Christian Science Monitor*, December 13, 1995, section 1, p. 2.

"The Cruelest Curse." *The Economist*, February 22, 2001.

Daniels, Anthony. "We All Make Mistakes (Joe Slovo Interview)." *The Spectator,* November 14, 1992.

Davidow, Mike. "Strengthening the Party: The Key to Soviet Stability" *African Communist* Second Quarter, no. 125 (1991).

Davis, Gayle. "SACP Jogs Debate on Macro-Economic." ANC website, August 30, 1996.

"De Klerk's Challenge Must Be Answered." *African Communist* Second Quarter, no. 121 (1990).

Doerner, William. "The Red and Black." *Time*, March 2, 1987, p. 36.

Donnelly, Lynley. "NPC: Diagnosis Before Treatment." *Mail & Guardian,* June 10, 2011.

Dyer, Gwynne. "Socialism with a Human Face: Another God That Failed." *Baltimore Sun*, November 18, 1992.

Edgar, Robert. "Notes on the Life and Death of Albert Nzula." *The International Journal of African Historical Studies* 16, no. 4 (1983): 675–79.

"Eighth Party Congress—A Party Triumph." *African Communist* First Quarter, no. 128 (1992).

"The Ekurhuleni Declaration of the Alliance." Africa News Service, April 10, 2002.

Ellis, Stephen. "The ANC in Exile." *African Affairs* 90 (July 1990): 439–47.

"Ex-Apartheid Party to Merge with ANC in South Africa." Shortnews.com. August 8, 2004.

"For a Democratic Victory and Advance to Socialism: The 7th Congress of the SACP." *African Communist* Third Quarter, no. 118 (1989).

"Forbes Economic Series." ANC website, 1997.

Fortescue, Dominic. "The Communist Party of South Africa and the African Working Class of the 1940s." *The International Journal of African Historical Studies* 24, no. 3 (1991): 418–512.

Francis, Samuel. "Communism, Terrorism, and the African National Congress." *Journal of Social, Political, and Economic Studies* (Spring 1986).

Frost, Meryn. "Joe Slovo and the Fate of Communism." *South Africa Foundation Review* 16, no. 5 (May 1990).

"Full Zuma Judgment." News24, September 13, 2008.

"FW, There's One Thing on Which We Agree..." *African Communist* First Quarter, no. 128 (1992).

Gann, L.H. "Moscow and Pretoria: A New Course?" *The Journal of Modern African Studies* 27 (June 1989): 341–46.

Gina, Cedric. "Numsa: Our Problems with the NDP." *Mail & Guardian*, April 26, 2013.

Goodman, David. "Rethinking Socialism." *Dollars and Sense*, July 1991.

Gordin, Jeremy. "On Zuma's Communist Past." PoliticsWeb, November 13, 2009.

"Govt's Economic Plans 'Will Undermine RDP Objectives.'" ANC website, July 1996.

"'Guard Against BEE-Fronting.'" *Mail & Guardian*, November 26, 2010.

Gwala, Harry. "Let Us Look at History in the Round." *African Communist* Fourth Quarter, no. 123 (1990).

_____. "A Party of the Working Class, or an Amorphous Mess." *African Communist* Fourth Quarter, no. 127, 1991.

Hani, Chris. "Chris Hani." *African Communist* First Quarter, no. 128 (1992).

Halloran, T. "The True Face of F.W. de Klerk." *African Communist* Fourth Quarter, no. 119 (1989).

Heerden, Dries van. "Future of the ANC/SACP Alliance." *South Africa Foundation Review*, March 1993.

Hlongwave, Sipho. "National Development Plan Is Not Finished Yet." *Bday*, June 12, 2013.

"Internationally: Aluta Continua." *African Communist* Second Quarter, no. 125 (1991).

Jensen, Hogler. "Pretoria Sees Red." *Maclean's*, August 5, 1990, p. 30.

Jobarteh, Udey. "On Socialism and Pseudo-Socialism." *African Communist* Third Quarter, no. 122 (1990).

"Jobless and Joyless." *The Economist*, February 22, 2001.

Johns, Sheridan. "The Comintern, South Africa, and the Black Diaspora." *The Review of Politics* 7, no. 2 (April 1975).

Johnson, R.W. "A World Apart: The ANC Pleads for Western Aid While the Communist Party Remains True to Its Stalinist Past." *New Statesman & Society* 3 (August 3, 1990a): 18–20.

_____. "Dirty Realism." *New Statesman & Society* 3 (August 17, 1990b): 14–16.

Johnson, Timothy. "'The Path to Power' Program of the South African Communists." *Political Affairs*, April 1990c.

Karis, Thomas. "South African Liberation: The Communist Factor." *Foreign Affairs* 65 (Winter 86/87): 267–87.

Keller, Bill. "South Africa's Communists Arise, and the West Yawns." *New York Times*, January 30, 1994.

_____. "South Africa's Communists Navigate a New Politics." *New York Times*, September 19, 1992.

Keyter, Elise. "RDP Criticised." *RDP News* no. 8 (August 1995).

Kitshoff, Michael Casparus. "The Role of Religious Education in Building a Nation in Multiethnic South Africa." *Religious Education* 89 (Summer 1994): 313–37.

Kofi, Explo. "Don't Forget the Machinations of Imperialism." *African Communist* Fourth Quarter, no. 123 (1990).

Laurence, Patrick. "Comrades and Capitalists." *African Report* 35 (September/October 1990): 39–42.

Le Roux, Frieda Elizabeth. "The Provision of Low-Cost Housing in South Africa: A Wicked Problem with a Systems Theory Solution." *SUNScholar,* 2011.

Lebedev, Yuly. "Nov. 7: Some Repentant, Others Defiant." *Current Digest of the Soviet Press* 43, no. 45 (December 11, 1991): 2–3.

Letsoalo, Matuma. "Zuma Tells NDP Critics to Choose Their Word." *Mail & Guardian* 23 Mar 2013 12:22.

Lodge, Tom. "Post-Modern Bolsheviks: SA Communists in Transition." *South Africa International* 22, no. 4 (April 1992).

Lubisi, Cassius. "Buthelezi and the 'Zulu Kingdom.'" *African Communist* Third Quarter, no. 134 (1993).

Mabhida, Moses. "At the Center of Liberation Struggles." *World Marxist Review* 27 (January 1984): 19–25.

MacLeod, Scott. "The Party's Not Over." *Time,* August 6, 1990, p. 33.

MacRobert, Don. "Break the Circle of Non-Reconstruction." *Weekly Mail & Guardian,* February 9, 1996.

Maharaj, Mac. "Now Mbeki Savages SACP." O'Malley: The Heart of Hope. July 3, 1998.

"Malema: 'Minister Manuel Has No Plan.'" *Mail & Guardian,* June 22, 2011.

Manamela, Buti. "Attack on SACP a 'Red Herring.'" *The Star,* May 10, 2013.

Mandela, Nelson. "Address to the 9th Congress." *The African Communist* Second Quarter, no. 141 (1995).

_____. "Speech to the SACP 9th Congress." *African Communist* First Quarter, no. 141 (1996).

"Mandela Hails South Africa Election Results." CNN, June 6, 1999.

Manning, Robert. "Eurocommunism: Ten Years Later, Down and Almost Out." *U.S. News and World Report,* July 14, 1986, pp. 32–33.

"Manuel Back under Spotlight After BEE-Comments Report." *Mail & Guardian,* March 14, 2011.

Mao Tse-Tung. "Quotations from Mao Tse Tung." Marxists.org, 2012.

Marrian, Natasha. "Cosatu Says NDP Threatens SA's 'Progressive Advances.'" *Bday,* June 7, 2013.

Masondo, Amos. "Renewal—The Numsa Route?" *African Communist* Second Quarter, no. 132 (1993).

Mayekiso, Mzwanle. "Heat, Light and Civil Society." *African Communist* Third Quarter, no. 134 (1993).

McGreal, Chris. "South Africa in Turmoil as Mbeki Heads for Defeat." *The Guardian* (UK), December 15, 2007.

"Members of the Interim Leadership Group." *African Communist* Fourth Quarter, no. 123 (1990).

Mkhula. "Moscow Tragedy." *African Communist* First Quarter, no. 128 (1992).

Mkokeli, Sam. "Cronin to Turn Down Nomination to ANC Executive." *BDay Live,* December 13, 2012.

Mokgabuti, Tishidi. "South Africa: The National Development Plan." *Mondaq,* May 23, 2013.

Molaba, Theo. "Letter of Resignation." *African Communist* Fourth Quarter, no. 135 (1993).

Molapo, Ben. "Manufacturing a Reformist ANC." *African Communist* Second Quarter, no. 125 (1990).

Monare, Moshoeshoe. "SACP Fires Rare Broadside at Mbeki." *Post,* May 18, 2006.

Montague, Richard. "Marx and Lenin's Views Contrasted." World Socialism.org, 2013.

Monteiro, Tony. "Joe Slovo's 'Has Socialism Failed?'" *Political Affairs,* March 1990.

"Motlanthe Says SACP Needs Political Education." *SABC,* June 21, 2012.

Mufson, Steven. "Uncle Joe." *The New Republic*, September 28, 1987, pp. 20–23.

Muravchik, Joshua. "Mandela in America." *Commentary*, October 1990, pp. 11–18.

Murphy, Jerome. "Apartheid's Legacy to Black Children." *Phi Delta Kappan* 73 (January 1992): 367–74.

"Nationalization Won't Help the Poor." *Times-Live*, November 13, 2013.

"No to Mindless Privatisation." *African Communist* Second Quarter, no. 141 (1995).

Nqakula, Charles. "Harry Gwala—Man of Steel." *African Communist* Third Quarter, no. 142 (1995).

Nzimande, Blade, and Mpune Sikhosana. "Civil Society and Democracy." *African Communist* First Quarter, no. 128 (1992).

Oberdorfer, Don. "Soviet 'Collapse' Shifts the Axis of Global Politics." *Washington Post*, September 1, 1991, section A, p. 35.

O'Grady, Kevin. "Dissatisfaction with ANC, but No Gain for Its Rivals." ANC website, 1997.

Ottaway, David. "An Integration Effort Gone Awry." *Washington Post*, January 26, 1992, section A, p. 21.

_____. "Signs of ANC–Communist Party Split Emerging in S. Africa." *Washington Post*, October 2, 1990, section A, p. 12.

"Our Eighth Congress." *African Communist* Fourth Quarter, no. 127 (1992).

Ozinsky, Max. "A Brief History of the Programmes of the SACP." *African Communist* Fourth Quarter, no. 127 (1992).

Ozinsky, Max, and Ebrahim Rasool. "Developing a Strategic Perspective for the Coloured Areas in the Western Cape." *African Communist* Second Quarter, no. 132 (1993).

"The Painful Privatisation of South Africa." *The Economist*, September 9, 1999.

"Path to Power." *The African Communist* Third Quarter, no. 118 (1989).

Pearce, Justin. "Analysis: SA's Zuma in the Dock." BBC News, October 10, 2005.

"Popular Power: The Supreme Goal." *World Marxist Review* 29 (September 1986): 58–59.

Puddington, Arch. "South Africa's Uncle Joe." *National Review*, July 23, 1990, p. 41.

"The Racist Regime Admits the Communists Can Never Be Destroyed." *World Marxist Review* 30 (September 1987): 66–70.

Radosh, Ronald. "Red Hills of Africa." *The American Spectator*, September 1992, pp. 44–47.

Radu, Michael. "The African National Congress: Cadres and Credos." *Problems of Communism* (July–August 1987).

"Reconstruction and Development Programme (Fourth Draft)." *African Communist* Third Quarter, no. 134 (1993).

"The Red Flag's Black Outpost." *The Economist*, October 28, 1989, p. 51.

"The Red Shadow in the South." *The Economist*, July 26, 1986, p. 35.

Revel, Jean-François. "The Myths of Eurocommunism." *Foreign Affairs*, January 1978.

Roji, Sknjana. "Disregarding the Lessons of History." *African Communist* First Quarter 1992, no. 128 (1993).

"Russia Moves to Relaunch CPSU." *African Communist* Third Quarter, no. 130 (1992).

"SACP Divided on Zuma." *Mail & Guardian*, December 20, 2007.

Schuman, Michael. "Can Asian-Style Capitalism Save the West?" *Time*, March 25, 2012.

Slovo, Joe. "Beyond the Stereotype: The SACP in the Past, Present, and Future." *African Communist* Second Quarter, no. 125 (1991).

_____. "Cracks in the Racist Power Bloc." *World Marxist Review* 30 (June 1987): 13–21.

_____. "Political Report." *African Communist* First Quarter, no. 128 (1992).

_____. "Shared Values: Socialism and Religion." *African Communist* First Quarter, no. 136 (1994).

_____. "We Are an Extended Family." *African Communist* Fourth Quarter, no. 119 (1989).

"South Africa: Affiliates Seek End to ANC Alliance as White Minority Rule Ends." *International Labour Review* 132, nos. 5–6 (1993): 556–57.

"South African Unemployment Rate." *Trading Economics,* 2013.

Stevens, Simon. "Perestroika and the South African Revolution." *African Communist* Second Quarter, no. 121 (1990).

Steyn, Lisa. "National Development: ANC Sticks to the Plan." *Mail & Guardian,* December 21, 2012.

"Structural Adjustment Programs." World Health Organization website, 2013.

Tamukamoyo, Hamadziripi. "Why the National Development Plan Benefits South Africa's Working Class." *ISS,* May 21, 2013.

Taylor, Paul. "2 Convicted in S. African Assassination." *Washington Post,* October 15, 1993, section A, p. 32.

Teitelbaum, Salomon M. "Parental Authority in the Soviet Union." *American Slavic and East European Review* 4, nos. 3–4 (December 1945): 54–69.

Tetekhin, Slava. "Perestroika in the Soviet Union." *The African Communist* First Quarter, no. 124 (1991).

Tloome, Dan. "The Racist Regime Admits the Communists." *World Marxist Review,* September 1987.

Tomilson, Richard. "South Africa: Competing Images of the Post-Apartheid State." *African Studies Review,* September 1988, pp. 35–60.

Trewhela, Paul. "Jacob Zuma in Exile: Three Unexplored Issues." PoliticsWeb, February 15, 2009.

Tutu, Mbeki. "Controversy." *Centre for Civil Society.* 11/23/2206.

Ungar, Rick. "Glenn Beck and the General Electric Communist Conspiracy." *The Policy Page,* September 4, 2009.

Vena, Vuvu. "BEE 'Is Not Meant for the Select Few.'" *Mail & Guardian,* March 15, 2011.

"The Way Forward for South Africa." *Political Affairs,* January 1992.

"We Have to Move House." *African Communist* Third Quarter, no. 122 (1990).

Wheatcroft, Geoffrey. "What the ANC Really Stands For." *Wall Street Journal,* April 21, 1994, section A, p. 16.

"Where Communism Is Still in Fashion." *The Economist,* December 4, 1991, p. 47.

"Whites Bar Blacks from South Africa School." *Boston Globe,* February 17, 1995, p. 8.

"Who Is Thabo Mbeki?" *The Economist,* October 30, 1997.

Wines, Michael. "Leadership Battle Grips South Africa's Dominant Party." *The New York Times,* December 17, 2007.

"World War II: Operation Barbarossa." *The Atlantic,* July 24, 2011.

Wren, Christopher. "South African Communist on the Air." *New York Times,* July 20, 1993.

"The Wrong Joe." *The Economist,* August 4, 1990, p. 32.

"Your Future Lies with Democracy." *World Marxist Review* 30 (June 1987): 21–22.

"Yuri Andropov." *The Cold War Files,* 2013.

"Zuma Calls for More Foreign Investment." *SANews,* September 29, 2010.

"Zuma Calls for Redefining of BEE." *Mail & Guardian,* December 30, 2010.

"Zuma Sworn in as SA's Fourth Democratic President." SABC. May 9, 2009.

Miscellaneous Documents

"9th Congress AT." 9th Party Congress of the SACP audiotapes, volumes 1–22, 1995.

9th Congress: Draft Strategy. SACP website, 1995.

Advance to Power—75 Years of Struggle. ANC website, 1987.

"ANC Manifesto." ANC website, 1995.

"ARM AT 1995" ARM interview, 1995.

"AWB and HNP AT 1995." AWB and HNP audiotapes, volumes 1–5, 1995.

Baqwa, S. "Successes of Law Enforcement Against Corruption." ANC Newslist, October 10, 1995.

"Base Document." ANC website, 1994.

Berg, Owen van den, and Dirk Meerkotter. "Action Research in South Africa: Classroom Transformation in a Political Cauldron." Conference paper, 1993. Annual Meeting of the American Educational Research Association (Atlanta, GA, April 12–16, 1993).

"Botha on Trial" (*Daily News*, NPR Radio, 1/22/98).

"The World Factbook: South Africa." The World Factbook, 2013.

"Commentary on the 1996/97 Budget." ANC website, 1997.

"The Communist Party (KPD)." Spartacus Educational, 2013.

"Cronin AT, 1995." Audiotapes, volumes 1–3, 1995.

"Crossing Madiba Cost Jordan His Job." ANC press release, April 4, 1996.

"Declaration of the 13th Congress of the South African Communist Party." SACP website, July 2012.

"The Declaration of the Tripartite Alliance Summit—'Ekurhuleni II.'" ANC website, April 23, 2005.

"Education." South African Government Information, 2013.

"Freedom Front Manifesto." ANC website, 1995.

"Housing." South African Government Information, 2013.

Kautsky, John. "Marxism and Leninism." Unpublished manuscript, 1990.

Mandela, Nelson. "Speech by President Nelson Mandela at the 9th Congress of the South African Communist Party." ANC website, April 7, 1995.

"Morogoro Document." ANC website, 1995.

"National Party Manifesto." National Party website, 1995.

"November 1995 Election Results." ANC website, 1996.

"PAC Chairman Steps Down." ANC Press Release, May 1996.

"PAC Interview, AT 1995." Pan Africanist Congress audiotapes, tapes 1–3, May 1995.

"A Policy Framework for Education and Training." African National Congress Education Department, January 1994.

"Political Report to the 13th Congress of the South African Communist Party." SACP website, July 2012.

"Ready to Govern." ANC Policy Guidelines for a Democratic South Africa Adopted at the National Conference, May 28–31, 1992.

"SACP 10th Congress." SACP website, July 1998.

"SACP 10th Congress Declaration." SACP website, July 1998.

"SACP 10th Congress Resolutions." SACP website, July 1998.

"SACP 11th Congress Political Report." SACP website, July 2002.

"SACP 11th Congress Resolutions." SACP website, July 2002.

"SACP 12th Congress Resolutions." SACP website, July 2007.

"SACP The South African Road to Socialism." SACP website, July 2007.

Slovo, Joe. "Has Socialism Failed?" SACP website, 1990.

_____. "SACP 70th Anniversary, 1921–1991." London: SACP, 1991.

"Socialism Is the Future, Build It Now!" SACP website, 1995.

"South African Schools Act." ANC website, 1996.

"State of the Economy: Legacy of Apartheid: Inequality and Slow Growth." ANC website, 1994.

"Strategic Perspectives." SACP website, 1995.

"Tactics Document." SACP website, 1995.

"Umkhonto we Sizwe (MK) in Exile." South Africa History Online, 2012.

United Nations Centre Against Apartheid. Statements at the International Conference on the Alliance Between South Africa and Israel. Vienna, July 11–13, 1983.

"Vote ANC!" Election pamphlet, April 2009.

"White Paper." ANC website, 1994.

"The Write Stuff." ANC website, 1995.

Index